Bertil Ohlin (1899–1979)

# Pioneers in Economics

*Series Editor:* Mark Blaug

Professor Emeritus, University of London
Consultant Professor, University of Buckingham
Visiting Professor, University of Exeter

This important series presents critical appraisals of influential economists from the 17th century to the present day. It focuses in particular on those economists who were influential in their own time and whose work has had an impact – often inadequately recognized – on the evolution and development of economic thought. The series will be indispensable for a clear understanding of the origin and development of economic ideas and the role played by the leading protagonists of the past.

A full list of published titles in this series is printed at the end of this volume.

# Bertil Ohlin (1899–1979)

*Edited by*

Mark Blaug

*Professor Emeritus,*
*University of London*

An Elgar Reference Collection

Published by
Edward Elgar Publishing Limited
Gower House
Croft Road
Aldershot
Hants GU11 3HR
England

Edward Elgar Publishing Company
Old Post Road
Brookfield
Vermont 05036
USA

A CIP catalogue record for this book is available from the British Library

A CIP catalogue record for this book is available from the US Library of Congress



ISBN 1 85278 507 1

# Contents

# Acknowledgements

The editor and publishers wish to thank the following who have kindly given permission for the use of copyright material.

Duke University Press for articles: Bertil Ohlin (1978), 'On the Formulation of Monetary Theory', *History of Political Economy*, **10** (3), Fall, 353–88; Otto Steiger (1978), 'Substantive Changes in the Final Version of Ohlin's 1933 Paper', *History of Political Economy*, **10** (3), Fall, 389–97; Hans Brems (1978), 'What was New in Ohlin's 1933–34 Macroeconomics?', *History of Political Economy*, **10** (3), Fall, 398–412; Don Patinkin (1978), 'Some Observations on Ohlin's 1933 Article', *History of Political Economy*, **10** (3), Fall, 413–18; Hans Brems (1978), 'A Comment', *History of Political Economy*, **10** (3), Fall, 419; Otto Steiger (1978), 'Prelude to the Theory of a Monetary Economy: Origins and Significance of Ohlin's 1933 Approach', *History of Political Economy*, **10** (3), Fall, 420–46; William P. Yohe (1978), 'Ohlin's 1933 Reformation of Monetary Theory', *History of Political Economy*, **10** (3), Fall, 447–53; Otto Steiger (1981), 'Bertil Ohlin, 1899–1979', *History of Political Economy*, **13** (2), Summer, 179–88; Bertil Ohin (1981), 'Stockholm and Cambridge: Four Papers on the Monetary and Employment Theory of the 1930s', *History of Political Economy*, **13** (2), Summer, 189–255; Bent Hansen (1981), 'Unemployment, Keynes, and the Stockholm School', *History of Political Economy*, **13** (2), Summer, 256–77.

Every effort has been made to trace all the copyright holders but if any have been inadvertently overlooked, the publishers will be pleased to make the necessary arrangement at the first opportunity.

In addition the publishers wish to thank the library of the London School of Economics and Political Science and The Alfred Marshall Library, Cambridge University, for their assistance in obtaining these articles.

# Introduction

Bertil Ohlin first made a name for himself in 1929 by disrupting Keynes' treatment of the German transfer problem; that is, the problem of how Germany was to pay her World War I reparations. In effect, Ohlin argued the income-theory of the balance of payments (which Keynes later made his own), whereas Keynes oddly enough argued the old classical theory according to which price changes – and not income change – bring balance of payments into equilibrium. But Ohlin's reputation was only firmly secured by the publication of *Interregional and International Trade* (Harvard University Press, 1933; 2nd ed., 1967), a book which won him the Nobel Prize in Economics in 1977, shared jointly with James Meade. Starting from an article written in 1919 by his old teacher, Eli Heckscher, Ohlin developed the thesis that both interregional and international trade are devices for the spatial exchange of the goods and services produced by factors of production since these factors themselves are to a greater or lesser extent incapable of being moved in space – think of land as the classic case of an immovable factor – in consequence of which relative prices in different geographical locations depend on the relative scarcity of factor endowments in these locations.

To put it in the language of modern trade theory: countries (or regions) will export commodities which are produced with their relatively abundant factors of production, and will import those which are produced with their relatively scarce factors, so that international trade tends towards an equalization of factor prices between trading nations, which is not to say that they will be equalized in practice. This 'Heckscher-Ohlin Theorem', as it was soon to be called, entered almost immediately into the textbook literature, although not without a push from Samuelson in the 1940s and the stimulus of Leontief's apparent empirical refutation of the theorem in the 1950s. It is doubtful, however, whether any later textbook treatment improved on Ohlin's own masterful presentation: the theorem is laid out in the first two chapters; it is then modified and extended, dropping the assumptions that transport costs are zero, that there are no import duties, that economies of scale are absent, that the pattern of demand is identical everywhere, that capital as well as labour are immovable, and that exchange rates are freely flexible. By the end of the book, the entire range of international economic problems has been discussed; moreover, the intimate connections between location theory, regional economics and international trade have been brilliantly displayed.

Ohlin, however, has other claims to fame. In a number of publications, beginning with a 1927 pamphlet and ending with a report in 1934 to a Swedish government committee on unemployment, he anticipated almost totally Keynes' theoretical schema in the *General Theory* (1936), including Keynes' policy recommendations. (Thus, with Myrdal, we have two Swedish economists to have scooped Keynes.) Unfortunately, Ohlin's contributions were published in Swedish and remained untranslated. Thus, when he sought to remind the British Keynesians that they were not the only ones and not even the first ones in the field in 'Some Notes on the Stockholm Theory of Savings and Investment' (*Economic Journal*, March-June 1937), they greeted his claims with incredulity. In recent years, however, the Stockholm School in general and Ohlin in particular have finally received proper recognition for their pioneering contributions to modern macroeconomics.

Ohlin was born in Klippan (Sweden) in 1899, the son of a lawyer and police superintendent. He entered the University of Lund at the age of 16, transferring to the Stockholm School of Economics and Business Administration two years later. Graduating in 1919, he began working for his doctorate under Gustav Cassel. He spent a few months at Cambridge University and a year at Harvard before receiving his doctoral degree in 1924. From 1925 to 1930, he was a professor at the University of Copenhagen. In 1930 he returned to the Stockholm School of Economics to succeed Eli Heckscher, remaining there until his retirement in 1965. He was a member of the Swedish Parliament for 32 years, from 1938 to 1970, and a leader of the Swedish Liberal Party during its 23 years of opposition, from 1944 to 1967, serving as a Minister of Trade in the final years of World War II.

## Note

Several paragraphs in this Introduction were borrowed from my *Great Economists Since Keynes* (Wheatsheaf Books, 1985).

# [1]

*History of Political Economy 10:3*


## On the formulation of monetary theory*

*Bertil Ohlin, translated from the Swedish by Hans J. Brems and William P. Yohe*



### I. *Terminology*

§1. *Introduction.* What characterizes Wicksell's formulation of monetary theory is, first, that changes in the general price level are treated in the same way as changes in the prices of individual goods, and above all, second, the introduction of the concept of monetary equilibrium defined as the equality between saving and new investment; the equilibrating rate of interest is designated as normal and is assumed to conform to the real or natural rate, which is equal to the marginal productivity of capital in an economy without money.

Among these notions, the path-breaking concept which left its mark on postwar monetary theory is the lack of equality between saving and new investment as the "cause" of general price move-

BERTIL OHLIN *is Professor Emeritus at the Stockholm School of Economics.*

* "Till frågan om penningteoriens uppläggning," *Ekonomisk Tidskrift* 35, no. 2 (1933): 45-81. A few typographical errors have been corrected. Assistance from Moshe Apelblat, Carl G. Uhr, Björn Hansson, Don Patinkin, and Otto Steiger is gratefully acknowledged. Royall Brandis kindly read an earlier draft and caught several errors.

ments. In this respect there is agreement between the two leading participants in the monetary theory debate of the last decade, Cassel and Keynes. A rising price level results from the availability of credit, demanding capital goods, i.e., real investment, in excess of current saving. Falling prices result from the opposite situation. The rate of interest which generates equilibrium in the capital market is called normal.

Such a formulation of the theory directs its attention to the output of and the demand for capital goods, including change in the inventory of consumers' goods. If demand for consumers' goods is added on the demand side and the output of consumers' goods plus or minus inventory change is added on the supply side, then the equilibrium condition will be that aggregate income (spent on consumption plus saved) equals the value of aggregate output (consumers' goods plus capital goods), i.e., that all income is "spent."

The content of this theory obviously depends on the meaning attached to such categories as income, saving, real investment, and the price level.

§2. *Definitions*. What, then, is meant by income? In conventional reasoning the underlying notion is quite vague. Presumably net income generally means the value of the quantity of goods and services made available in a period for consumption and the "expansion" of productive capacity. Such a definition implies that income always equals expenditure and that net saving always equals the value of new investment. The capital-market equilibrium problem just mentioned simply does not arise. If lack of equality between saving and new investment is to be used in a description of changing prices, the terms must be so defined as to make such lack of equality possible. As will be shown below (§3), the necessary definitions will be quite troublesome to work with.

The very notion of an "unchanged" capital stock whose depreciation is always balanced by maintenance and replacement lacks precision, among other things because of the steady technological progress affecting the form of replacement (reinvestment). As a result, the expansion of productive capacity and with it net income will also lack precision. The expansion of the value of productive capacity is obviously no guide, for the value will fluctuate with the rate of interest and with expectations. Such fluctuations of value are best considered capital gains and capital losses of a character quite different from net income.

In the following I hope to show that business accounting may be profitably applied to determine net income and other concepts. Where to draw the line is obviously a bit arbitrary. But that is true of any procedure and will play merely a modest role in the price analysis to be presented.

The positive or negative net income emerging in business and individual accounting is arrived at by subtracting from gross income, i.e., the sum of all revenue, the expenditure related to products sold in the period in question. Such expenditure may be considered investment of capital in money form to be "freed," i.e., becoming disposable for new demand, when products are sold. To the extent such sums are spent productively—on raw materials, wages, machines—reinvestment is taking place. Part of such reinvestment is short-run, i.e., in goods and wages, often referred to as working capital, as distinguished from reinvestment in durable structures and the like, constituting fixed capital.

Relating expenditure to the products produced or sold in a period is, however, to some extent arbitrary. Many expenditures are related to the activities of several periods. Observe that at the beginning of a period durable capital goods exist and that during the period additional ones are acquired and will remain after the end of the period. Their depreciation is based upon the historical cost of acquisition and rests upon assumptions concerning an uncertain future, for example the useful life of the capital good. Later, when the period is seen in retrospect, it may turn out that certain goods should have been depreciated more rapidly, others less rapidly. Furthermore, depreciating on the basis of the historical cost of acquisition is a strange procedure if at the time of depreciation such structures happen to have entirely different, higher or lower, costs of reproduction. A remedy might be to use the latter as a basis for depreciation and to enter the difference between the remaining historical cost of acquisition and the reproduction cost on a capital-gain-and-loss account. Under falling prices of capital goods depreciation would become smaller and net income larger—or losses smaller—than according to the conventional procedure. But in the real world capital goods are not normally replaced by goods of the same character and having the same useful life as the depreciating ones, consequently the concept of reproduction cost will be very imprecise. Wherever drawn, the boundary line between the two parts of gross revenue, net income and freed capital, is highly arbitrary.

Another capital item is inventory of acquired and produced goods held at the beginning and the ending of the period. Again, it will hardly be profitable to try to improve on the accounting actually used by the business community. Admittedly the borderline between net income and freed capital, i.e., between new investment and reinvestment, may be drawn so as to understate net income in times of falling prices and overstate it in times of rising prices. But the boundary line is to some extent arbitrary in any event. Above all let us recall that in a study of prices what we are trying to explain by the generation of income among other things, are changes in the supply of and the demand for various goods and services. It will be to our advantage to apply the net income concepts reflected in accounting and therefore possessing a certain reality to the businessmen themselves. At the same time it should be borne in mind that such concepts may occasionally deviate somewhat from accounting data. In any event it is important to realize how the boundary line is drawn. Here, monetary theory would do well to start with gross revenue. Part of the latter is spent on demand for consumers' goods, another part—freed capital plus new saving—goes into reinvestment and new investment, i.e., constitutes investment demand.

What, then, is meant by gross revenue? Notice, first, that it applies to a past period and, second, that it is the sum of sales of all firms in that period. As has already been said, it is divided into two parts, i.e., net income and freed capital. The latter equals the sum of all costs related to the sales of the period and is usually spent as reinvestment in wages, raw materials, and semifinished goods, as well as in durable capital goods considered necessary to maintain productive capacity. To reinvestment also belong the costs of purchasing finished goods incurred by distribution.

Net income is gross revenue minus the costs related to it (the capital freed); many private individuals have no such costs, of course. New saving is the part of such net income not spent for consumption purposes in the period; it is applied to the expansion of productive capacity. "Waiting" (freed capital plus new saving) is the part of gross revenue not spent for consumption purposes in the period. Notice, first, that durable consumers' goods ("consumption capital objects") serve consumption for several periods and, second, that all goods other than retail sales for immediate consumption are purchased with waiting. Durable consumers' goods, for example, are paid for with own or borrowed waiting. Automobiles are often purchased on the instalment plan. The distributor uses his working capital to purchase all kinds of goods wholesale. The part of gross revenue not constituting waiting, then, is the part equaling the flow of nondurable or slightly durable consumers' goods and services ("means of consumption") sold by retailers and consumed in the period.[1]

1. Services rendered in a period by durable consumers' goods such as automobiles and furniture are left out of our reasoning to the extent they are not purchased and sold in the period. If they are, they are an item of consumers' goods.

The entire expenditure in a period is, as we have said, always equal to gross revenue. One man's purchase is another's sale. Consumption demand is equal to the flow of consumers' goods to consumers. The flow of all other goods is always equal to the flow of waiting, new and freed—*even if the money supply is changing*. Within such a system of definitions treating equilibrium in the same way as done by ordinary price theory, the Wicksell-Cassel-Keynes problem of capital market equilibrium does not arise.

Use the following symbols for period $x$. All magnitudes are flows[2] in terms of money. Gross revenue $=I_x^b$; gross expenditure $= U_x$; consumption demand $= K_x$ = consumers' goods for consumers; and waiting $= V_x$ = output for investment;[3]

$$I_x^b = U_x = K_x + V_x.$$

Net income $= N_x^i$; freed capital $= O_x$ = reinvestment (i.e., the sum of the costs of production of all goods sold in the period); new saving $= S_x$ = new investment;

$$I_x^b = N_x^i + O_x;\ V_x = O_x + S_x;\quad N_x^i = K_x + S_x.$$

Here net income and waiting are computed *net*. The former is the sum of positive individual incomes minus negative ones. Part of the supply of waiting consists of freed capital, another of net saving; the latter is arrived at after gross saving, i.e., the sum of all positive saving items, has been reduced by negative saving items, i.e., negative incomes (usually called "losses") and consumption credit. In the capital market will be supplied the part of freed capital not reinvested by the same firm. In addition, even if net new saving is zero, there will be a supply of new saving absorbed by consumption credit and the financing of negative income in other firms.

Net income may be divided into two parts, (1) nonfirm income constituting costs to the firm (like wages) and income to others; and (2) firm income, "profits," constituting the surplus of the firm over costs. This distinction, to which the English-language literature, e.g., Keynes, attaches decisive significance, is not too clear, however; for firms purchase from one another, and one firm's profit is another's

2. The capital values appearing in balance sheets play a secondary role in monetary theory. They do not represent "actual value" and enter the picture merely by affecting depreciation and other freeing of capital, i.e., the breakdown of $I^b$ into $N^i$ and $O$. Writing off the value of capital such as plant of obsolescent technical form will affect the breakdown.

3. All these magnitudes are obtained directly from accounts of transactions made, unlike the following magnitudes, which depend on estimates of the costs related to the production of the goods and services sold in the period.

cost. For this reason and for another now to be pointed out, it would be better to include profitability in the following manner.

Profitability notions are of interest to price theory because they motivate human economic action. Such action concerns the future and is only indirectly related to profitability computed *backwards*, i.e., the ratio of net income to capital invested by a firm. An entrepreneur purchasing a machine will do so because he expects the present worth of the discounted future revenues generated by this machine (its subjective capital value) to exceed the present worth of the costs incurred by the machine. In addition, he expects the present worth of the machine to exceed the present worth of any alternative use of the money involved. In other words, his purchase is not only a testimony to his expectation of a positive present net worth but also shows that the latter is deemed larger than that of other or later investments of an alternative character, i.e., excluded by the former investment. Often he may have no definite notion of the size of such present net worths but does consider it likely that the present net worth of one investment will exceed that of the others.[4]

Thus the extent and direction of demand is determined by profitability computed forward in time. The retrospective profitability of a machine now being retired plays no direct role—albeit occasionally an indirect one—in deciding on the expediency of acquiring a new one like it. Indeed, in many cases nobody bothers to compute the retrospective profitability of individual capital goods.

Analogously, expectations determine the direction and size of production, i.e., changes in supply.

But if so, what is the use of reasoning about net income and cost? Is not such reasoning redundant? The answer is No. Depreciation policies and other allocations of expenditure among periods as costs of products sold in each period largely do determine entrepreneurial notions of how gross revenue is divided into net income and freed capital. What is considered net income plays a decisive role in determining the direction and size of consumption demand. Similarly, the size of what is considered freed capital is significant for investment demand.

Along with a description of changes in supply,[5] a description of the generation of demand for various goods must lie at the heart of

4. The indefiniteness of his expectations should always be kept in mind when referring to subjective capital values.

5. In the present paper I am mainly concerned with the changes on the demand side. A more comprehensive formulation should consider the elasticity of supply to a greater extent than I have done.

every analysis of price changes. For the reasons given, such a demand analysis must be based upon an investigation of the composition of gross revenue, reasoning *backwards* in time, as well as upon an investigation of prevailing notions of profitability computed *forward* in time. That is the only way to explain changes in demand. Quite simply, the task is to record transactions period by period, relating them to one another, thus illuminating why they came into existence.

In the following pages I shall try to demonstrate the usefulness of the simple conceptual system presented above. To some extent it marks a return to an older procedure differing from postwar monetary theory. The waiting of a period has just been defined as identically equal to the real investment of the period. By contrast, as Myrdal points out, "the separation of saving and capital formation is . . . the very essence of modern monetary doctrine."[6]

## II. *The Stability of the Price System*

§3. The problem is to describe price changes over time, i.e., during a period or, if you like, from a subperiod at the beginning of the main period to a subperiod at the end of the main period, ignoring changes within the short subperiods. Under which conditions, one may ask, will the system maintain a certain stability characterized by specific relations between the situation at one time and that at a later time? Under which conditions will the price system be moving upward and downward?

The present section will examine the concept of intertemporal stability. To begin with, the term is taken to mean that certain kinds of price changes are excluded for as long as stability prevails. This type of reasoning is applied to the relation between gross revenue and certain expenditure, or between saving and the narrower category of expenditure designated new investment.

Suppose a divergence between revenue and expenditure or between saving and new investment is to be possible, and suppose a multi-period price stability condition is to be formulated accordingly[7] by relating the revenue of a period to the expenditure of the *same*

6. "Om penningteoretisk jämvikt [On the theory of monetary equilibrium], *Ekonomisk Tidskrift*, 1931 (printed in 1932), §13 [cf. *Monetary Equilibrium*, London, 1939, p. 90].

7. By stability Myrdal means something other than absence of changes in the price system from one period to another. His analysis refers to a *point of time*, has to do with absence of *tendencies* to certain price changes, and does not preclude major actual changes in price levels in periods of "monetary equilibrium." Lack of equality between saving and investment is possible for him, as it is to Lindahl, because both are looking *ahead* in time, i.e., are concerned with *planned* saving and investment.

period. One will then be forced to define revenue and income differently from the way it was defined above. They will have to be defined as referring fully or partially to sales made in the preceding period. For example, income may become fully or partially disposable only in the period subsequent to the period in which services were rendered (back pay); or business income earned in the production of period I may be transferred to period II, giving rise to demand by the firm and its owners in the latter period.[8] Thus, intertemporal relations are smuggled into the definitions, giving the impression that price stability is conditioned by a relation between revenue and expenditure *within the same period*. It is certainly more transparent to use terms making the stability condition explicit with respect to intertemporal relations. A person's expenditure in a period is then considered financed by his income in *that* period or with his capital freed in that period.

Underlying the notion of monetary stability is the idea that stability precludes specific differentials between later and earlier price results. Which differential? In any case, violent inflation or deflation, i.e., significant changes in prices or incomes. But equilibrium would be compatible with various changes in the direction of production. Monetary stability would exist when the prices and incomes of a period are at some sort of rest, despite steady changes in the conditions of production, in taste, etc., and consequently in the direction of production.

Could this notion of "rest" be given a more precise meaning? Various parts of the price system may shift relatively to one another. This applies to, say, relations between (1) factor prices, (2) rentals of older capital goods, (3) wholesale prices of new capital goods and consumers' goods, and (4) their retail prices. A price system being at rest would imply that some sum or weighted average or relation of prices or price differentials would not be changing. How such weights or relations should be designed is clearly a matter of convention. Prices were inflationary in 1917 and deflationary in 1930, but where to

8. This is the construction used in my recently published work, *Interregional and International Trade*, and in my discussion with Keynes on capital movements in the *Economic Journal*, 1929; Hammarskjöld's method (this journal 1932) appears to be a mixture of that type and that of Lindahl. (Since the present paper had been worked out before the publication of Hammarskjöld's paper, I have been unable to take account of the latter.) Finally one may proceed as Keynes does, by simply excluding part of profits, i.e., "windfalls," from income. Thus one has to distinguish no less than five categories of terminology. Keynes' method has the weakness that it loses sight of price changes offset by changes in factor prices and therefore leaving "windfalls" unaffected.

draw the line between inflation and deflation is a matter of convention. It may be drawn at will. But it should be drawn expediently for the problem under analysis.

Two conceivable stability requirements would be that net income or gross revenue—perhaps calculated per unit of labor—should not be changing rapidly. But intertemporal stability usually refers to a certain price level as measured by a price index. Such an index is often designed to reflect the wholesale or retail purchase prices of an entire basket of goods. The basket may be composed so as to represent (1) current consumption, (2) net income, or (3) gross revenue, i.e., total transactions. The goods and services included may differ, and their weights may differ. Stability required from one point of view may differ from that required from another.

Price stability in some sense is of course possible even when various parts of the price system are so related that, say, large negative incomes are being generated because certain prices are declining far more than are factor prices and contractual obligations, or because sales volumes are declining.

A sharp contraction of output at specific points may indicate a distortion of the price system—by which we mean the collection of prices and quantities entering into the static general-equilibrium scheme. A substantial change in specific prices may do the same. Such distortions may last a long time, and for as long as they last the price system may be stable from many points of view. Whatever is meant by stability clearly does not imply "normal" relations between price and quantity elements of the system. And it is not expedient to designate as "normal" a rate of interest[9] existing when certain relations are stable in contrast to the rate existing when a different part of the price system is stable or when no specified stability condition is met.

The price stability debate often follows avenues other than those suggested above. It often bears the stamp of the old classical notion that when individual market prices diverge from their stable normal level determined by relative costs, then supply reactions will quickly make them return to that level. No corresponding tendency to return is found in changes of the general price level upwards or downwards, i.e., in shifts of the entire price system. There is the following kernel of truth in this. When prices of individual goods are moving and corresponding cost elements fail to follow because of the nature of the

9. The present paper uses "rate of interest" as a summary expression for the terms of credit supply.

supply reactions affecting them, a tendency to return must result. Thus, among other things, the stability of long-run relative prices depends upon that of relative wages. By contrast, if all prices rise, then current and expected future costs will often be rising too. If so, the supply reactions tending to return prices to their original level will fail to materialize. Whether the degree of price stability is high or low, then, depends upon the relation between certain prices and other, relatively rigid, ones or rather upon the expectations of them.

If by stability one means a price situation prevailing for a long time without major change, then one must examine the presence or absence in such a situation of inherent tendencies toward essential price changes. Such an examination must allow not only for price and cost relations but also for quantity relations (such as labor flowing from one industry to another, unemployment rates, etc.), or rather, one must allow for planned investment and consumption demand as well as for available factor supply, for such plans could indicate pending price changes.[10] The question is to what extent a certain state of the price system carries in it the seed of more or less violent and significant changes to come.

Notice that all states carry in them the seed of some such changes. And notice that a state may continue for some time without major change, even though price and cost relations are such as to make significant changes inevitable. Imagine, for example, a deep depression in which everything is temporarily "frozen." Price instability, then, in the sense used here is not the same as the presence of tendencies toward *immediate* price change.[11]

### III. *The Morphology of the Price System*

§4. *Time-structure classification of the price system*. When describing price changes we apply various kinds of price index numbers. According to their time structure, Table 1 classifies flows of new goods and services on their way through the processes of production and distribution. The table allows for the character of available statistical data. Needless to say, goods may belong to several categories of the table. Changes of the price of leather may well be observed under I.B (automobile leather) as well as under II.B (shoe leather). But one might also classify every good according to its major use.

Demand for goods might expediently be divided into two parts, (1) demand by the distributor and (2) demand by the user (producer and

10. Presumably this is the core of Myrdal's formulation of monetary theory; cf. §11 below on "the driving force" of price movements.

11. On Myrdal's presentation, see further §§11–12.

consumer). Waiting is the source of all demand except the user's demand for consumers' goods (II.A). Waiting is also the source of hiring labor, land, and older capital goods for purposes other than direct and immediate consumption. The use of such factors might be included in Table 1 as I.C and II.C. Goods in the process of distribution as well as categories I.B and II.B in the hands of users for further processing are circulating capital. I.A. in the hands of users is fixed capital.

The term "durability" of a good refers to its useful life. The "storability" of a good, i.e., lending itself to storage, is a different matter. New investment during a period implies an expansion of the aggregate supply of all goods at the end of the period compared to its beginning.

Let us take a closer look at the relations among various parts of the mechanism. In a certain sense all production is aiming at consumption, i.e., at the production of finished consumers' goods. Consequently, in a *static* system (on the *time sequence* of price changes, see §6) the wholesale prices of all other goods and factors will reflect the wholesale prices of consumers' goods, and the wholesale prices of the latter will reflect their retail prices. The relation between prices at one stage of production (yarn) and the next (fabric) is obviously influenced by the necessary processing costs such as the price of the labor

*Table 1.* Flow of new goods and services

- I. Capital goods
  - A. Finished products (= capital instruments)
    - 1. Means of production
      - (a) Structures (ships, roads, canals)
      - (b) Equipment (machines, livestock)
    - 2. Durable consumers' goods (passenger cars, furniture)
  - B. Semifinished goods and raw materials

- II. Consumption goods[12]
  - A. Finished products (= means of consumption)
    - 1. Semidurable goods (shoes, clothes, books)
    - 2. Nondurable goods (food, tobacco, newspapers and magazines. Services, personal as well as rendered by durable consumers' goods
  - B. Semifinished goods and raw materials
    - 1. For semidurable goods (shoe leather, fabric)
    - 2. For nondurable goods (most agricultural products)

12. Notice that durable consumers' goods are not included in consumption goods.

and capital required. Under dynamic conditions these relations are by no means as rigid as under static conditions; production at the various stages has been known to result sometimes in positive, sometimes in negative income.

A closer examination of such matters usually takes its cue from Böhm-Bawerk's capital theory, the doctrine of time-consuming processes of production. Labor and nature are used for a longer or shorter period before finished consumers' goods emerge. The average of such periods is the "period of investment." The longer the latter, the more capital-intensive production will be, i.e., the larger will be the quantity of capital existing per unit of labor and nature. Real capital consists of all capital goods and all consumers' goods not yet ready for consumption, i.e., everything except consumers' goods in the hands of the ultimate consumer.

The length of the period of investment depends, first, on the period of production of goods and, second, on the useful life of durable capital goods (durable producers' as well as consumers' goods).[13]

The period of production is the period elapsing in the production of a raw material, as well as in its march through the process of production leading to ultimate consumption in the hands of the consumer. The length of this period depends upon the time required for conversion, transportation, and storage. Wheat is sown, harvested, transported, stored, ground, baked, and consumed in the form of bread. The period elapsing between the first and the last stage may be guessed to be 6 to 18 months after sowing.[14]

The useful life of buildings is perhaps fifty years or more, that of machines often about ten years, whereas their period of production is often not much longer than that of bread. Over the useful life of a durable capital good the original factors of production invested in it will successively "ripen" into consumers' goods.[15]

For the use of durable capital goods already existing or built this year, the expectations of interest rate and useful life underlying their construction no longer play any role. What matters is only the remaining useful life. Durable capital goods are a gift of the past to the present. In the economy of the present they have the same importance and place as exhaustible natural resources. By contrast, this

13. The useful life of semidurable consumption goods may be ignored.

14. Exactly where a process of production begins is, of course, highly arbitrary.

15. As already pointed out, in the breakdown of demand into consumption and investment demand a major role is played by previous conceptions underlying the depreciation policy adopted, which, to the extent it is not altered, will determine depreciation policies and with them current conceptions of net income.

year's use of labor, capital, and natural resources as a choice among alternative periods of roundabout production is influenced by current expectations of useful lives of alternative durable capital goods under consideration, as well as by current expectations of future prices, such as interest rates. Because the period of production is so short, the rate of interest is unimportant for the relation between prices of raw materials and finished goods. But the rate of interest is very important for the relation between the present worth of durable natural resources or capital goods, on the one hand, and the prices of finished consumers' goods and services, on the other hand. The present worth of immortal natural resources will tend toward the capitalized difference between product price and processing cost—assuming such a price and cost structure to prevail or assuming the risk of a declining difference between price and cost to be balanced by the chance of an increasing one (cf. waterfalls and electric energy). The lower the rate of interest, the higher the prices of goods at early stages will tend to be relative to finished consumers' goods and expectations of other things as well. That is why a reduced rate of interest will improve the profitability of very durable capital goods, making it profitable to extend the planned average period of investment of factors of production used (labor, capital, and natural resources).[16] For example, more durable goods (machines and durable consumers' goods) are produced than before, and their planned useful lives are longer than before.

The length of the average period of investment adopted at a given time, i.e., the character and expected useful lives of investment goods, will obviously influence future productive capacity, i.e., the supply conditions of later years. This is a phenomenon not to be ignored in an analysis of a price sequence. It does, however, in my opinion play a limited direct role in the short run. The Vienna school, it seems to me, definitely exaggerates its significance. In the following pages this matter will not be discussed. I merely wish to indicate its place in price analysis.

Call the wholesale price level of consumers' goods (finished current consumers' goods) $p^k$. Take semifinished goods and raw materials for such goods together in one group and call its wholesale price $p^{kr}$. Call the price level of finished capital goods $p^i$, and that of corresponding semifinished goods and raw materials $p^{ir}$.

With waiting $V$ is demanded (1) consumers' goods by the distribu-

16. This concept is applicable under dynamic conditions—unlike the total average period of investment for all capital existing.

tion sector, (2) other goods by "users" (producers and consumers) as well as by the distribution sector. Let $V^k$ be distributors' demand for consumers' goods. If the quantity of such goods is $v^k$, then $V^k/v^k = p^k$. If $V^k$ is subtracted from $V$, the remainder may be divided into three parts, i.e., (1) demand for semifinished goods and raw materials for consumers' goods $V^{kr}$; if their quantity is $v^{kr}$, then $V^{kr}/v^{kr} = p^{kr}$; (2) demand for semifinished goods and raw materials for capital goods $V^{ir}$; if their quantity is $v^{ir}$, then $V^{ir}/v^{ir} = p^{ir}$; (3) demand for finished capital goods $V^i$; if their quantity is $v^i$, then $V^i/v^i = p^i$. In addition, $V^a$ and $V^p$ are used to demand factors of production for productive purposes. Call the quantity of labor $f^a$ and the hiring price of labor $p^a$. Call the quantity of older capital goods and natural resources $f^p$ and their hiring price $p^p$. Then $V^a = f^a p^a$ and $V^p = f^p p^p$.

Finally, one must consider the demand for consumers' goods $K$ and their retail prices $p^d$. Call the various interest rates $S_1$, $S_2$, etc., and the change in inventory of finished current consumers' goods $v^I$. Then:

| | Investment Demand | Consumption Demand |
|---|---|---|
| | $V = V^{kr} + V^{ir} + V^i + V^k + V^a + V^p$ | $K$ |
| Price levels . . . | $p^{kr}, p^{ir}, p^i, p^k, p^a, p^p$ | $p^d$ (retail price) |
| Quantities . . . | $v^{kr}, v^{ir}, v^i, v^k, f^a, f^p$ | $v^k + v^i$ |

The weights used in the computation of price indices represent the actual quantities produced or sold.[17] The question is how these prices and quantities vary with shifts within the price structure. In other words, the latter could be described by accounting for the former.

The majority of such index numbers are available or could be computed, even if not exactly, from available data. But it is regrettable that capital-market data on issues, bank deposits, etc., cannot be used to check the data on various $V$ items available in the transactions index, i.e., the index on the sum of business transactions.

In addition to the various price indices and their corresponding transaction indices, quantity indices ($v$) should, of course, be computed wherever possible in order to check the computations of $V$ and $p$. If possible, inventory holdings should be broken down into producers, distributors, and users.

17. Except for consumption goods and certain capital goods, only a small part of such transaction of goods takes place in retail trade. Thus $p^k$, $p^{kr}$, and $p^{ir}$ are largely wholesale prices. Any $p$ except $p^a$ and $p^p$ may be replaced by two price indices, i.e., (1) distributor's purchase price and (2) distributor's selling price. In addition the various kinds of $V$ and $v$ could be split in an analogous way and distributor's inventory change included.

For better insight into the process of price movement it will be necessary to study what lies behind the changes of demand items as well as of available quantities of goods. On the demand side the circumstances to watch are the following: (1) the consumption demand depending upon, first, changes in net income appearing in accounting and, second, human expectations (thus it is important to have data illuminating changes in net income $N^i$ and its component parts, e.g., wage income $L$); and (2) investment demand, which is hardly influenced by net income as recorded in cost accounting. Data on past profitability always deserve some attention, but profitability expectations are certainly more important; the latter may be illuminated by capital-value statistics, especially the trend in stock-market prices.

§5. *Exchange-structure classification of the price system.* A description of a price sequence cannot confine itself to such an analysis of *total* demand and supply at every stage of the production process. Goods at the same stage must be classified by industry, and changes in industry supply and demand must be observed. For example, along with rising output of food may go declining farm gross revenue and demand (cf. the situation in 1928–1929). As distinct from the changes treated above in terms of a conceptual apparatus referring to the time structure of the price system,the changes now to be considered might be called changes in the *exchange structure* of the price system. They have to do with exchange relations among industries. To illustrate them the following data will be required.

(1) Output volume, capacity utilization, inventory, prices and wages within industries such as agriculture, trade, transportation, raw materials production, fabricating industry, and construction.
(2) The distribution of net income in each industry among owners of the factors of production, labor on one side and owners of land and capital on the other; furthermore the distribution between active and passive capitalists.
(3) Costs of living.
(4) Productivity changes.
(5) Output volume, capacity utilization, inventory, and prices in monopolized industries relative to other industries.
(6) The volume, composition, and prices (including exchange rates and tariffs) of international trade.
(7) International capital movements.

It would be impossible to describe a price sequence such as that of the last four years without treating such exchange relations, as well as changes in the time structure of the price system. For illumination I refer to the League of Nations report, *The Course and Phases of the World Economic Depression* (Geneva, 1931), ch. 6, A–C.

When trying to describe a sequence, we shall find the *timing* of the various changes to be of obvious significance.

§6. *The time sequence of price changes.* Perhaps it is most expedient to illuminate this matter by some examples.

Imagine that people decide to reduce their saving sharply, so demand for consumers' goods will rise. The primary effect upon goods of which inventories are held will not be rising retail prices ($p^d$) but rather rising sales at unchanged prices. Retailers will increase their orders with manufacturers. It will depend upon the idle capacity and the unfilled orders of the latter whether factory prices will rise immediately. In any event manufacturers will increase their orders for semifinished goods and raw materials. Thus investment demand will rise. In some markets, pricing is such that a rising demand will immediately lead to rising price. But even if delayed, most wholesale prices will rise before retail prices do. As a result, prices at the "earlier" stages cannot properly be regarded as reflections of changes in retail prices. In this respect reminiscences of a static Böhm-Bawerk formulation have left their mark on, e.g., Lindahl's presentation.[18]

The decision to reduce saving may not be accompanied by a tightening of credit. If so, investment demand will at first be allowed to go on as usual, assuming an increasing money supply or an increasing velocity of circulation, and the rising investment demand of the consumers' goods industries will eventually bring about an increase in total investment. Total saving, then, is not reduced but on the contrary increased, despite the fact that consumption is up. What makes this possible is expanding output.

If, on the other hand, the decision to reduce saving results in a *simultaneous* contraction of investment demand and expansion of consumption demand, e.g., because bankers immediately restrict their credits, it is uncertain whether eventually aggregate demand will rise or fall. Among other things, the outcome depends on how much investment demand will rise in consumers' goods industries and fall in capital goods industries as a result of the primary change in demand.

Take another example. In a depression imagine a general wage cut of 10 percent in all industries, immediately reducing labor's consumption demand. If at the same time firms impressed with the improved profitability prospects expand their investment demand by the same

18. *Penningpolitikens medel* [The means of monetary policy], ch. 2.

amount, aggregate demand will not fall. Then average profitability will indeed improve and may indirectly stimulate investment demand. On the other hand, if no immediate tendency to expand firm investment demand arises, the wage cut reduces total consumption demand by as much as the cut in wage costs. Prices will tend downwards, and profitability will deteriorate. The deteriorating profitability in consumers' goods industries is at first balanced by improvement in the capital goods industries, but according to established accounting methods the falling prices will reduce the profitability of investment and eventually tend to reduce investment demand as well.

An unusually large harvest in, say, wheat in a number of producing countries will often depress the price of wheat so much that the value of the harvest is reduced. The investment demand of wheat traders in money terms will then be reduced. Immediately disposing of less money than usual, farmers will reduce their demand. A compensating increase in consumer demand for bread, because bread is now cheaper, will not materialize at once. It may be some time before millers reduce the price of flour and bakers the price of bread; they are carrying earlier inventory purchased at old, higher prices and so far have had no increase in their net incomes. As a result, the reduced demand of farmers is not offset by an increase anywhere else.

Under a sharply reduced food supply such as occurred in Sweden in 1917, food prices will rise more than in proportion to the reduction of supply because of the low elasticity of demand. Consumers will have less money left to purchase other goods, but, anticipating higher future incomes, farmers may simultaneously increase their demand. If so, the rising price will not be offset by falling prices of other goods, hence the general price level has been raised more than in proportion to the reduction of supply.[19]

By now it should be sufficiently clear that the effects of a given primary change will differ widely if the secondary reactions occur in one time sequence rather than another. Obviously, different alternatives imply differences in money supply or the velocity of circulation. The changes in the latter will depend upon the time intervals elapsing between one change in the price system and the next. Those time intervals are not primarily determined by money and banking condi-

19. This case and others were discussed in the Nationalekonomiska klubben [Economics Club] towards the end of the war. Cf. Davidson, "Valutaproblemets teoretiska innebörd" [The theoretical nature of the exchange-rate problem], esp. p. 123 (*Ekonomisk Tidskrift*, 1920) and Wicksell, "De skandinaviska kronorna" [The Scandinavian Crowns] (*Ekonomisk Tidskrift*, 1925) [translated as an appendix to *Interest and Prices*, London, 1936].

tions, but rather by industrial organization, shifts in the exchange structure, etc., and it is not expedient, therefore, to discuss them in terms of "the velocity of circulation of money." It is an entirely different matter that the responses of the money and banking system, such as an increase in the stock of notes in circulation, may bring about changes in credit policies significantly influencing the later course of events.

Simple quantity-theoretical formulae ignoring the timing of events may serve as an overview. But many problems will completely elude such schematic treatment. In any event it will still remain to treat the development of separate categories of the price system, classified according to its exchange and time structure, and to allow for the time sequence of the changes.

As examples of parts of such an analysis some cases of rising and falling prices will now be examined.

## IV. *An Analysis of Some Price Movements*

§7. *A process of rising prices*. A price change implies that demand is changing in a different way from supply. There may be a multitude of reasons why this may happen to a single good. The same applies to a group of goods. From the point of view of monetary policy an interesting case is the autonomous reduction of the rate of interest by the central bank (both the discount rate and the bond rate) in a situation in which (1) various price indices have remained the same for some time and (2) the productive capacity of most industries is not fully utilized. Under such circumstances what are the effects of the reduction of the rate of interest?

Investment in durable capital goods will appear more profitable; demand for such goods $V^{i}$ will rise, and their prices $p^{i}$ will tend to rise. As a result output will rise by better utilization of productive capacity. Demand for labor will also rise, i.e., more workers are employed, and productive capacity is better utilized. Furthermore, demand for raw materials and semifinished goods for capital goods ($V^{ir}$) is growing; prices of such raw materials and semifinished goods tend to rise.

This process implies that not only gross revenue but also net income is growing. For one thing, more labor is employed, raising the total wage bill; for another, business income is up, both because of better utilization of durable capital goods and natural resources and because of the tendency of prices to rise.

The probable effect of higher net income is growing demand ($K$) for consumers' goods in retail trade. Retailer demand ($V^{k}$) will be growing more or less in proportion—if wholesale prices of consumers' goods ($p^k$) begin to rise, probably more than in proportion. Output ($v^k$) will rise and, often somewhat later, a price increase (higher $p^k$) will materialize. Retail prices ($p^d$) will rise, usually still later.

The increasing demand for consumers' goods will quickly call forth increasing demand for raw materials and semifinished goods. Demand ($V^{kr}$) is rising, and so is probably the quantity ($v^{kr}$): rising prices ($p^{kr}$) will be the result. The price increase will very likely occur at a time when the increased demand for consumers' goods in retail trade has not yet raised retail prices of goods of which inventory is carried, but has so far merely increased the demand of retailers and manufacturers. Such demand increase is not caused by an anticipation of rising wholesale prices of consumers' goods ($p^k$) but will of course be magnified to the extent such an anticipation exists. Even without an increase in finished-goods prices, expanding output will improve profitability because overhead costs per unit of output are being reduced by rising sales. Needless to say, what applies to a finished-goods manufacturer with respect to his raw materials will apply to any producer with respect to his earlier stages of production.

As a result of all this, the acquisition of capital goods serving the production of consumers' goods, as well as raw materials and semifinished goods for the latter, will look even more profitable than before. Demand for capital goods and their corresponding raw materials and semifinished goods is growing further, and price movements are further strengthened. The demand for capital goods to produce capital goods and their raw materials and semifinished goods is certainly growing, too.

How profitable the acquisition of new durable capital goods will appear, and how much their prices will be pushed up, are of course highly dependent upon the wage rates generated by the process described. If wage rates are rising by the same percentage in all industries, new machines, etc., will become more profitable in consumers' goods industries than if at the same overall wage increase only an insignificant wage increase has occurred in those industries.

Simple rules about the strength of price movements at various points hardly apply.[20] But a valid generalization on timing would perhaps be that during the early part of a period of rising prices every producer and middleman will demand goods in excess of his sales, so demand and price will tend to be growing more rapidly for raw ma-

20. Lindahl gives his reader an impression of a precision not at all corresponding to reality. See *Penningpolitikens medel*, ch. 2.

terials, i.e., goods at earlier stages, than for finished manufactures. The growth of demand will be accelerating "backwards." Notice in particular that, for example, the price of durable capital goods turning raw materials into semifinished goods relative to the price differential between raw materials and semifinished goods will depend not only upon the level of other processing costs but also, among other things, upon expected future price relations. For changes in that relation, then, no simple rule will hold. The capital good is going to serve in future periods, too, and expectations differ in different circumstances. Given present and anticipated cost-price relations, elements of price rigidity may give rise to price differences interpreted as positive or negative present net worth of new plant.

Certainly the market value of existing plant and titles to it (corporate stock) will rise. Business income prospects for the future will be more optimistic, because variable costs usually are rising less rapidly than prices (the wage lag) and because overhead costs per unit produced are falling. Such income prospects for the future are discounted to the present by applying discount rates lowered by the reduction of the rate of interest. The income prospects are a matter of expectations. Such expectations may be very vague, and the present worth of capital goods arrived at by discounting them is therefore rarely quantitatively fixed. All one can say is that, to every stockholder, it will exceed the book value of his stock. For the analysis of the pricing of goods and services in the process of production and distribution all this is of merely indirect significance. But it may be of interest per se because it illuminates other aspects of pricing.

In summary, net income is rising due to (a) increasing output and rising prices of consumers' goods, (b) increasing output (beyond acquisitions for replacement) and rising prices of capital goods, and (c) possibly rising inventory of other goods. Furthermore, income as recorded in accounting is rising because capital goods and inventory enter the balance sheet at higher prices in the closing balance than in the opening one. Such a price difference may not, from certain points of view, be income, but it is treated as such in accounting and hence considered as such by the business community.

If it is generally assumed that the reduced rate of interest has come to stay, i.e., a further reduction is considered as likely as an increase; and if there are no reasons to expect long-run investments to become less profitable than at current price relations, then the prices of capital goods are up relative to those of consumers' goods, i.e., the former prices are rising more rapidly than the latter. This is the result not only of the reduction of the rate of interest but also, often overlooked, of the better utilization of the capacity of capital goods, which—if not considered temporary—does make long-term investments appear more profitable. Under such assumptions about expectations, the prices of capital goods, and probably also of the raw material and semifinished goods going into them, will have risen relatively more than the prices of consumers' goods over the entire process of rising prices; i.e., the former have run ahead of the latter. The tendency to increasing output of capital goods will generate increasing income in the capital-goods industries, which, in turn, will increase the demand for consumers' goods, as well as the income generated in the consumers' goods industries. Real investment will then appear even more profitable, and demand for capital goods will rise even further, etc. The price system is spiraling upwards. Notice that the process does not imply any actual *relative* enlargement of real investment, i.e., a different direction of production. Lindahl's conclusion to the contrary—emphasized by Myrdal—follows from his very special assumption that businessmen expect current prices of consumers' goods and capital goods to continue. Under such expectations no income increase could occur in capital goods industries unless the direction of production changed.[21]

Under plausible assumptions, the rising prices of capital goods imply that the prices of the semifinished goods and raw materials in the capital goods industries will be rising more rapidly than those of the consumers' goods industries, unless the elasticities of supply are very different and special. If the rising prices continue for so long that virtually all labor is employed, labor may possibly migrate from consumers' goods industries to capital goods industries. If, on the other hand, after prices have been rising for a while, the price relations so favorable to long-term investment are no longer expected to last, demand for capital goods may be rising less rapidly than demand for consumers' goods, and labor may migrate in the opposite direction. No price relation between different industries common to all cases of rising prices will be found to exist. At the risk of some repetition we shall illuminate this by discussing a case different from the autonomous reduction of the rate of interest.

Rising prices in general[22] imply that the demand for goods and

21. See *Penningpolitikens medel*, p. 35.

22. Meaning a rising price level as measured by a general price index for sales of new goods and services in a period, i.e., an average of the price index numbers mentioned in §4; weights are in accordance with quantities sold. In the following pages, wherever the term "price level" appears without qualifications it should be understood in this sense.

services is rising more rapidly than the quantities supplied. *One* possibility is that so many entrepreneurs find immediate real investment profitable that investment is growing (to such entrepreneurs the difference between the subjective capital value and the estimated cost of real investment is positive and not expected to become larger in the future). Another possibility is that demand for consumers' goods is rising. The necessary and sufficient condition for a process of rising prices is that the sum of those two kinds of demand is rising relative to output.

The present section will assume output to expand in response to growing demand. Even without growing demand for investment purposes, rising prices are possible if demand for consumption purposes is growing. This assumes that improving profitability prospects will fail to raise many more subjective capital values over the rising cost of real investment than before.[23] Such an assumption may be satisfied if many entrepreneurs considering long-term investments expect profitability to deteriorate in the future, for example, because they expect the price rise to be interrupted or expect costs to rise rapidly. In other words, demand for long-term investment purposes may conceivably be falling in the face of rising consumers' goods prices. By contrast, unless the business community is expecting immediately falling prices, there will usually be a growing demand for short-term investment purposes like purchases by retailers or purchases by manufacturers of semifinished goods.

Admittedly a general price index may be rising in the face of falling or stationary investment demand only for a shorter period—for example, during several months of doubt in the business community bringing price increases of durable goods to a halt, while prices of less durable goods keep rising. In most cases the expansion of demand will apply both to consumers' goods and to short-term and long-term investment, but the prices of long-term investment may very well be rising *less rapidly* than those of consumers' goods. In other words, prices may well keep rising even though the prices of consumers' goods are ahead, while the prices of producers' goods are lagging behind. The assumption must be the entrepreneurial expectations mentioned above. What generates the upward movement of prices may, for example, be the sharp reduction of the intention to save discussed above (§6). Demand for consumers' goods will then rise, and their prices rise, thus expanding employment and perhaps raising

23. More precisely, the condition is that the sum of investments whose present net worth is positive and cannot be raised by delaying the investment is not growing.

the wages of the workers producing consumers' goods at various stages. In such industries the incomes of both labor and entrepreneurs will rise, and the demand for consumers' goods will further expand. In this situation demand will rise for durable capital goods and indirectly for other capital goods, their prices will tend to rise, capacity will be better utilized, and incomes shoot upwards. This will, in turn, generate expanded consumption demand, which feeds new investment demand, etc. If wages are flexible (for example, indexed), if entrepreneurs are realizing that the improved profitability manifesting itself in their accounting is to some extent "fictitious," merely depending on closing-balance values being expressed in money of less purchasing power than opening-balance values, and if, finally, entrepreneurs expect rising prices to be of limited duration, being followed by falling ones, then the structure of price movements just discussed is by no means unlikely.[24] A price rise of this type need not at all be less rapid than that of the other type.

Admittedly, at certain phases the prices of long-run investment (new durable capital goods) are usually rising more rapidly than are the prices of consumers' goods. But at certain phases prices of raw materials and semifinished goods going into capital goods will be rising most rapidly of all, not because purchases of such goods constitute a *longer*-term investment (in the Austrian sense) but because of the phenomenon pointed out above, i.e., that the growth of demand will be accelerating backwards. For the same reason prices of short-run investments (raw materials for consumers' goods, e.g., cotton, wool, wheat, hides) will sometimes rise very rapidly. To offer simple rules for the relative magnitude of price movements is impossible. A study of the conditions for the generation of investment demand should also allow for the profitability prospects of short-run investment, e.g., in inventory, and should not confine itself solely to the relation between cost and subjective value of durable capital goods, which, as shown above has a rather elastic tie to the rate of interest and the prices of consumers' goods. One should not, by the way, forget that the elasticity of supply responses differs for different goods, but this is not to be explored in the present paper.

As already pointed out, price changes of older capital goods have an indirect significance for the demand for newly produced goods and

24. The reasons why Wicksell and his followers concluded that producers' goods must lead the cumulative price movement were that (1) they concentrated their attention on the special case of an autonomous reduction of the rate of interest (see, e.g., Myrdal, "Om penningteoretisk jämvikt," §43), (2) they assumed wages, and with them consumption demand, to be rigid.

services flowing into and out of the process of production. In certain cases, houses for example, the tie between the values of older and newer units is close. But in other cases, older units are not priced separately, but enter as component parts of an entire firm; this is true of machines, for example. The pricing of entire firms materializes in the market value of corporate stock plus liabilities adjusted for changes on the asset side of the balance sheet. In times of generally rising prices such values of firms usually rise, but rarely more rapidly than the prices of consumers' goods.[25] Among other things, wage trends and expectations are decisive; the value of a firm represents a capitalization of nonlabor income. Continually rising prices of goods are not incompatible with upward and downward fluctuations of the value of a firm.

Clearly, variations in the values of firms have only a very indirect tie to investment demand. New firms acquiring their entire equipment are not in all respects comparable to old firms; and the major part of real investment does not consist of the formation of new firms, but rather of investment in replacement and expansion by old firms.

Everything taken into account, it seems clear that the development of price relations is far more varied than is claimed by neo-Wicksellian theory (Lindahl's, as well as Hayek's), resting on a rather one-sided consideration of the tendency of a reduction of the rate of interest to raise certain capital values. The same is presumably true of the development of price relations under assumptions not treated above.

Finally, a word should be added on the so-called "forced saving," supposedly generated by rising prices. Generally rising prices probably in most cases imply that the output of real capital is larger than it would have been under price stability. From the point of view of saving, the larger real capital formation is primarily caused by the fact that persons whose incomes are growing, first, for a while may be underestimating the growth of their incomes (stockholders do not know the profits of the current year) and, second, may wish to save a larger share of their profits than before. In certain cases they are almost forced to do so, because firms may be concealing part of their profits. On the other hand, the saving of persons whose incomes are not growing is reduced because of rising costs of living, but it is easy to imagine that the tendency to reduce saving is weaker than the

25. Considering changes on the supply side, an approximately exact measure of the value of firms is not within reach. It is doubtful whether even in 1918 values of firms were rising more rapidly than prices of consumers' goods.

tendency to raise it. It is somewhat misleading to describe saving under rising prices as "forced saving."

An essential distinction holds between the case in which investment is growing because, to begin with, individuals decide to save a larger share of their income and that share is then invested and, on the other hand, the case in which investment demand grows, under an unchanged intention to save. Here, credit expansion, a higher velocity of circulation, and rising prices will follow. Hand in hand with these things, saving will be rising. Differences in the timing of investment decisions and saving decisions will result in different price movements. But to me things are not clarified by saying that in case 2 investment exceeds saving.

§8. *A process of falling prices*. A process of rising prices must come to a halt either because of declining demand for some group of goods or because of some rapid expansion of supply, for example, the dumping of inventory into the market.

In many cases the shock originates in a reduction of $V^i$, quickly pulling a reduction of $V^{ir}$ with it. The circumstances underlying such a reduction of $V^i$ are a major problem of business-cycle theory, but will not be discussed in the present essentially formal analysis. Profitability may deteriorate and subjective capital values fall for a thousand and one reasons without anyone knowing exactly by how much they have fallen.[26]

The reduced output and declining price of capital goods and the raw materials and semifinished goods going into them will reduce net income and with it consumption demand ($K$), but not necessarily in the same proportion. The result is a reduced output of consumers' goods and a tendency to falling prices, rapidly spreading to several raw materials and semifinished goods. Under these circumstances the profitability of real investment is reduced, and $V^i$ and $V^{ir}$ will fall further.

A detailed analysis of different processes of falling prices would be redundant, since the earlier reasoning applies *mutatis mutandis*. Only one aspect, capital consumption, will have to be considered.

If the price fall is sharp and protracted, the output of capital goods

26. It would hardly be practical to force an analysis of all such circumstances into an analysis of a discrepancy between some natural rate or profit rate and the money rate of interest. Declining "confidence" in the future cannot be put into a calculating machine grinding out how much the natural rate of interest has been reduced. To try to fix quantitatively the present net worth of a planned investment serves no good purpose. It will suffice to observe quantitative changes in demand. See Part VII, below.

may fall short of what is considered to be depreciation of fixed capital. In addition, inventory may be falling. In such cases capital is wearing down. Even though depressed, consumption is in excess of net income.

Looking at the behavior of individuals and firms, we observe, first, that many firms have negative profits. Second, some individuals have no income or very small income and hence are consciously eating up past savings. Third, owners may have no clear conception of the decline of their share of profits. By eating up corporate dividends paid out of last year's profits but exceeding this year's, stockholders are, in effect, eating up past savings.

In practice the reduction of real investment implies an equally large reduction of new investment; since depreciation of fixed capital is hardly reduced, prevailing accounting principles consider reinvestment to be almost as large as before. The reduction of new investment equals the reduction of net new saving. The latter is the sum of all new saving (gross saving) minus consumption credits and negative incomes. Partly, the latter are generated by the decline of real investment. In addition, individual incomes and with them gross saving are declining. The decline of net new saving is the result of both tendencies.[27]

Growing negative incomes and declining individual incomes are two sides of the same process, i.e., declining net income. How much of the latter is to be classified as declining individual income and how much as growing negative income depends on, among other things, industrial organization, e.g., wage flexibility. In a study of a process of deflation both matters deserve attention.

Had purchases been larger, losses would have been smaller and the sum of individual incomes larger. A definite opportunity for an expansion of demand restoring monetary equilibrium, as claimed to exist by Wicksellian theory, will not be found. The more demand is rising, the more positive incomes will rise and negative incomes fall.

27. A process of deflation is characterized not only by the fact that part of gross saving is offset by negative incomes but fully as much by a declining gross saving.—The idea expressed in Wicksellian theory by saying that investment is falling short of saving in my own terminology by no means implies an investment demand so low that negative incomes are generated, reducing net saving below gross saving. Notice that negative incomes occur even under rising prices; consequently, investment *always* falls short of gross saving.—In a discussion [Carl] Iversen has claimed that my "gross saving" is identical to what Scandinavian economists used to mean by "saving," when discussing lack of equality between saving and investment. But that cannot be true, for investment supposedly may *exceed* saving. In Wicksell and others it must surely be some kind of *net saving* which in periods of falling prices is falling short of new investment.

Output and prices are rising simultaneously, the former up to a certain point.

When prices have been falling for a while, investment demand and consumption demand may stop falling and the price fall come to an end. The reason may be that consumption demand cannot easily contract beyond a certain point, and its resilience will check the tendency to declining investment demand. But if the resilient consumption demand is caused by wage rigidity, thus jeopardizing profitability prospects, investment demand may well fall more than it would have done had consumption demand contracted further. To analyze alternative cases of this type is one of the most urgent tasks of business-cycle theory.

Neo-Wicksellian theory habitually expresses as follows the conditions for an interruption of the price decline. Since investment is too low relative to saving, either more must be invested or less saved. But such reasoning is conclusive only if income is thought of as given and independent of what is happening within the period.[28] In that case, the alternatives laid down simply imply an increase of either investment demand or consumption demand. But if income is falling, aggregate demand and prices may fall. A correct formulation would quite simply be that the price fall will tend to be ending whenever aggregate demand is growing relative to supply.

What is the effect of a higher intention to save, i.e., a reduction of the fraction of income spent on consumption?

Keynes' theory attaches great weight to the fact that even if the increased saving is fully invested, i.e., if there is a reduction of consumption demand and an increase of investment demand, prices of consumers' goods will surely fall, but those of capital goods will not necessarily rise. Presumably the latter are determined quite differently from the former.

Such a paradoxical conclusion arises because the term "fully invested" is taken to include purchases of *non-newly produced* capital goods even when the sellers of these goods fail to spend their sales proceeds on investment. The term thus includes both true investment and an "investment transfer." Applying my own terminology, it is clear that from the point of view of pricing of the flow of newly

28. Behind such an implicit assumption we find the hidden idea that the income disposable for demand in a period partly depends upon the production of the preceding period. This was the idea underlying Scandinavian postwar discussion of monetary theory. Hammarskjöld's analysis and extension of that idea thus represents a smaller deviation from Wicksell than do the formulations by Keynes, Lindahl, Myrdal, and myself. Cf. §3 above.

produced capital goods, a reduction of investment demand has occurred; part of gross waiting has given rise to no true investment demand at all but merely to an investment transfer. Negative incomes are being generated, and the net supply of waiting is reduced relative to the gross supply.

Price formation of capital goods is influenced, then, not only by the subjective capital values of those who demand and own newly produced units of capital goods but also by the subjective capital values of owners of older units of capital goods. Whenever the latter fall below market prices, the older units will be sold. Such supply of older units will affect the pricing of new ones by influencing the demand for the latter via the size of gross waiting and the share of it constituting net waiting.

To a lesser extent the same is true of the pricing of other kinds of goods of which inventory is carried and may be dumped on the market.

Such questions are thus easily treated without changing the formal monetary theory scheme offered above.[29]

A much disputed question is what happens in a process of falling prices if the intention to save is reduced and consumption demand ($K$) increased. Wholesale prices of consumers' goods ($p^k$) and of raw materials and semifinished goods related to them ($p^{kr}$) will tend to rise. But what happens to the demand for capital goods and to their prices? The answer must, of course, depend upon expectations, i.e., views on profitability prospects held by entrepreneurs and potential buyers of durable consumers' goods. Profitability prospects are very likely judged to be improving, and investment demand is higher than it would otherwise have been. If the tendency toward increasing demand is strong enough to more than offset existing downward tendencies, i.e., if investment demand is increasing, then the prices of capital goods as well as consumers' goods must go up.

Rising consumption demand does not at all mean falling net saving, which equals new real investment. On the contrary. Aggregate demand and gross income will be rising *more* rapidly than consumption demand. Consequently, gross saving will be rising while negative incomes are falling. Net saving, then, will be rising for a twofold reason.

It appears that measures which will expand or reduce demand at

29. Anyone who wishes to do so may think through the opposite process in which holders of bank deposits exchange the latter for capital goods, thus raising the prices of old and new units of such goods. From the point of view of the market for new units, this implies a rising investment demand.

one point in the price system, if not offset by changing demand at other points, will tend to push the entire price system upward or downward. Only a closer examination can clarify the conditions under which, say, expanding demand at one point (i.e., expanding one of the *V*'s) will induce decreased demand at a different point and thus set off a counteracting force. In other words, relations among changes of various kinds of demand (*V* and *K*) are important, not just changes in aggregate demand. Certain kinds of expanding demand, influencing the direction of production, probably carry in them the seeds of a reversal, e.g., a reduction of investment demand. A case-by-case study is called for, allowing for, among other things, situations differing with respect to unused capacity and higher or lower degrees of price rigidity. Such a study should not overlook the significance of various economic policy measures, monetary policy as well as fiscal and other policies. A study of such phenomena is a primary task for a business-cycle theory studying both "monetary" and "real economic" forces and integrating them into a unified theory.

## V. *The Rate of Interest*

§9. The conclusions emerging from the preceding analysis have far-reaching implications for the theory of interest, and they deserve emphasis. According to the static theory of distribution the rate of interest is determined by the supply of and the demand for saving. By Wicksell and later by Cassel such a rate of interest was identified with the rate guaranteeing monetary equilibrium, i.e., keeping the price level constant. This very integration of distribution theory with monetary theory has been considered one of Wicksell's most valuable accomplishments.

If, as we did above, we apply an equilibrium concept similar to that of conventional price theory, we shall always have equilibrium in the capital market, i.e., between waiting and investment, regardless of how the central bank fixes the money rate of interest. In contrast to legislation fixing a ceiling rate of interest and similar interference in pricing having the same effect as ceiling prices of goods, the central bank interferes by affecting not merely price but also supply of and demand for credit.

If under otherwise equal circumstances the central bank fixes an essentially higher interest structure in one case than in another, price developments will certainly differ. Consequently, income, saving, and investment will differ. Per se, one interest structure is no more normal than the other. As we have said, any rate of interest indicates equilibrium in the capital market simply because net saving and investment always adjust so as to be equal.

Assume that different interest rates are quoted in the capital market for different kinds of loan transactions and that those rates alone regulate supply and demand. How are their levels determined? What is being supplied and demanded are rights to dispose of sums of money. A supplier is anybody who wishes to lend money he has received in one of two ways, (1) by selling older capital goods, securities, titles, and the like, or (2) by selling goods and services on their way in the flow of the production process. The latter source of supply equals the part of gross revenue not financing current consumption. Certainly part of this waiting is demanded for reinvestment by those supplying it, and to that extent no lending transaction is taking place.

At first sight, transactions listed under item (1) might seem unable to affect the level of the interest rates. Each transaction generates as much demand for capital disposal as supply of it or, more correctly expressed, supply is transferred from one person to another. This, however, may shift supply curves of various kinds of capital disposal—long-term and short-term, for example—and with them the rates of interest. Even if there were only a single rate of interest, it could be affected, for the holder of money always has the choice between supplying it and hoarding it. (Cf. what was said above on the pricing of capital goods.)

The reason why every interest rate is an equilibrium rate is that the more the credit demand and lending are expanding, the more the sources of waiting listed under item (2) are growing (except to the extent that new means of payment are borrowed for hoarding). The question is merely how prices and quantities transacted will develop under alternative interest policies, given the assumptions on the intention to save and the like.

That the rate of interest plays a major role in determining the demand for investment was uncovered by Wicksell's analysis founded on that of Böhm-Bawerk. Already the Classicists realized the fact but did not examine the nature of the relationship. Such a fact finds its place just as well in the present formulation of monetary theory and has nothing at all to do with the concept of a "normal" rate of interest.

If it is desired to call one particular price development more "stable" than others, then the interest policy generating it will of course appear more "normal" than a policy leading to sharply rising or sharply falling prices. In other words, if a deflation such as that of 1931 is considered "unnatural," then the accompanying interest policy will also be unnatural; measures designed to lower interest rates and to counteract deflation will not be "artificial," but on the contrary make interest policy more natural. Which interest rate is natural can—from the point of departure mentioned—be judged only by the resulting price development.

The philosophy of science offers no reason why price movements or anything else should be singled out for special attention. What matters is simply what one finds it practical to mean by "stable" and "normal" in economic life (see §3 above). An analysis of dynamic processes based upon the conceptual apparatus of the monetary theory described above is not tied down by the introduction of notions of monetary equilibrium and a corresponding interest policy. Such notions are dangerous, among other things because they let alternative interest policies appear artificial. What is a natural or an artificial policy can only be judged by examining to what extent the policy will bring within reach economic results which for one reason or another are considered desirable.

### VI. *Conclusion*

§10. In order to test the applicability of the formulation of monetary theory just described we ought now to examine the functioning of alternative monetary mechanisms (money and banking systems) under alternative assumptions and under alternative price movements. But that will have to wait for another time.

The purpose of the present attempt at a formulation of the theory different from the neo-Wicksellian one has been to construct a simpler and more practical conceptual apparatus.[30] Among other things, I have tried:

(1) To get away from the income concept, inapplicable in any statistical analysis, employed by Lindahl and Myrdal.[31]

(2) To hint at a more generally valid but also, if it were to be elaborated further, a more case-by-case-oriented description of price movements than Lindahl's analysis, based on far too special assumptions, of a Wicksellian so-called cumulative

30. We have tried to suggest how the more profound understanding of the nature of price movements gained from Wicksellian theory could be presented, more completely and correctly, in a form easier to handle and lending itself to an analysis of statistical data available, among other places, in business accounting. Those who have become accustomed to Wicksellian terminology will find the latter the simpler one, of course. But a study of the extensions of Wicksellian theory by Hammarskjöld, Lindahl, Keynes, and Myrdal will weaken the belief in its ease of handling.

31. See §12 below.

process. As it turned out, such a process is possible without any redirection of production from consumers' goods to capital goods or vice versa. It also turned out that the former goods could lead the development of price just as well as the latter ones.

(3) To show how the accomplishments of Austrian capital theory concerning the time structure of pricing could be incorporated, more completely than Wicksell did, by an expedient classification of commodity flows enabling us to judge the price trends of the latter by already available or easily computed index numbers. In this way it would become possible to consider within a unified theory the significance of so-called monetary as well as so-called real factors in the business cycle. This would be an attempt to work out one of Wicksell's ideas in a different way than Hayek did.

(4) To make clear that the exchange structure and above all the time sequence of price movements, now attracting so much attention in recent discussion of the present depression, lie at the heart of monetary theory—just like the time-structure analysis of interest, capital values, etc.[32]

(5) To show that the notion of a normal or equilibrium rate of interest found in static price theory is misleading in the analysis of dynamic processes.[33]

For a fully satisfactory solution of these problems, as we have already said, a complete monetary theory would have to be worked out, and its value would have to be tested by a case-by-case analysis using statistical data.

## VII. *Appendix: A Critique of Neo-Wicksellian Monetary Theory*

§11. *The driving force of a price movement.* The question of the driving force behind price movements has been much discussed in monetary theory. Wicksell, Cassel, and Keynes alike appear to find it in a lack of equilibrium in the capital market, and postwar discussions

32. It might seem redundant to make such a point. But the fact is that these points of view have been almost entirely ignored in the standard works on monetary theory.

33. Despite the essential dissimilarities between Lindahl's formulation and my own—and their results—there can be no doubt that his *Penningpolitikens medel* has heavily influenced my exposition above, especially with respect to item (5). To some extent the same is true of Myrdal's *Prisbildningsproblemet och föränderligheten* [The Problem of Price Formation and Changeability] and to a large extent of numerous oral discussions with him. Sven Brisman's critical examination of galley proofs has clarified a number of points.

have generally accepted this point of view. Let us look a little closer at the meaning of this conception of a driving force.

A wholesale price index of the usual kind will be rising because the demand for goods in wholesale trade is rising relative to supply. For simplicity's sake assume the latter to remain largely unchanged for a period. Then prices are rising because the sum of the demand for capital goods and consumers' goods is rising. Alternative cases are conceivable: (1) both categories of demand are rising; (2) one category is rising while the other is unchanged; (3) one category is rising more than the other is falling.

What are the circumstances influencing investment demand? A great many, of course. A businessman purchasing a machine or building a structure expects it to bring him more than it costs. Its subjective capital value, determined by his expectations, exceeds its cost. Thus he is counting on a positive present net worth. This is certainly a necessary but not a sufficient condition for the purchase to materialize. He may, for example, anticipate a future reduction of the cost (price) of the good, but no corresponding fall in its subjective value. In that case he will postpone his purchase. The same is true if he expects the subjective capital value of a later time to be larger without a corresponding increase in cost. For example, even when unable to fully utilize this capacity, an entrepreneur may wish to take advantage of current low prices to expand his capital equipment. But he will postpone his purchase if he expects the subjective capital value to be rising (because an expansion now would not generate revenue until later) while expecting no offsetting increase in cost.

As for demand for consumers' goods in retail trade, it will depend, among other things, upon individual conceptions of current and future income. But it will also be affected by individual conceptions of the status of assets. Finally notice that consumption demand depends upon expected prices; for example, an anticipated price fall may have a restraining effect on purchases.

Furthermore, it must be emphasized that, in order to purchase, one must either dispose of money or purchase on credit. Many individuals wishing to purchase for investment or consumption purposes do not satisfy these conditions. An individual wishing to borrow for consumption or investment may be unable to put up adequate collateral and hence is unable to purchase. The reason why aggregate demand is growing in a period is that all such factors, psychological and others, are making it grow.

To say with Cassel and Wicksell that prices are rising because lending is exceeding saving and hence aggregate demand is growing, is a far from satisfactory formulation—as Myrdal has shown. In my own terminology the underlying idea may be expressed as follows. Economic conditions like credit terms and expectations are making demand grow relative to supply. No explanation of why this is happening is offered by referring to the relative amount of credit. An explanation must include an account of the factors influencing various components of the demand for goods. It is debatable whether, when treating certain problems such as questions of discount policy, it may be said that demand is rising because credit policy is satisfying the condition that demand is rising; that is what Wicksell and Cassel are saying. To say so may be expedient in certain cases, because credit policy is something that can readily be modified. But certainly no new element of an explanation has been provided by such a statement. One merely succeeds in calling attention to the particular fact that a change in credit policy may produce a change in demand and price movements. On the other hand, in other cases this may be a disadvantage. Which terminology is the better may in the present context be left open. The main point is that even when revised, completed, and complicated in Myrdal's way, the talk about lack of equilibrium in the capital market as the cause of rising prices, i.e., as the "driving force," explains nothing more than saying that demand for investment purposes or for consumption or both is growing relative to the flow of production of goods and services. No matter which terminology is used, special cases will equally require further illumination. When one is providing such illumination, it serves no good purpose to press the analysis of several kinds of demand changes into the straitjacket of seeing everything in terms of the relation between a "normal" rate and the actual money rate. Such a terminological straitjacket would seem impractical if, for example, any form of credit rationing were applied or if loans were refused because bankers were taking a pessimistic view of the quality of collateral offered.

§12. *Is statistical observation of Myrdal's monetary equilibrium possible?* For a judgment of the most practical terminology, available opportunities for statistical observation may be relevant. As Myrdal himself points out, theory should pose the questions that might be answered by the data.

How do three alternative ways of formulating a modified Wicksellian monetary equilibrium condition stand up, i.e. (1) equality between the supply of and the demand for waiting, (2) equality between the normal rate and the money rate of interest, (3) a price level satisfying certain conditions?

Let me start with the last formulation. An analysis of the first two conditions has led Myrdal to the conclusion that they will be satisfied if the stable price level is of a special kind: "According to the two equilibrium conditions analyzed earlier, the 'price level' to be stabilized in order to maintain monetary equilibrium under the impact of primary changes in the conditions of price formation would be the expression of general price movements to be found from an index computation weighing individual prices by, first, their relative importance in entrepreneurial profitability estimates and, second, their specific inverse speeds of reaction."[34] The complete impossibility of computing such an index is apparent. Consequently, from a study of actual price trends one would never be able to find their relation to monetary equilibrium as defined above. For that reason Myrdal falls back on an alternative expression of monetary equilibrium, i.e., "equality between capital values and the cost of reproduction of real capital." This expression is derived from the required equality between the normal rate and the money rate of interest—magnitudes that cannot be captured statistically. Index numbers would, then, have to be computed for both items of the alternative expression. Should "these index series run parallel, monetary equilibrium would prevail. Divergence between them would reflect a divergence between money rate and natural rate."[35] The question arises: "How does one handle the case, regularly encountered, in which *the profitability divergence differs among firms* or is even positive in one firm and negative in another? What principle may be offered for weighing divergences between our indices in different industries?"[36] "The weighing . . . should be done in accordance with *the effects, estimated in money terms, of the divergence upon the magnitude of real investment*. The weights would vary from one industry to another and would also vary with the sign, width, and trend of the divergence. The correct way to get at such *elasticity coefficients of real investment with respect to profitability changes* would be a statistical study of industry behavior over the business cycle."[37]

Evidently such coefficients would refer solely to the situation at a certain time. The weights would have to be done over every time one had observed how real investment had developed in the immediate past and one would be trying to estimate how the profitability divergences would now be affecting investment plans. In other words,

34. Myrdal, "Om penningteoretisk jämvikt," §26 [cf. *Monetary Equilibrium*, 1939, pp. 136–137; in this, §§39–41 have been omitted].

35. Ibid., §39.

36. Ibid., §40.

37. Ibid.

from observed changes in investment one would draw inferences about changes in a divergence index defying statistical observation. What purpose is then served by the construction of such an index? It conveys nothing more than a summing of investment plans. A certain value of it would not at all indicate that some cumulative process was on its way.

Presumably the idea pursued in such language is that as long as a divergence index has a certain value, e.g., as long as planned saving is falling short of planned new investment, a price movement will continue. It would be simpler to say that as long as the sum of planned investment demand and consumption demand exceeded planned supply, the price level would be rising. But such a statement amounts to referring to a point of time that which might more simply, and more amenably to statistical analysis, be referred to a period of time; i.e., as long as aggregate demand is rising relative to aggregate supply, the price level will be rising.

Myrdal seems to be aware of the impossibility of computing a divergence index, for he proceeds to discuss the possibility of statistically observing waiting and real investment, i.e., the relation between them. Notice that in his terminology these terms refer to human plans for the future; waiting is the part of expected future gross revenue not to be spent on current consumption. For his equilibrium criteria not to become practically useless Myrdal must adopt the optimistic position that "beyond question, relatively simple observations could make available statistical data capable of illuminating how the important relation between the magnitudes real investment and free waiting is developing."[38] I for one have difficulty seeing how such magnitudes, existing only in the human mind, could possibly lend themselves to statistical observation. The conclusion must be that in any actual situation, such as now, no one can establish whether or not monetary equilibrium in Myrdal's sense is prevailing. Myrdal's reconstruction of Wicksellian theory does not, it seems to me, satisfy his own requirement of all theory, i.e., that theory should provide the questions answered by the data. However, we should be grateful for his mapping of the paths and the results to which a consistent extension of one variety of Wicksellian thought would lead. In my view the result is such as to urge us to explore alternative paths that we could follow without losing the large domains won by Wicksell's formulation.

38. Ibid., §41.

# [2]

*History of Political Economy 10:3*


# Substantive changes in the final version of Ohlin's 1933 paper

*Otto Steiger*

Until recently, it was widely believed that Bertil Ohlin's paper appearing in the summer of 1933 was strongly influenced by the publication in March and April of Keynes' *The Means to Prosperity*.[1] Thanks to an early draft of the article found in the papers of the late Professor Erik Lindahl, we now know that Ohlin's ideas had been worked out in virtually identical form to the published version no later than February 26, 1933, so that he could not have been influenced by Keynes' pamphlet.[2] In my 1976 article, I gave page references for all the major revisions, additions, and deletions in the final version of "Till frågan om penningteoriens uppläggning" vis-à-vis the earlier draft, which was entitled "Till penningteoriens centralproblem" (On the Central Problems of Monetary Theory). I did not, however, reproduce any of these changes. The most significant ones appear in Tables 1, 2, and 3 below.

OTTO STEIGER *is Professor of Economics at the University of Bremen.* *He acknowledges the assistance of William P. Yohe in the organization of his material for publication.*

1. This view had its origin in Karl-Gustav Landgren's book *Den 'nya ekonomien' i Sverige* (The "New Economics" in Sweden) (Stockholm, 1960), ch. 8.
2. Otto Steiger, "Bertil Ohlin and the Origins of the Keynesian Revolution," *History of Political Economy* 8 (1976): 353–54.

*Table 1.* Major revisions in Ohlin's 1933 paper

| 1932 DRAFT | 1933 FINAL VERSION |
| --- | --- |
| Postwar monetary theory—as represented by, e.g., Cassel, Keynes, and Wicksell—has focused on the study of equilibrium in the capital market, defined as agreement between saving and real investment. It has been assumed that such an equilibrium would keep the price level constant, whereas a rise in the price level would be the result of the fact that *more* money was placed at the disposal of the demand for capital goods, i.e., real investment, than corresponded simultaneously to current saving. A price fall would follow from the opposite situation. The interest rate which produces equilibrium in the capital market has been denoted as normal. Sometimes it has been assumed to conform to the marginal productivity of real capital, usually designated as the natural or real rate of interest. [P. 1 of script.] | What characterizes Wicksell's formulation of monetary theory is, first, that changes in the general price level are treated in the same way as changes in the prices of individual goods, and above all, second, the introduction of the concept of monetary equilibrium defined as the equality between saving and new investment; the equilibrating rate of interest is designated as normal and is assumed to conform to the real or natural rate, which is equal to the marginal productivity of capital in an economy without money.<br>Among these notions, the path-breaking concept which left its mark on postwar monetary theory is the lack of equality between saving and new investment as the "cause" of general price movements. In this respect there is agreement between the two leading participants in the monetary theory debate of the last decade, Cassel and Keynes. A rising price level results from the availability of credit, demanding capital goods, i.e., real investment, in excess of current saving. Falling prices result from the opposite situation. The rate of interest which generates equilibrium in the capital market is called normal. [Pp. 353–54; page numbers refer to the translation above.] |
| But that is true of any procedure and will play but a modest role in the price analysis persistently built on change of demand[i] and presented in the following. | But that is true of any procedure and will play merely a modest role in the price analysis to be presented. [P. 354–55.] |

[i]This change depends in the first hand on expectations about the future, of course, which thus become a central

| | |
|---|---|
| instrument in price analysis. It is the merit of Myrdal to have emphasized this aspect. [P. 2 of script.] | |
| The flow of all other goods is equal to the flow of waiting, new and freed. [P. 6 of script.] | The flow of all other goods is always equal to the flow of waiting, new and freed—*even if the money supply is changing*. [P. 357.] |
| $I^p_x = U_x = P_x = K_x + V_x \cdot$ [P. 6 of script.] | $I^p_x = U_x = K_x + V_x \cdot$ [P. 357.] |
| —should not be changing. [P. 12 of script.] | —perhaps calculated per unit of labor—should not be changing rapidly. [P. 361.] |
| If one wants to study in detail the changes in the mechanism of price formation, one is forced to take into account not only the various price index numbers but corresponding transaction indices, which illuminate the various $V$ as well as $K$; and along with this the various quantity indices ($v$) should, of course, be computed wherever possible. It is also important to know to what extent demand leads to changes in inventory holdings and how these are broken down into producers, distributors, and users. [P. 19 of script.] | In addition to the various price indices and their corresponding transaction indices, quantity indices ($v$) should, of course, be computed wherever possible in order to check the computations of $V$ and $p$. If possible, inventory holdings should be broken down into producers, distributors, and "users." [P. 366.] |
| What purpose is then served by the construction of such an index, which conveys nothing more than the data of real investment that can be observed and added up directly? One does not penetrate deeper into these relations by complicating the problem. [P. 48 of script.] | What purpose is then served by the construction of such an index? It conveys nothing more than a summing up of investment plans. A certain value of it would not at all indicate that some "cumulative" process was on its way. [P. 388.] |

*Table 2.* Major deletions from the 1932 draft

| *In 1932 draft—not in 1933 final version* | *Page number in original (Swedish) script* | *Page number of Sections in Column 1 in translation if not deleted* |
|---|---|---|
| A detailed analysis of this phenomenon would make it necessary to develop a complicated and, in the world of business, very strange system of concepts. The usefulness of this in an analysis of price movements, the central problem of monetary theory, I think is very small. | 2 | 354 |
| On practical grounds usually even "semi-durable" consumption goods are included, for example, shoes and clothing. The division of gross revenue into waiting (demand for investment) and demand for consumption, like the division in freed capital and net income, obviously is rather indeterminate. | 6 | 356 |
| output $= P_x$ | 6 | 357 |
| In making use of the conceptual scheme presented above, the problem cannot be elaborated in this way. Look, e.g., at the development of total expenditures $U_x$. If $U_{x+1} < U_x$, then $I^b_{x+1} < I^b_x$ and $< P_{x+1} < P_x$. (It is very likely that $V_x = V_{x+1}$ and nevertheless $U_{x+1} < U_x$. The fall of expenditures then implies that $K_{x+1} < K_x$, i.e., that consumption demand has fallen.) If expenditures during a period are equal to gross revenues of the *preceding* period ($I^b_x = U_{x+1}$), then $I^b_x = I^b_{x+1}$ and $U_x = U_{x+1}$. | | |
| (e.g., $I^b_x = I^b_{x+1}$ or $I_x = U_x +_1$). | 11 | 359 |
| I cannot discover that the neo-Wicksellian school has given further illumination of these relations by the concept normal rate of interest. | 13 | 362 |
| Furthermore, a fall in investment demand in both sectors of production soon will occur, because a minor sum is paid for wages. | 23 | 369 |

*Table 2.* Major deletions from the 1932 draft (*continued*)

| *In 1932 draft—not in 1933 final version* | *Page number in original (Swedish) script* | *Page number of Sections in Column 1 in translation if not deleted* |
|---|---|---|
| . . . to a unified theory.[1]<br><br>[1]A more detailed discussion of such a theory does not fit into the scope of this essay; its purpose is to demonstrate that a simple approach to monetary theory makes it feasible to treat the important problems, which the neo-Wicksellian school handles by a much more complicated apparatus. The essay does not attempt to solve these problems but wants to describe—for the purpose of exemplification only—some cases of rising and falling prices. | 38 | 381 |
| Many things support characterizing stability by a development which can be assumed to continue for a long time and in the same way without a further change in the situation. In this case one has to obey not only price movement but also quantity changes in different sectors from one point of time to another. Changes in quantities, as well as in prices, can bear the potential for future disturbances, i.e., violent and significant changes. Certain conclusions, however, can in this case be drawn by the relations of prices and costs and quantities, existing at a given moment (data on profitability and percents of unemployment), or rather by the existing plans for investment and consumption demand,[1] for they can bear witness to coming disturbances.<br><br>[1]It is chiefly this aspect which is central in Myrdal's approach to monetary theory. | 40 | 382 |

*Table 3.* Major additions to the 1933 version

| *Additions* | *Page number of addition in translation* |
|---|---|
| To begin with, the term is taken to mean that certain kinds of price changes are excluded for as long as stability prevails. [P. 9 of script.] | 359 |
| Suppose a divergence between revenue and expenditure or between saving and new investment is to be possible and . . . [P. 10 of script.] | 359 |
| A person's expenditure in a period is then considered financed by his income in *that* period or with his capital freed in that period. [P. 11 of script.] | 360 |
| The price stability debate often follows avenues other than those suggested above. [P. 13 of script.] | 361 |
| Whether the degree of price stability is high or low, then, depends upon the relation between certain prices and other, relatively rigid, ones or rather upon the expectations of them.<br>If by stability one means a price situation prevailing for a long time without major change, then one must examine the presence or absence in such a situation of inherent tendencies toward essential price changes. Such an examination must allow not only for price and cost relations but also for quantity relations (such as labor flowing from one industry to another, unemployment rates, etc.) or rather one must allow for planned investment and consumption demand as well as for available factor supply, for such plans could indicate pending price changes.[10] The question is to what extent a certain state of the price system carries in it the seed of more or less violent and significant changes to come.<br>Notice that all states carry in them the seed of some such changes. And notice that a state may continue for some time without major change, even though price and cost relations are such as to make significant changes inevitable. Imagine, for example, a deep depression in which everything is temporarily "frozen." Price instability, then, in the sense used here is not the same as the presence of tendencies toward *immediate* price change.[11] [P. 13 of script.] | 362 |
| Consequently, in a *static* system (on the *time sequence* of price changes, see § 6) . . . [P. 14 of script.] | 363 |
| . . . but according to established accounting methods the falling prices will reduce the profitability of investment and eventually tend to reduce investment demand as well. [P. 23 of script.] | 369 |

*Table 3*. Major additions to the 1933 version (*continued*)

| *Additions* | *Page number of addition in translation* |
| --- | --- |
| An essential distinction holds between the case in which investment is growing because, to begin with, individuals decide to save a larger share of their income, and that share is then invested, and, on the other hand, the case in which investment demand grows under an unchanged intention to save. Here, credit expansion, a higher velocity of circulation, and rising prices will follow. Hand in hand with these things, saving will be rising. Differences in the timing of investment decisions and saving decisions will result in different price movements. But to me, things are not clarified by saying that in case 2 investment exceeds saving. [P. 34 of script.] | 377 |
| Neo-Wicksellian theory habitually expresses as follows the conditions for an interruption of the price decline. Since investment is too low relative to saving, either more must be invested or less saved. But such reasoning is conclusive only if income is thought of as given and independent of what is happening within the period.[28] In that case, the alternatives laid down simply imply an increase of either investment demand or consumption demand. But if income is falling, aggregate demand and prices may fall. A correct formulation would quite simply be that the price fall will tend to be ending whenever aggregate demand is growing relative to supply.<br>What is the effect of a higher intention to save, i.e., a reduction of the fraction of income spent on consumption?<br>Keynes' theory attaches great weight to the fact that even if the increased saving is fully invested, i.e., if there is a reduction of consumption demand and an increase of investment demand, prices of consumers' goods will surely fall, but those of capital goods will not necessarily rise. Presumably the latter are determined quite differently from the former.<br>Such a paradoxical conclusion arises because the term "fully invested" is taken to include purchases of *non-newly produced* capital goods even when the sellers of these goods fail to spend their sales proceeds on investment. The term thus includes both true investment and an "investment transfer." Applying my own terminology, it is clear that from the point of view of pricing of the flow of newly produced capital goods, a reduction of investment demand has occurred; part of gross waiting has given rise to no true investment demand at all but merely to an investment transfer. Negative incomes are being generated, and the net supply of waiting is reduced relative to the gross supply.<br>Price formation of capital goods is influenced, then, not only by the subjective capital values of those who demand | 379–80 |

(*continued*)

*Table 3.* Major additions to the 1933 version (*continued*)

| *Additions* | *Page number of addition in translation* |
|---|---|
| and own newly produced units of capital goods but also by the subjective capital values of owners of older units of capital goods. Whenever the latter fall below market prices, the older units will be sold. Such supply of older units will affect the pricing of new ones by influencing the demand for the latter via the size of gross waiting and the share of it constituting net waiting. To a lesser extent the same is true of the pricing of other kinds of goods of which inventory is carried and may be dumped on the market. Such questions are thus easily treated without changing the formal monetary theory scheme offered above.[29] [P. 37 of script.] | |
| Rising consumption demand does not at all mean falling net saving, which equals new real investment. On the contrary. Aggregate demand and gross income will be rising *more* rapidly than consumption demand. Consequently, gross saving will be rising while negative incomes are falling. Net saving, then, will be rising for a twofold reason. [P. 37 of script.] | 380 |
| That the rate of interest plays a major role in determining the demand for investment was uncovered by Wicksell's analysis founded on that of Böhm-Bawerk. Already the Classicists realized the fact but did not examine the nature of the relationship. Such a fact finds its place just as well in the present formulation of monetary theory and has nothing at all to do with the concept of a "normal" rate of interest. [P. 40 of script.] | 382 |
| Presumably the idea pursued in such language is that as long as a divergence index has a certain value, e.g., as long as planned saving is falling short of planned new investment, a price movement will continue. It would be simpler to say that as long as the sum of planned investment demand and consumption demand exceeded planned supply, the price level would be rising. But such a statement amounts to referring to a point of time that which might more simply, and more amenably to statistical analysis, be referred to a period of time; i.e., as long as aggregate demand is rising relative to aggregate supply, the price level will be rising. [P. 48 of script.] | 388 |

*Additions to notes*

5. In the present paper I am mainly concerned with the changes on the demand side. A more comprehensive formulation should consider the elasticity of supply to a greater extent than I have done. [P. 9 of script.]

7. By stability Myrdal means something other than absence of changes in the price system from one period to another. His analysis refers to a *point of time*, has to do with absence of *tendencies* to certain price changes, and does not preclude major actual changes in price levels in periods of "monetary equilibrium." Lack of equality between saving and investment is possible for him, as it is to Lindahl, because both are looking *ahead* in time, i.e. are concerned with *planned* saving and investment. [P. 10 of script.]

8. This is the construction used in my recently published work, *Interregional and International Trade*, and in my discussion with Keynes on capital movements in the *Economic Journal*, 1929; Hammarskjöld's method (this journal 1932) appears to be a mixture of that type and that of Lindahl. (Since the present paper was worked out before the publication of Hammerskjöld's paper, I have been unable to take account of the latter.) [P. 10 n.1 of script.]

27. A process of deflation is characterized not only by the fact that part of gross saving is offset by negative incomes but fully as much by a declining gross saving.—The idea expressed in Wicksellian theory by saying that investment is falling short of saving in my own terminology by no means implies an investment demand so low that negative incomes are generated, reducing net saving below gross saving. Notice that negative incomes occur even under rising prices; consequently, investment *always* falls short of gross saving.—In a discussion [Carl] Iversen has claimed that my "gross saving" is identical to what Scandinavian economists used to mean by "saving," when discussing lack of equality between saving and investment. But that cannot be true, for investment supposedly may *exceed* saving. In Wicksell and others it must surely be some kind of *net saving* which in periods of falling prices is falling short of new investment. [P. 36 of script.]

28. Behind such an implicit assumption we find the hidden idea that the income disposable for demand in a period partly depends upon the production of the preceding period. This was the idea underlying Scandinavian postwar discussion of monetary theory. Hammarskjöld's analysis and extension of that idea thus represents a smaller deviation from Wicksell than do the formulations by Keynes, Lindahl, Myrdal, and myself. Cf. § 3 above. [P. 37 of script.]

29. Anyone who wishes to do so may think through the opposite process in which holders of bank deposits exchange the latter for capital goods, thus raising the prices of old and new units of such goods. From the point of view of the market for new units, this implies a rising investment demand. [P. 37 of script.]

# [3]

*History of Political Economy 10:3*


# What was new in Ohlin's 1933–34 macroeconomics?

*Hans Brems*

The purpose of the present paper is twofold. First, I shall try to summarize what was new in Ohlin's 1933 article [14] on the formulation of monetary theory. This summary can be brief—and should be, now that the article has, at long last, been translated into English. Second, I shall try to review Ohlin's as yet untranslated 1934 book [15] on monetary policy, public works, subsidies, and tariffs as measures against unemployment. My review should give an impression of what the entire book was like but will naturally pay particular attention to the relation between the 1933 article and the 1934 book and to points at which the latter broke new ground. At such points I shall, as far as possible, let Ohlin speak for himself in direct translation.

## I. *Ohlin's 1933 Article*

To Bertil Ohlin in 1933, physical output was a variable. Its variations are described explicitly in the core of his 1933 article, i.e., §§ 6 through 8. Section 6 deals with the time sequence of price changes and examines the case of a sharp reduction of the propensity to save. The result of such a reduction may be expanding physical output, expanding employment, and a higher volume of saving. Section 7 on a process of rising prices, too, "will assume output to expand in response to growing demand." In § 8 output contracts in response to contracting demand.

So far Ohlin anticipated Keynes' *General Theory*. But he went beyond it in two respects.

First, Ohlin never used a Keynesian static equilibrium of physical output—often illustrated by the 45°-line diagram—in which output less than equilibrium will lead to inventory depletion, and output greater than equilibrium to inventory accumulation. Ohlin's physical output

HANS BREMS *is Professor of Economics at the University of Illinois at Urbana-Champaign.* *For friendly criticism and prodding he is indebted to Don Patinkin, for encouragement and comments to Paul A. Samuelson, and for endorsement of interpretation to Bertil Ohlin, letter of December 2, 1977.*

was not an equilibrating variable in such a static equilibrium. But Ohlin did see a feedback mechanism: his physical output responds to demand. In doing so, it generates new income, hence new demand. Thus, in Ohlin's saving example in § 6 referred to above, his physical output will rise as a result of the increased consumption demand, and there will be a feedback from physical output via income generated by it to new consumption demand. There will also be a feedback via induced investment. In Ohlin's own words, "the rising investment demand of the consumers' goods industries will eventually bring about an increase in total investment. Total saving, then, is not reduced, but on the contrary increased, despite the fact that consumption is up. What makes this possible is expanding output." Ohlin sees the feedback, then, but his feedback is not telescoped into an instant static equilibrium along an output axis the way the Keynesian feedback is in the 45° diagram. Ohlin's feedback takes place along a time axis, the way Wicksell's interaction between prices and income did at parametric output in *Interest and Prices* [21]. The difference between Wicksell's and Ohlin's cumulative processes is that the former was an interaction between prices and income only, the latter an interaction among price, physical output, and income. Like all Swedish theorists of his generation, Ohlin was brought up on Wicksell, hence had a head start in dynamics and was convinced of its power. He concludes his § 6 by saying: "By now it should be sufficiently clear that the effects of a given primary change will differ widely if the secondary reactions occur in one time sequence rather than another." Perhaps the most valuable contribution of Ohlin's 1933 paper lies in its explicit analysis of such time sequences.

Second, Keynes put greatest emphasis on physical output and paid less attention to prices: he came around to them in his chapter 21, "The Theory of Prices," [7], 292–309, and observed that "instead of constant prices in conditions of unemployment, and of prices rising in proportion to the quantity of money in conditions of full employment, we have in fact a condition of prices rising gradually as employment increases." [7], 296. But the chapter came after the party was almost over: chapter 21 is the last of the main body of *General Theory*. To Ohlin, prices did not come in as an afterthought. From the outset his prices were always varying in response to his demand *along with* his physical output. This points to a present-day inflation-unemployment tradeoff.

In one respect Ohlin failed to go beyond Keynes. As Wicksell and Keynes had done, Ohlin analyzed the investment-interest relationship. But that was as far as the three of them went. They did not see

Fisher's [3] distinction between a "money" rate (the rate of interest in terms of gold) and a "real" rate (the rate of interest in terms of wheat or of goods in general), playing a role in monetarist writing from Turgot [19] to Mundell [11]. Keynes knew Fisher's work but was not impressed.[1] Ohlin never mentioned it. Keynes had the better excuse: he paid less attention to prices anyway. But to Ohlin, prices were always varying along with physical output.

## II. *Ohlin's 1934 Book*

On April 14, 1934, Ohlin's report to the Swedish Unemployment Committee[2] was submitted to the King by the secretary of the Committee, Dag Hammarskjöld. As a volume in the findings of the committee, the report was published a few months later by the Royal Printing House under the title *Penningpolitik, offentliga arbeten, subventioner och tullar som medel mot arbetslöshet* (Monetary Policy, Public Works, Subsidies, and Tariffs as Measures Against Unemployment).

The book had three parts. Part I was an expansion of the 1933 article. Part II was a systematic and clear analysis of monetary policy, public works, subsidies, and tariffs as measures to generate an economic expansion. Part III—the shortest of the three—dealt with measures to cope with structural unemployment in specific industries or geographical regions.

### *Chapter 1. Principles of monetary theory*

The 1934 book may be viewed as an application of the 1933 article to problems of employment policy. Ohlin himself must have viewed it in this way, or he would not have devoted his entire 77-pages-long Part I of his 176-page book to an expanded reproduction of his 1933 article. The early methodological and terminological parts of the article are reproduced almost verbatim in Chapter 1.

But in that chapter, two things happened to what in Ohlin's 1933 article had been called "the intention to save" ("sparviljan"). First, the equivalent term "propensity to save" ("sparbenägenhet")[3] was

1. In ch. 17 of *General Theory* [7], 222–229, Keynes did consider "own rates" of interest like a wheat rate of interest, a copper rate of interest, etc., and discussed their carrying-cost and liquidity aspects. In ch. 11 [7], 142–43, Keynes discussed Fisher's [3] aspect of such "own-rates" but remained unconvinced.

2. On the committee, its findings, and its impact, see Uhr [20].

3. The Swedish word "sparbenägenhet" is composed of "spar[a]" ≡ to save and "benägenhet." To neutralize my bias as an economist, I consulted my Swedish-English dictionary and found three English equivalents offered for the word "benägenhet," i.e. disposition, inclination, and propensity. The latter offering was

added; second, the two were formally defined as follows:

> The "intention to save" and "propensity to save" of an individual or a firm are defined as their planned savings ratio, i.e., the relation they intend to maintain between new saving and net income. This intention to save is a function of, among other things, expected future income and the level of the rate of interest. The planned savings ratio is something entirely different from the relation in ex-post account between, on the one hand, net new saving, equaling new investment, and on the other hand net national income; the latter relation could be called "a national new investment ratio." [15], 20n.

The reason why the 1934 book offered explicit definitions of certain terms left undefined in the 1933 article is probably that the book was addressing a wider audience than the article was. In accordance with Swedish constitutional practice the book was a public document, whereas the article was meant for professional colleagues only.

*Chapter 2. The character of processes of expansion and contraction*

In Chapter 2 the mechanisms of expansion and contraction are set out once again, but more completely so, with more cases examined, and with more definitional help to the reader.

Explicit definitions of the key concepts of expansion and contraction are offered in the opening lines of the chapter:

> In the following we shall mean by expansion a rising real net income and by contraction the opposite. Real net income reflects the volume of productive activity. But there is much to be said for measuring the latter by the change in real net income *plus* the allowance for wearing down fixed productive equipment,[4] i.e., "value added by manufacture,"[5] adjusted for price changes. For neither net real income nor the quantity of manufacturing are index numbers readily available. Consequently, as an aggregate expression for the volume of productive activity it is customary to use an index number for the volume of gross output, as measured by the usual index numbers for the volume of output in manufacturing, agriculture, transportation etc. [15], 24.

---

exemplified by "benägenhet för att ljuga" ≡ propensity to lie, and "benägenhet för dryckenskap" ≡ propensity to drink.

4. I.e., capital consumption allowances.

5. Ohlin uses the English words.

Having thus defined his terms "expansion" and "contraction," Ohlin carefully specifies his initial conditions: expansionary measures will be analyzed on the background of a depression in which

> Productive capacity in the majority of firms within manufacturing, transportation, and trade is merely incompletely utilized, e.g., output falls short of 80 to 90 per cent of what it might have been at practically the same fixed capital equipment and at the existing labor force in the various industries, perhaps after some migration of labor from one to the other. [15], 25.

Thus defined and thus starting, processes of expansion and contraction are then analyzed in much the same way they were analyzed in §§ 6, 7, and 8 of the 1933 article—removing the last doubts that to Ohlin, physical output was a variable to be explained and to be affected by public policy.

The remainder of Chapter 2 is devoted to a study of money and capital markets similar to that offered in the 1933 article. But the chapter offers a first glimpse of the liquidity trap—to be elaborated in Chapters 3 and 4. Ohlin asks if monetary policy, in its efforts to reduce the interest rate, might encounter a floor to the latter. Ohlin finds such a floor:

> Rather than buying or owning bonds which have risen to a price considered unreasonable and expected soon to fall, capitalists will deposit their money, even on non-interest-bearing accounts. [15], 42.

*Chapter 3. Various types of conditions for expansion*

The chapter opens with a seven-page survey of business-cycle theory not found in the 1933 article. Ohlin observes that the volume of productive activity fluctuates more for capital goods than for consumers' goods. And he continues:

> It is clear that the business cycle implies changes in the *quantity relations* of the economy. . . . A special quantity relation which seems to play a major role in the character of processes of expansion and contraction has to do with the rate of growth of the total productive apparatus on the one hand and the size of it in industries producing durable capital goods on the other. For the rate of growth of the former to rise from 5 per cent per annum to 10 per cent per annum, the capacity of the latter industries must double if already fully utilized. But durable capital goods are also produced for replacement purposes. If average replacement amounts

to 5 per cent per annum, then the increase of the rate of growth of the total productive apparatus mentioned above—which is not the same as that of output itself—would require a 50 per cent increase of the output of durable capital goods: the annual output of new durable capital goods must rise from 10 to 15 per cent of the existing productive apparatus. [15], 50–51.

Here, then, is the accelerator. Section 7 in the 1933 article had described a cumulative process of expansion but had not tried to explain why such a process should come to an end. In Chapter 3 Ohlin now uses the accelerator to explain why it should: the accelerator links investment demand to the *growth* of output, whereas the propensity to save links saving to the *level* of output. Those are very special conditions, and output may not satisfy them. Ohlin's intuitive reasoning about this matter on pages 52–53 is reminiscent of the discussion fourteen years later of a Harrod [5] unstable, knife-edge, growth path.

Ohlin did not consider the accelerator his own discovery. On page 51 he refers to the Frisch-Clark discussion of it in the 1931–32 *Journal of Political Economy*. He must have known Clark's 1917 article [1] and must have heard about the accelerator from his teacher Cassel. But the ease with which Ohlin fits the accelerator into his Chapter 3 is nevertheless interesting. First it shows once again that to Ohlin, physical output was a variable. Can anything be more physical than the accelerator? Second it shows that Ohlin's macroeconomics was dynamic. Let physical investment, capital stock, and output be $I$, $S$, and $X$, respectively; let a parametric capital coefficient be $b$, and our behavior relationship be $S = bX$. We explain investment by differentiating that behavior relationship with respect to time: $I \equiv dS/dt = bdX/dt$. But as soon as we are differentiating with respect to time, we are doing dynamics. Can anything be more dynamic than the accelerator?

The remainder of Chapter 3 is an account of ways in which an expansion might be generated in an economy left to itself. An expansion might, for example, be generated by improved expectations or by a lower propensity to save. The latter case was examined in § 6 of the 1933 article, and the book repeats the examination.

Could an expansion also be generated by, say, a wage reduction or a higher propensity to save? The article did not examine these cases, but the book does. What they have in common, Ohlin says, is that both reduce consumption demand. A wage reduction reduces consumption demand and cost alike. Consequently, if prices should fall correspondingly, a decline in physical consumption could be avoided and profit margins would have remained the same. If prices did not fall correspondingly, profit margins would be up, but physical consumption would be down. In a closed economy, Ohlin concludes, a wage reduction will hardly be capable of starting an expansion.

A higher propensity to save is even less likely to do so. It would reduce consumption demand without reducing cost. Physical consumption would be down without any improvement in profit margins. But wouldn't investment be induced by a lower rate of interest? At this point the liquidity trap makes it second appearance. The relevant interest rate may encounter a floor:

> It is not a limited *total* amount of credit that keeps the rate of interest from falling to zero; many capitalists hold their money as demand deposits at zero interest rate. What is decisive for the rate of interest in this range is the limited amount of credit that capitalists are willing to "tie" to a specific placement such as bonds. If the effective bond yield falls below a certain level, that amount of credit will be reduced and fall short of the supply of bonds, and the yield will again rise. [15], 69.

*Chapter 4. Monetary policy measures*

The chapter opens with a clear but traditional analysis of the mechanism through which central-bank discount policy affects other rates of interest, prices, and the propensity to save. Then follows an equally clear analysis of open-market operations and their effects upon liquidity and lending rates of commercial banks and savings banks. The treatment is traditional until Ohlin discusses the effect of open-market operations upon bond prices. Here the liquidity trap makes its third and full appearance:

> Of great importance for the efficacy of buying and selling bonds by the central bank is the development of bond prices, i.e., the effective long-term rate of interest. How much the purchase of a certain amount of bonds will raise their prices depends first and foremost on the willingness of bondholders to sell, i.e. their supply curve. If there are many who believe that the declining yield will be temporary and who will therefore sell their bonds at once after an insignificant increase in bond prices, then the latter will indeed be insignificant. If, on the other hand, bondholders hold on to their bonds and merely supply a small quantity when prices are raised, then the price increase may become significant. [15], 85.

Like Keynes two years later, Ohlin sees a floor under the bond rate of interest: that rate is partly determined by what asset holders expect it to be. Ohlin's conclusion is the same as that of Keynes: whatever the central bank intends to do, it should do boldly and firmly, and it should declare its intention to do it.

Ohlin does not confine himself to monetary policy in a closed economy but carefully explores open-economy aspects of an expansionary monetary policy. There will be negative effects upon the balance of payments, both because expanding output at home will reduce the balance of trade, and because a lower interest rate will encourage short-term capital export. Under a gold standard the central bank has little room for maneuver vis-à-vis such negative effects. The best it can do is to widen the gap between the selling and buying price of gold, thus pushing the gold points farther apart. But under a paper standard the central bank may let prices of foreign currencies rise. The effect upon the balance of trade will be positive: export will be stimulated and import discouraged. The effect upon short-term capital movements will depend upon expectations. Under a gold standard such movements are stabilizing, but under a paper standard they may be de-stabilizing and become, as Ohlin puts it (page 93), "the masters rather than the servants of exchange policy." Only a central bank possessing ample exchange reserves can remain in control. Such a central bank can steer expectations by operating in the forward exchange market.

Everything taken into account, then, is monetary policy a potent policy instrument? Ohlin sees two obstacles. The first is the liquidity trap now making its fourth appearance (on page 96): "There is a limit below which it is difficult to reduce the rate of interest for long and medium-long loans." The second obstacle is the exchange situation: Does an ample exchange reserve exist? If not, will the country get away with an isolated devaluation or will it merely escalate the devaluation race?

A deep and widespread depression may leave monetary policy impotent. The trick must be, Ohlin says, to avoid getting into such a depression in the first place. That can only be done by preventing the expansion from going too far: "That an automobile is stuck in a ditch does not mean that keeping it on the road lies beyond the powers of good driving." [15], 96.

*Chapter 5. Public works*

Ohlin examines public works as follows. Let the monetary policy permitted by the balance-of-payments constraint be unable to stimulate private investment. Let the government undertake some investment project—say highway construction or electrification of state railroads—which does not compete with private investment. Let the project be financed in a way—say central-bank discounting of treasury bills—which does not deprive private investment of finance.

Such public works will generate incremental income. With two leakages, i.e., import and saving, such incremental income will generate incremental consumption demand. The incremental consumption demand, in turn, will generate new incremental income to be spent subject to the same two leakages. The stage is set for the dynamic multiplier.

In its simplest possible form the dynamic multiplier would nowadays be set out as follows. Let consumption and income be $C$ and $Y$, respectively. Let a parametric propensity to consume be $c$. Let income generated at time $t - 1$ be spent on consumption at time $t$: $C(t) = cY(t - 1)$. Let public works at time $t$ generate the direct increment $dY(t)$ to income $Y(t)$. Let the public works have been going on for $n$ periods. In addition to the direct increment $dY(t)$ at time $t$ there will then be an indirect spillover of $cdY(t - 1)$ from public works at time $t - 1$, another indirect spillover of $c^2dY(t - 2)$ from public works at time $t - 2$, . . ., and a last indirect spillover of $c^ndY(t - n)$ from public works at time $t - n$, when they started. Let public works have been stationary; then $dY(t) = dY(t - 1) = dY(t - 2) = \cdots = dY(t - n)$. At time $t$ the sum of all direct as well as spillover incremental income is

$$(1 + c + c^2 + \cdots + c^n)dY(t) = \frac{1 - c^{n+1}}{1 - c}\,dY(t)$$

This is exactly what Ohlin says in a numerical example in which $c = \frac{1}{2}$, $dY(t) = 20$ million kronor, $n = 3$, and the length of the unit period is three months:

> Imagine that the average "delay" among consumers—the "time lag"[6] of consumption response—is three months and that half the income—of labor, entrepreneurs, and taxpayers—buys Swedish goods, while the remainder buys imported goods or is saved. Then an income of $a$ kronor in the first quarter will generate incomes of $a/2$, $a/4$, and $a/8$, etc., in the following quarters. If in each and every quarter of 1933, public works in Sweden would have directly generated 20 million kronor then the sum total of indirect income increments in the fourth quarter, generated by

6. Ohlin uses the English words.

consumption responses to the public works undertaken in the preceding three quarters, would be 10 + 5 + 2½ million kronor (p. 105).

In the fourth quarter, then, the sum of all direct as well as spill-over incremental income is 20 + 10 + 5 + 2½ = 37½ million kronor—which is, of course, exactly the sum of our geometric progression for $n = 3$.

Like the accelerator, the multiplier was old hat in 1934. On page 103 Ohlin refers to Kahn's celebrated, then three-year-old article [6]. But what Ohlin does and does not do with his multiplier in Chapter 5 says something about his method of analysis. The reader will notice three things.

First, the reader will notice the way Ohlin uses the income-consumption lag. This makes his use unequivocally dynamic. Second, the reader will notice Ohlin's use of a finite value of the number of periods considered: $n = 3$. Ohlin never bothers to find the limit of his geometrical progression for $n$ approaching infinity. That limit would have been a multiplier of $1/(1 - c) = 2$, i.e., 20 million kronor's worth of expenditure would have generated 40 million kronor's worth of income! That limit would have been the static multiplier used by Keynes [7], 115. Why didn't Ohlin even bother to find it? Ohlin's strong sense of realism probably told him two things: public works don't last forever, so $n$ doesn't go to infinity; anyway the important thing is that after merely three quarters, 37½ million kronor's worth of income has been generated. The difference between 40 and 37½ was not important to Ohlin.

The third important thing about Ohlin's use of the multiplier is his afterthoughts: the mechanical consumption-demand multiplier is merely one part of the story; there are other important repercussions. One is inventory adjustment: How soon do retailers, wholesalers, and manufacturers replenish depleted inventory? Another is investment in plant and equipment: How soon does rising demand necessitate such expansion? The answers will depend upon expectations and confidence. Ohlin discusses such speeds of reaction at length: his multiplier approach is thoroughly dynamic.

The remainder of Chapter 5[7] asks such questions as: Should public works be financed by borrowing or by taxes? Tax financing would

7. From now on our review of Ohlin's 1934 book will be very brief. Our primary interest has been Ohlin's theoretical innovation, and the remainder of the book specifies policy recommendations and is well summarized by Uhr [20], particularly 107–110.

reduce consumption and thus defeat the purpose of public works. If financed by borrowing, should public works be financed by the central bank or by the private capital market? Government bonds sold in the private capital market might depress bond prices and thus discourage private investment. What is the cost of public works to the economy? If the resources absorbed by them would otherwise have been idle, the cost is zero. How can public works be productive if they aren't profitable? If they absorbed resources taken out of better uses, they would be unproductive or indeed counterproductive. But if the resources would otherwise have been idle, public works are productive as soon as they produce anything of use. Don't public works financed by borrowing mean living now at the expense of the future? Public works do not mean capital consumption. On the contrary future capital stock is increased by highway construction or electrification of state railroads, and the future will be better off, not worse off, for it.

Ohlin's answers to such questions would be standard textbook answers today, but in 1934 they were new.

*Chapter 6. Subsidizing private production*

Subsidizing private investment has effects upon output and income very similar to those of public works. But other effects are different.

First, subsidies leave more room for selective private initiative: projects closest to being profitable will be the first ones activated by subisidies. Second, the government outlay on subsidies is a fraction of total outlay. Consequently it matters less whether that outlay is financed by borrowing or taxation. Third, subsidies do not create future government assets like highways or electric state railroads. Consequently traditional fiscal principles would suggest tax financing.

Subsidies raise problems of their own. A subsidy favoring one industry may jeopardize another, competitive, industry. There is always the danger of corruption. But to a civil service with a corruption threshold as high as the Swedish one, Ohlin dismisses the corruption problem as an administrative one.

*Chapter 7. Tariff policy and capital movements*

Ohlin aptly characterizes the effects of a higher tariff in terms of his theoretical apparatus developed in Chapters 4 and 5. In terms of Chapter 5 a higher tariff will raise the multiplier by reducing the import leakage. In terms of Chapter 4 it will ease the balance-of-payments constraint upon monetary policy. Indeed filling the space, now less constrained, will to some extent be automatic: as we know, every central-bank purchase of foreign exchange from exporters will expand the money supply, and every sale to importers will reduce it. Consequently, a tariff reducing import more than export will expand central-bank assets and with them the money supply. In other words, the monetary effect of a higher tariff is much the same as that of open-market bond purchases by the central bank.

Public works raised an important fiscal problem. Like subsidies, tariff policy merely raises a minor one. Indeed, inelastic import demand may even raise government revenue! Whether government revenue is down or up, it will have repercussions upon output and income. Such repercussions will have to be examined, Ohlin adds.

Long-term tariff policy might be designed to be countercyclical, i.e. protectionist in depressions, free-trade in booms—helping to keep expansions from going too far.

### *Chapter 8. Expansion, structural change, and unemployment*

Ohlin's last chapter examines measures to help specific industries suffering from short-run problems like dumping or violent world-market price falls or from long-run ones like lagging technology or declining demand. The chapter is less macroeconomic than the previous ones and neither introduces nor applies new theoretical tools.

## III. *Retrospect*

### *The critics of the Stockholm School*[8]

The two leading critics of the Stockholm School, Lerner [9] and Landgren [8], share, first, the use of a static Keynesian equilibrium as their standard of comparison, second, a strong conviction of its superiority to dynamics as a practical tool of analysis, and third, great lucidity in setting out their argument. But their native tongues differed. Ohlin's 1933 article and 1934 book were accessible to Landgren only.

Both for that reason and because his article [9] was a review article of translations of Lindahl's and Myrdal's work, Lerner never mentioned Ohlin. As for Lindahl and Myrdal, the verdict was that they had been "caught up with and overtaken by Mr. Keynes." [9], 591. We can only guess whether Lerner would have included Ohlin in that verdict, had he known Ohlin's work. He might have liked Ohlin's explicit use of physical output as a variable. But he would have liked Ohlin's dynamics no better than he liked Lindahl's and Myrdal's on which he said,

8. Paul Samuelson encouraged me to do this section.

> For practical purposes, compromises and simplifications have to be made, and when this has been done, it seems to me that little if anything has been gained as compared with the simplifications and compromises of equilibrium analysis. . . . [9], 589.

Twenty years after Lerner, the late Karl-Gustav Landgren [8] offered his comprehensive re-appraisal of the Stockholm School. Very briefly expressed, his verdict was that the Stockholm School neither anticipated nor appreciated Keynes' breakthrough. But Landgren does single out Ohlin as the shining exception. He alone "carried out a Keynesian revolution in Swedish economics." [8], English-language summary, 299. Such treatment might seem gratifying to Ohlin until one examines Landgren's documentation. Landgren, no friend of dynamics, ascribes to Ohlin a rather un-Ohlinian static-equilibrium determination of income and output. As Fernholm [2] pointed out in his comprehensive review article, this is a misrepresentation of Ohlin. To his theoretical misrepresentation Landgren added a historical one, less gratifying to Ohlin: Ohlin must have seen the Keynesian light only after reading Keynes' March 1933 letters to the London *Times*, assembled in the April 1933 pamphlet *The Means to Prosperity*. Steiger [17] [18] has shown that Ohlin's manuscript was completed in the fall of 1932. The debate was rounded off by Lundberg's [10] balanced and elegant article entitled, in English translation, "On Comprehending Keynes and Understanding Others."

*My own conclusion*

In his 1933 article Ohlin applied two Keynesian tools of analysis, i.e. (1) physical output as a variable and (2) the propensity to save. In his 1934 book Ohlin's emphasis on physical output as a variable became stronger and more explicit. In retrospect, Ohlin sees nothing strange in this. In a letter to this writer of December 2, 1977, he writes, in English translation,

> I am also happy that you emphasize so strongly that the quantity of aggregate output and employment were variables in my 1933–34 thinking. The very assignment given by the Unemployment Committee referred to the quantity of employment, and it would have been downright impossible not to consider the latter a variable and with it national income in terms of quantity side by side with the price level and income in terms of value.

In his 1934 book Ohlin applied two additional Keynesian tools of analysis, i.e. (3) liquidity preference and (4) the multiplier, and finally a non-Keynesian one, i.e. (5) the accelerator.

Liquidity preference must have been discovered by Ohlin. Indeed, glimpses of it are found even in his pre-1933 writings such as his paper at the Scandinavian economists' 1931 meeting [12] and his League of Nations report [13] in the same year.

The accelerator and the multiplier were discovered by others, but Ohlin's use of them shows how dynamic his macroeconomics was. The accelerator is inherently dynamic and incompatible with a static equilibrium, and Keynes never mentioned it. But if Keynes could do without it, his followers could not. Lerner and Landgren notwithstanding, "the economist has no choice but to study dynamics," as Samuelson once put it. In the very year of *General Theory*, Harrod [4] gave the accelerator a prominent place in his *Trade Cycle*. Prompted by Alvin Hansen, Samuelson [16] three years later dynamized the Keynesian system by his celebrated interaction between the multiplier and the accelerator.

Unlike the accelerator, the multiplier is not inherently dynamic. A static multiplier may be formulated and was—by Keynes. As shown above, one may find the limit of my geometrical progression for $n$ approaching infinity. That limit is the static multiplier $1/(1 - c)$ used by Keynes [7], 115. For such a multiplier Ohlin had no use. He never bothered to find the limit $1/(1 - c)$. His sense of realism must have told him that public works don't last forever, so $n$ doesn't go to infinity. Instead, Ohlin discussed speeds of reaction at length.

Ohlin used his five tools to derive some strikingly Keynesian policy conclusions. In times of underutilized capactiy and unemployment a government should not try to encourage a wage reduction or a higher propensity to save. Instead, it should conduct

(1) A monetary policy of open-market operations designed to depress the rate of interest—subject to a liquidity-trap constraint and a balance-of-payments constraint;
(2) A policy of public works, generating income magnified by the multiplier;
(3) A policy of—much less expensive—subsidies to private investment doing the same;
(4) A policy of raising tariffs, thus enlarging the multiplier and easing the balance-of-payments constraint upon monetary policy.

All this was in the 1934 book. Much of the necessary analytical apparatus was explicitly present in Ohlin's 1933 article. But not all. Was the rest of it implicit in that article—trying to get out of its cocoon and succeeding in doing so in 1934? Or was the rest new and independent theory? We do not know, but what matters is that by 1934 both Keynesian theory in a dynamic form and Keynesian policy conclusions had been anticipated by Ohlin.

## REFERENCES

[1] Clark, J. M. "Business Acceleration and the Law of Demand: A Technical Factor in Economic Cycles." *Journal of Political Economy* 25 (March 1917): 217–35.

[2] Fernholm, T. "Idéutveckling, ekonomisk politik och ekonomisk teori." *Ekonomisk Tidskrift* 62 (Sept. 1960): 161–84.

[3] Fisher, I. "Appreciation and Interest." *Publications of the American Economic Association* 11 (Aug. 1896): 331–442.

[4] Harrod, R. F. *The Trade Cycle*. Oxford, 1936.

[5] Harrod, R. F. *Towards a Dynamic Economics*. London, 1948.

[6] Kahn, R. F. "The Relation of Home Investment to Unemployment." *Economic Journal* 41 (June 1931): 173–98.

[7] Keynes, J. M. *The General Theory of Employment, Interest and Money*. London, 1936.

[8] Landgren, K.-G. *Den 'nya ekonomien' i Sverige. J. M. Keynes, E. Wigforss, B. Ohlin och utvecklingen 1927–39*. Uppsala, 1960.

[9] Lerner, A. P. "Some Swedish Stepping Stones in Economic Theory." *Canadian Journal of Economics and Political Science* 6 (1940): 574–91.

[10] Lundberg, E. "Om att begripa Keynes och att förstå andra." *Ekonomisk Tidskrift* 62 (Sept. 1960): 195–205.

[11] Mundell, R. A. *Monetary Theory: Inflation, Interest, and Growth in the World Economy*. Pacific Palisades, 1971.

[12] Ohlin, B. "Den internationella penningpolitiken och dess inverkan på konjunkturutvecklingen." *Nordiska nationalekonomiska mötet*, June 1931.

[13] Ohlin B. *The Course and Phases of the World Economic Depression*. Geneva, 1931.

[14] Ohlin, B. "Till frågan om penningteoriens uppläggning." *Ekonomisk Tidskrift* 35 (1933): 45–81.

[15] Ohlin, B. *Penningpolitik, offentliga arbeten, subventioner och tullar som medel mot arbetslöshet*, Statens offentliga utredningar 1934:12. Stockholm, 1934.

[16] Samuelson, P. A. "Interactions Between the Multiplier Analysis and the Principle of Acceleration." *Review of Economic Statistics* 21 (May 1939): 75–78.

[17] Steiger, O. *Studien zur Entstehung der Neuen Wirtschaftslehre in Schweden*. Berlin, 1971.

[18] Steiger, O. "Bertil Ohlin and the Origins of the Keynesian Revolution." *History of Political Economy* 8 (Fall 1976): 341–66.

[19] Turgot, A. R. J. "Réflexions sur la formation et la distribution des richesses." *Ephémérides du citoyen*, Nov. 1769–Jan. 1770. English translation, *Reflections on the Formation and the Distribution of Riches*, New York, 1898.

[20] Uhr, C. G. "Economists and Policymaking 1930–1936: Sweden's Experience." *History of Political Economy* 9 (Spring 1977): 89–121.

[21] Wicksell, K. *Geldzins und Güterpreise*. Jena, 1898. English translation, *Interest and Prices*, London, 1936.

# [4]

*History of Political Economy 10:3*


## Some observations on Ohlin's 1933 article

*Don Patinkin*

Bertil Ohlin's 1933 article "Till frågan om penningteoriens uplägg- ning" plays a crucial role in the perennial debate about the relationship between the "Stockholm School" and Keynes' *General Theory*.[1] Non-Scandinavian economists can accordingly only be very grateful to Hans Brems and William P. Yohe, as well as the editors of *HOPE*, for having made this important article available to them in an English translation.

I would like now to take advantage of this occasion to make some observations on the basic question which has arisen with respect to Ohlin's article: namely, the extent, if any, to which it anticipates the *General Theory*.[2] In order to do this, let me first emphasize that the distinctive contribution of the *General Theory* is not the advocacy of public-works expenditure as a major means of reducing unemployment. The *General Theory* is, as its name indicates, a book concerned with theory. It contains practically no discussion of policy. And in particular it contains only brief, passing discussions of the policy of public-works expenditures. Furthermore, Keynes could not have seen the novelty of his book as lying in its advocacy of such a policy; for already in 1929, in his influential election pamphlet with Hubert Henderson entitled *Can Lloyd George Do It?* Keynes had been an out-

DON PATINKIN *is Professor of Economics at the Hebrew University of Jerusalem and Ford Foundation Visiting Research Professor at the University of Chicago.*

1. This debate has been vigorously renewed since the provocative study by Karl-Gustav Landgren (1960) and the subsequent critique by Otto Steiger (1971). In the English summary at the end of his book, Landgren (1960, pp. 297–301) has expressed his views on Ohlin's 1933 article; and in a recent article in this journal, Steiger (1976) has extended and in part revised that part of his monograph which deals with Ohlin and Keynes (ibid., p. 364 n.).

2. This and the following three paragraphs draw freely on my forthcoming paper "On the Relation Between Keynesian Economics and the 'Stockholm School' " (1978), in which I made use of an unpublished translation of Ohlin's article prepared for me by Moshe Apelblat, a student at the Hebrew University of Jerusalem. See also my *Keynes' Monetary Thought* (1976), pp. 64–68. (This book will be referred to henceforth as *KMT*.)

I might also note that I hope to deal with this question in greater detail on some future occasion.

standing and forceful proponent of this policy. Correspondingly, the advocacy per se of public-works expenditure was not the purpose of the *General Theory*; rather it was to provide a theoretical underpinning for such a policy.

This underpinning consisted of a model whose distinctive feature was not only a basic concern with the analysis of output, but even more so the assignment of an equilibrating role to variations in output. In particular, the *General Theory* showed how a (say) initial situation of excess aggregate supply causes a decline in output which (by virtue of a marginal propensity to consume of less than unity) is greater than the resulting decline in aggregate demand, so that the economy is eventually brought to a position of unemployment equilibrium in which the excess supply has been eliminated.

This analytical framework can be instructively contrasted with that of Keynes in his *Treatise on Money* (1930). Here the major concern—as expressed in the so-called "fundamental equations"—was with the determination of the prices of consumption and investment goods as contrasted with their respective costs of production, and the effects of the resulting profits (or losses) in these industries in increasing (or decreasing) their respective outputs. Thus there is a concern with output—but it is derivative from the concern with prices. And what is even more important, either there is no reference to a feedback mechanism by which changes in output directly affect demand, or when there is (viz., *Treatise,* 1: 159–60) it is implicitly based on the assumption that a (say) decrease in output generates an equivalent decrease in demand, and so does not affect the disequilibrium situation.[3]

If we examine Ohlin's 1933 article from this viewpoint, it is clear that its central concern is far closer to that of the *Treatise* than of the *General Theory*. For like Keynes of the *Treatise*, Ohlin in his article is primarily concerned with changes in prices, and discusses changes in output only as derivative from them. Indeed, at several points in his discussion (pp. 354, 357, 379, 384, and notes 8 and 28), Ohlin refers implicitly to Keynes'. *Treatise* and compares his conclusions with those of the *Treatise*—which he includes in what he denotes as the "neo-Wicksellian theory."

At the same time I must emphasize that Ohlin's 1933 article is a decided improvement over the *Treatise*. First, it avoids the mechanical and artificial analysis which was the frequent outcome of the "magic formula mentality" with which Keynes applied his so-called

3. For further details, see *KMT*, pp. 67–68.

"fundamental equations."[4] Second, and related to the preceding point, Ohlin's 1933 article makes more use than the *Treatise* of the feedback effects of a change in output on aggregate demand; but once again what primarily concerns Ohlin are the consequent effects of the resulting changes in excess demand on prices (cf. pp. 377, 379, 381). There is no recognition of what I have singled out as the major contribution of the *General Theory*: namely, the fact that changes in output per se affect the extent of the excess demand.

At first glance, the following passage in Ohlin's paper might (as Hans Brems has implied on page 399 of his article) seem to contradict this conclusion:

> Imagine that people decide to reduce their saving sharply, so demand for consumers' goods will rise. . . . The decision to reduce saving may not be accompanied by a tightening of credit. If so . . . the rising investment demand of the consumers' goods industries will eventually bring about an increase in total investment. Total saving, then, is not reduced but, on the contrary, increased, despite the fact that consumption is up. What makes this possible is expanding output [Ohlin 1933, p. 368].

But if we read this passage against the background of the earlier literature, it will be seen that it does not differ fundamentally from Keynes' imprecise contention in *Can Lloyd George Do It?* (1929) that an increase in investment in public works will generate corresponding savings—in part "by the very prosperity which the new policy will foster" (*JMK* IX, p. 120). Indeed, one of the major contributions of Richard Kahn's subsequent multiplier article was the rigorous demonstration of this proposition (Kahn 1931, pp. 16–19; see also Warming 1932, pp. 215–16, and Kahn 1932, pp. 494–95).[5]

In brief, I do not believe that Ohlin in the aforementioned passage from his 1933 paper is saying anything more than what Kahn said in his 1931 multiplier article and in its 1932 sequel; and, for reasons that I have explained elsewhere, I do not believe that Kahn's multiplier article represents an anticipation of the *General Theory* (*KMT*, pp. 69–71; see also Patinkin 1977, pp. 18–20).

Let me end this discussion of Ohlin's 1933 article by noting that the concluding section of this article records Ohlin's "revealed choice" of what he regarded as the major objectives of his article; and

4. *KMT*, ch. 6.

5. Cf. Kahn's recent statement that this is the way he himself regards his article (Patinkin and Leith 1977, p. 147).

that with the exception of the first objective which he lists (which deals with the definition of income), all of the others have to do primarily with prices.

I turn now to Ohlin's 1934 book. Here I am faced with the great drawback of not being able to read it either in the original or in translation. But if I rely on the summary of this book which Hans Brems has provided in his contribution to the Symposium in this issue of *HOPE*, then I suspect that if I could read this book, I would have the same disagreement with Brems about it as about Ohlin's 1933 paper—which we have both read (even if I have done so only in translation). For one thing, Brems emphasizes that the basic analytical framework of Ohlin's 1934 book did not differ substantially from that of his 1933 article. Furthermore, and more specifically, there is no indication in Brems' summary that Ohlin's book contained the central innovative feature of the *General Theory* whose absence in the 1933 paper I have already noted: namely, the fact that variations in output per se affect the extent of excess demand in the commodity market.

I must also confess that my reluctance to accept Brems' claims for Ohlin's 1934 book has been reinforced by the fact that in some instances they are clearly exaggerated. Thus in his summary of this book, Brems (p. 411) tells us that "liquidity preference must have been discovered by Ohlin"; but the well-developed beginnings of this theory are already in Keynes' *Treatise* (1: 127–29).[6]

Again, Brems tells us (p. 408) that the arguments that Ohlin made for public-works expenditures as a means of offsetting unemployment "would be standard textbook answers today, but in 1934 they were new." I doubt if Ohlin himself would make such a claim: for in his own recent discussion of these questions he has emphasized that Swedish economists in the early 1930's (including himself) were "stimulated by Keynes's expansionist attitude in 1928–29" (Ohlin 1974, p. 898b). In this context, Keynes' already-mentioned *Can Lloyd George Do It?* (1929)—with its argument that "it is precisely *with* our unemployed productive resources that we shall make the new [public-works]investments" (*JMK* IX, p. 120)—was particularly influential. Furthermore, Steiger (1976, p. 351) refers to a review-essay which Ohlin wrote in August 1932 in which he cited with approval

6. For further details, see *KMT*, pp. 37–39. Note that I am referring here to liquidity preference, and not to the "liquidity trap"—which, to the best of my knowledge, is not referred to in the *Treatise*. I should, however, also emphasize that Keynes did not regard the "liquidity-trap" argument as an important element of the *General Theory* (*KMT*, pp. 111–14).

Keynes' statement (in an article by him which had just been published) that "there will be no means of escape from prolonged and perhaps interminable depression except by direct State intervention to promote or subsidize new investment" (Keynes 1932, p. 85). Finally, though Steiger (1976, pp. 353–54) convincingly demonstrates that Ohlin wrote a preliminary draft of his 1933 paper—"in the main identical with [the published version]"—before he read Keynes' vigorous advocacy of public works in his articles on *The Means to Prosperity* (1933), Ohlin had surely read these articles by the time he wrote his 1934 book: for Landgren (1960, p. 297) refers to Ohlin's "penetrating account of these articles" in a Swedish Liberal newspaper in April 1933.

Brems concludes his article (p. 412) with the statement that "by 1934 Keynesian theory in a dynamic form and Keynesian policy conclusions had been anticipated by Ohlin." But Brems' list of such "policy conclusions" consists of (1) "open-market operations designed to depress the rate of interest"—which, of course, had long-since been a central part of the Wicksellian tradition, and which had also been espoused by Keynes as the major policy-message of his 1930 *Treatise*; (2) "a policy of public works" and (3) "subsidies to private investment"—and in the preceding paragraph I have said enough about Keynes' priority (relative to Ohlin) on both these points; and, finally, "a policy of raising tariffs"—which Keynes, to the great consternation of his academic colleagues, had already advocated in 1931 (Harrod 1951, pp. 489–98). In brief none of the "Keynesian policy conclusions" which Brems lists had actually been "anticipated" by Ohlin in his 1934 book; correspondingly, I am unable to accept without further evidence Brems' parallel claim that Ohlin's 1934 book had also "anticipated" Keynesian theory.[7]

## BIBLIOGRAPHY

Brems, Hans. "What Was New in Ohlin's 1933–34 Macroeconomics?" *History of Political Economy* 10 (1978): 398–412.
Harrod, Roy F. *The Life of John Maynard Keynes*. London, 1951.
Kahn, Richard R. "The Relation of Home Investment to Unemployment." *Economic Journal* 41 (1931): 173–98. As reprinted in Kahn 1972, pp. 1–27.

7. This note was written while serving as Ford Foundation Visiting Research Professor at The University of Chicago. I would like to acknowledge the aid received from NSF Grant #SOC77-12212. My thanks too to my research assistant, Clark Nardinelli, and to Beverly Griffith for typing this note through its various drafts.

———. "The Financing of Public Works—A Note." *Economic Journal* 42 (1932): 492–95.

———. *Selected Essays on Employment and Growth*. Cambridge, 1972.

Keynes, John Maynard. *A Treatise on Money, Vol. 1: The Pure Theory of Money*. 1930. As reprinted in Keynes' *Collected Writings*, Vol. V.

———. *A Treatise on Money, Vol. 2: The Applied Theory of Money*. 1930. As reprinted in Keynes' *Collected Writings*, Vol. VI.

————. The World's Economic Crisis and the Way of Escape." In Arthur Salter et al., *The World's Economic Crisis* (London, 1932), pp. 69–88.

———. *The Means to Prosperity*. 1933. As reprinted in Keynes' *Collected Writings*, Vol. IX, pp. 335–66.

———. *The General Theory of Employment, Interest, and Money*. 1936. As reprinted in Keynes' *Collected Writings*, Vol. VII.

———. *Collected Writings*. London, 1971–1973.

——— and Hubert Henderson. *Can Lloyd George Do It? An Examination of the Liberal Pledge*. 1929. As reprinted in Keynes' *Collected Writings*, Vol. IX, pp. 86–125.

Landgren, Karl-Gustav. *Den 'nya ekonomien' i Sverige: J. M. Keynes, E. Wigforss, B. Ohlin och utvecklingen 1927–1939 (The "New Economics" in Sweden: J. M. Keynes, E. Wigforss, B. Ohlin and the Development 1927–1939)*. Stockholm, 1960.

Ohlin, Bertil, "Till frågan om penningteoriens uppläggning" (On the Question of the Method and Structure in Monetary Theory). *Ekonomisk Tidskrift* 35, no. 2 (1933): 45–81. As translated by Hans Brems and William P. Yohe under the title "On the Formulation of Monetary Theory." *History of Political Economy* 10 (1978): 353–88.

———. *Penningpolitik, offentliga arbeten, subventioner och tullar som medel mot arbetslöshet* (Monetary Policy, Public Works, Subsidies and Tariffs as Remedies for Unemployment). Arbetslöshetsutredningens betänkande, II, bilagor, band 4, Statens offentliga utredninger 1934: 12. Stockholm, 1934.

———. "On the Slow Development of the 'Total Demand' Idea in Economic Theory: Reflections in Connection with Dr. Oppenheimer's Note." *Journal of Economic Literature* 12 (1974): 888–96.

Patinkin, Don. *Keynes' Monetary Thought: A Study of Its Development*. Durham, N.C., 1976.

———. "The Process of Writing the General Theory: A Critical Survey." In Patinkin and Leith 1977, pp. 3–24.

———. "On the Relation Between Keynesian Economics and the 'Stockholm School.' " *Scandinavian Journal of Economics* 80 (1978), forthcoming.

——— and J. Clark Leith, eds., *Keynes, Cambridge and the General Theory: The Process of Criticism and Discussion Connected with the Development of the General Theory*. London, 1977.

Steiger, Otto. *Studien zur Entstehung der Neuen Wirtschaftslehre in Schweden: Eine Anti-Kritik*. Berlin, 1971.

———. "Bertil Ohlin and the Origins of the Keynesian Revolution." *History of Political Economy* 8 (1976): 341–66.

Warming, Jens. "International Difficulties Arising Out of the Financing of Public Works During Depression." *Economic Journal* 42 (1932): 211–24.

# [5]

Excerpt from *History of Political Economy*, **10** (3), 419

A COMMENT

Having seen the proofs of Patinkin's January 1978 comments on my Ohlin interpretation, I do not wish to revise the latter. An honest disagreement remains on what constitutes a feedback. For Patinkin, to qualify as a feedback the feedback must be telescoped into an instant static equilibrium along an output axis, the way the Keynesian feedback is in the celebrated 45° diagram. Ohlin's feedback, which takes place along a time axis, does not qualify. For me it not only does but is the better one of the two. Let the reader decide for himself!*

HANS BREMS

* Don Patinkin has asked us to say that he does not accept this characterization of his position.—ED.

# [6]

*History of Political Economy 10:3*


# Prelude to the theory of a monetary economy: origins and significance of Ohlin's 1933 approach

*Otto Steiger*

## I. *Introduction*

§1. There is good cause for satisfaction that Bertil Ohlin's 1933 essay in the *Ekonomisk Tidskrift*, "Till frågan om penningteoriens uppläggning" (On the Formulation of Monetary Theory), has been made available to an international public in this issue of *HOPE*. For the article fills an important gap in our knowledge not only about a famous period in the history of Swedish monetary economics—the time of the early Stockholm School, formed by the neo-Wicksellians Erik Lindahl, Gunnar Myrdal, and Bertil Ohlin—but also about the origins of modern macroeconomics, i.e., the years before the publication of John Maynard Keynes' *General Theory* (1936).[1]

OTTO STEIGER *is Professor of Economics at the University of Bremen.*

1. The relationship between Keynes' *General Theory* and the early Stockholm School has been discussed in the following works:

(i) K.-G. Landgren, *Den 'nya' ekonomien i Sverige. J. M. Keynes, E. Wigforss, B. Ohlin och utvecklingen 1927–39* (The 'New' Economics in Sweden: J. M. Keynes, E. Wigforss, B. Ohlin, and the Development 1927–39) (Stockholm and Uppsala, 1960);

(ii) "Stockholmsskolan: Idéer, tillkomst och utveckling. Ett symposium" (The Stockholm School: Ideas, Origin, and Development: A Symposium), *Ekonomisk Tidskrift* 62 (1960): 159–205, 296–300, with contributions by T. Fernholm, E. Wigforss, E. Lundberg, and G. Lindahl;

(iii) O. Steiger, *Studien zur Entstehung der Neuen Wirtschaftslehre in Schweden. Eine Anti-Kritik* (Berlin, 1971);

(iv) C. G. Uhr, "The Emergence of the 'New Economics' in Sweden: A Review of a Study by Otto Steiger," *History of Political Economy* 5 (1973): 243–60;

(v) B. Gustafsson, "A Perennial of Doctrinal History: Keynes and 'the Stockholm School,'" *Economy and History* 16 (1973): 114–28;

(vi) B. Ohlin, "On the Slow Development of the 'Total Demand' Idea in Economic Theory: Reflections in Connection with Dr. Oppenheimer's Note," *Journal of Economic Literature* 12 (1974): 888–96;

(vii) O. Steiger, "Bertil Ohlin and the Origins of the Keynesian Revolution," *History of Political Economy* 8 (1976): 341–66;

(viii) B. Ohlin, "Some Comments on Keynesianism and the Swedish Theory of Expansion Before 1935," in D. Patinkin and J. C. Leith, eds., *Keynes, Cambridge and the General Theory: The Process of Criticism and Discussion Connected with the Development of the General Theory* (London, 1977), pp. 149–65;

§2. Up to the present the only contributions of the Swedish neo-Wicksellians that have been made available to the English-speaking world are those of Lindahl (1929) and Myrdal (1932, 1933) in *Studies in the Theory of Money and Capital* and *Monetary Equilibrium*, respectively, both published in 1939.[2] Apart from the Scandinavian countries, almost nothing is known of Ohlin's achievements in the field of monetary economics. His famous 1934 report to the Swedish Committee on Unemployment[3] was mentioned in various papers on the Stockholm School, but no detailed account of it was given until Karl-Gustav Landgren's 1960 treatise—in Swedish—on the New Economics in Sweden. Ohlin's 1933 essay in the *Ekonomisk Tidskrift*, which is the forerunner of the 1934 report, was up to its discovery by Landgren, as far as I know, named only once: in Brinley Thomas's 1936 work *Monetary Policy and Crises: A Study of Swedish Experience* (p. 97 n.1).

§3. On the other hand, Bertil Ohlin's short presentation of Swedish monetary theory, his "Some Notes on the Stockholm Theory of Savings and Investment" in the *Economic Journal*, 1937, was hardly sufficient to fill the gap. On the contrary, in a certain respect these "Notes" were rather confusing, because they suffered from two facts: (i) their publication one year after the *General Theory* gave them a flavor of an *ex post* construction—at least they were interpreted in that way by many authors—and (ii) they gave no clear account of what in the Stockholm theory really was the achievement of Ohlin and in what respect it differed from or coincided with the contributions of Lindahl and Myrdal and other Swedish economists named in the "Notes." It is to be hoped that the publication in English of the 1933 article will be the first step in clearing up these confusions. To complete our knowledge of Swedish monetary theory of the early thirties, however, an English edition of Ohlin's 1934 report is also necessary. There is good cause to hope that it will appear in the not too distant future.[4]

---

(ix) D. Patinkin, "On the Relation Between Keynesian Economics and the 'Stockholm School,' " *Scandinavian Journal of Economics* 80 (1978): 135–43.

(x) B. Ohlin, "Keynesian Economics and the Stockholm School: A Comment on Don Patinkin's Paper," *Scandinavian Journal of Economics* 80 (1978): 144–47.

2. Note that the English translations of the original Swedish or German texts are, to no small extent, revisions; therefore I refer to both the English and Swedish or German texts. For a more detailed bibliographical account see my article in *History of Political Economy*, pp. 354ff.

3. See below, Part II, §§14–16. An extensive summary of the report is given in Hans Brems' contribution to the Symposium, below in this journal, "What Was New in Ohlin's 1933–34 Macroeconomics?"

4. Ohlin has informed me that a translation is being prepared and that it will be

## II. *Understanding Ohlin's Conceptual Apparatus*

§4. What, at least at first glance, may look very strange to a contemporary economist reading Bertil Ohlin's 1933 paper is the complete neglect of technical monetary details in the conceptual apparatus used; the quantity of money is scarcely even mentioned, and one may wonder, therefore, what Ohlin's approach actually has to do with monetary theory. To understand the significance of his conceptual apparatus, I think, one has to go back to the works of Lindahl and Myrdal from which it evolved.

§5. Erik Lindahl's approach to monetary theory, as developed in his 1929 work *Penningpolitikens medel*, marked a decisive break with Knut Wicksell's famous theory of changes in the general price level, i.e., the value of money. Lindahl accomplished this break by completely abandoning the starting point of the Wicksellian analysis, the monetary mechanism itself. Lindahl had observed the fact that Wicksell, despite his critique of the quantity theory of money, had used his approach to underpin and extend the central reasoning of the quantity theory. By using Wicksell's suggestion of a "perfect credit system" Lindahl showed that the Wicksellian approach did not lead to a theory of the value of money which is generally valid, because it could not explain changes in the general price level in a society with no cash holdings.

§6. Thus, the problem of explaining changes in the value of money had to be attacked from another starting point, which Lindahl found in a general theory of prices, extended to *dynamic* conditions.[5] This theory, therefore, had to analyze not only relative prices in a given state of equilibrium in a certain period but also movements in the price level in a process in *time*. Lindahl assumed that these movements are influenced by the *expectations* of individuals in the economy and that the process in question can be divided into different periods. Without applying concepts connected with the quantity theory, such as the volume of money, the velocity of circulation, and

---

published in 1979. Immediately after its publication in April 1934, Brinley Thomas, who had stayed in Stockholm from October 1933 to April 1934 to examine the Swedish recovery program, intended to carry out a translation; however, this was never realized—see Landgren, p. 219 n.10.

5. Important elements of this dynamic analysis, in particular with regard to the significance of uncertainty for investment decisions, had already been developed in the following works of Myrdal and Lindahl respectively: (i) *Prisbildningsproblemet och föränderligheten* (The Problem of Price Formation and Changeability) (Uppsala and Stockholm, 1927); (ii) "Prisbildningsproblemets uppläggning från kapitalteoretisk synpunkt" (The Place of Capital in the Theory of Price), *Ekonomisk Tidskrift*, 31 (1929): 31–81; translated as Part III of *Studies*.

other technical monetary details, Lindahl treated his monetary problem by analyzing changes in different macroeconomic variables, measured in *monetary units*. He started his approach in the following way:

> In explaining the factors determining changes in the price level, it is convenient to start from the fact that in each period the portion of the total nominal income that is not saved is equal to the total quantities of goods and services consumed during the period, multiplied by their prices. This may be expressed in the form:
>
> $$E\,(1 - s) = PQ,$$
>
> where $E$ denotes the total nominal income, $s$ the proportion of this income which is saved, $P$ the price level for consumption goods and $Q$ the quantity of such goods in a certain period [*Penningpolitikens medel*, p. 12; quotation is from *Studies*, p. 142].

§7. Lindahl's treatment of these monetary macroeconomic variables can be characterized as a *casuistic* reasoning which makes use of "type models" like the Wicksellian process. He thus applied a method which can be described as a process or period analysis combined with intertemporal equilibrium:

> In order to analyze such a dynamic process, we imagine it to be subdivided into *periods of time* so short that the factors directly affecting prices, and therefore also the prices themselves can be regarded as unchanged in each period. All such *changes* are therefore assumed to *take place at the transition points between the different periods*. The development of prices can then be expressed as a series of successive price situations. We assume further, that in each of these short periods of time individuals have full knowledge of the prices ruling during the period, and that they allow their actions concerning supply and demand to be determined by these prices, which are therefore consistent with their actions. The price situations will then be equilibrium states in the sense that there will be equality between supply and demand during the period. The formation of prices can in this way be expressed in a system of equations for each period. Changes in the various prices and in the price level from one period to another will depend on changes in the factors determining prices, which are assumed to take place in the transition between the different periods. Thus, *a movement in the price level is connected with changes in the variables of the equation* $E\,(1 - s)/Q$. It has to be noted that gains and losses of individuals which are

the result of changes at the transition points between the periods, cause a change of the total national income (*E*)—for each period counted as the accrued interest on the average total capital value during the period—which is equal to the interest on the amount of gains and losses respectively [*Penningpolitikens medel*, pp. 31 f.; my italics; cf. the revised version in *Studies*, pp. 158 f.].

§8. The primary objective of Lindahl's monetary approach was to explain changes in the level of prices and not in the level of physical output (real income). In spite of this, his analysis resulted in achievements which are important for modern macroeconomics: (i) the use of the Keynesian tool of "the propensity to save" (*s*) leads to a definite distinction between saving and investment, both considered as expected values;[6] (ii) this distinction makes it necessary to divide aggregate income into saving and consumption demand, and aggregate output into investment and the production of consumption goods; (iii) the assumption of unused resources is introduced; i.e., changes in physical output (and hence real income) and employment are considered; (iv) the "paradox of saving" is solved, according to which a reduction in saving results in increased savings.

Furthermore, Lindahl's complete abolition of technical monetary details, including the quantity of money, signified that the plans and motives of the economic individuals, especially with regard to investment demand, had to be considered as a central instrument of analysis in his monetary approach. It enabled Lindahl to apply the tool of the propensity to save, which protected his theory from the fate of Keynes' *A Treatise on Money* (1930), where, as Don Patinkin has recently shown in his brilliant analysis, *Keynes' Monetary Thought* (1976), "the traditional quantity theory does indeed remain valid" (p. 46). It must, however, be emphasized in this context that despite the above results, especially his use of the Keynesian tools of the variations of physical output and the propensity to save, Lindahl's monetary approach did not contain "the distinctive analytical contribution of the *General Theory*" (Patinkin).[7] This means that Lindahl was not concerned with changes in output (income) "as an *equilibrating force* with respect to aggregate demand and supply—or, equivalently, with respect to saving and investment" (*Keynes'*

6. Lindahl's *s*, his "propensity to save," is a *planned* savings ratio which relates savings to *expected* income. There is no reason why the plans to save and the plans to invest should coincide.

7. "On the Relation Between Keynesian Economics and the 'Stockholm School,' " p. 139.

*Monetary Thought*, p. 14). What Lindahl's analysis instead showed was how changes in the *distribution* of income—not in its aggregate value—equilibrated saving and investment (*Penningpolitikens medel*, p. 41; cf. *Studies*, p. 174).[8]

§9. The importance of the results of Lindahl's monetary approach was first recognized to its full extent and formulated in the way shown above by Gunnar Myrdal in his essay "Om penningteoretisk jämvikt" (On Monetary Equilibrium), *Ekonomisk Tidskrift*, vol. 33, nos. 5–6 (1931; printed in 1932). This study can be said to represent first and foremost a deepening of Lindahl's treatment of changes in the value of money, and hence it used the same type of casuistic reasoning and also neglected completely technical monetary details. Nevertheless, Myrdal was vehemently opposed to the *method* applied by Lindahl, i.e., the intertemporal equilibrium period analysis, which he denounced as "meaningless": "The only possibility of studying a [dynamic] process . . . is, of course, to analyze *tendencies of a* certain situation and/or *movements from one situation to another*, i.e., *during a certain period*" (p. 230; Myrdal's italics; deleted, in both "Der Gleichgewichtsbegriff"[9] and *Monetary Equilibrium*).

§10. In his extensive discussion of Myrdal's *Monetary Equilibrium* in 1941 (cf. "On the Concepts and Methods of the Stockholm School", *International Economic Papers*, No. 3, 1953), Tord Palander characterized this method as an "instantaneous analysis" or rather a "*period analysis for a single period, using a very special concept of the period*" (p. 10). The significance of this for Myrdal's monetary approach becomes evident from the following summary of his conceptual apparatus used in "Penningteoretisk jämvikt." This

8. The equilibrating role of changes in total income with respect to saving and investment is, however, implicit in Lindahl's reasoning on "The Significance of the Relation Between Saving and Investment" in his mimeographed draft "A Note on the Dynamic Pricing Problem," which he sent to Keynes in 1934. This note is reproduced in my *Studien zur Enstehung der Neuen Wirtschaftslehre in Schweden*, pp. 204–11; with regard to the saving/investment relation see esp. pp. 208–10. Cf. further in this context Lindahl's discussion of the possibility of a systematic use of changes in the budget balance as a means to stabilize economic fluctuations in the following works: (i) *Penningpolitikens medel*, ch. 2, §8 on "The Influence on the Price Level by Means of Public Finance" (pp. 63–68); not translated in *Studies*; (ii) "Offentliga arbeten i depressionstider" (Public Works in Times of Depression), *Nationalekonomiska Föreningens Förhandlingar*, 1932, pp. 127–37, 163f. (iii) "Arbetslöshet och finanspolitik" (Unemployment and Fiscal Policy), *Ekonomisk Tidskrift*; Vol. 37, nos. 1 and 2, esp. Sections I (pp. 1–5) and VI (pp. 26–36); cf. the revised version in *Studies*, pp. 356–67.

9. The German version of the 1932 essay was entitled "Der Gleichgewichtsbegriff als Instrument der geldtheoretischen Analyse," in F. A. Hayek, ed., *Beiträge zur Geldtheorie* (Vienna, 1933), pp. 361–487.

paragraph is reproduced *in extenso*, not only because it formed the starting point for Ohlin's own conceptual apparatus but also because the version used in "Der Gleichgewichtsbegriff" was quite different and because it was completely deleted in *Monetary Equilibrium*:[9a]

> Now, it only remains . . . to try to generalize our conclusions. . . . For a more definite confirmation of the results of our analysis we ought to show that both equations of equilibrium—the equation for the profitability of investment and the equation for the situation on the capital market—usually correspond to each other. Let us . . . make use of some simple algebraic symbols. All quantities are *aggregate sums* for all entrepreneurs in a certain society, and they are, as usual in this work, expressed in *monetary units*. All quantities refer to a particular *instantaneous state of price formation*. This means that quantities which cannot be directly classed as instantaneous capital values are sums of individual expectations of income, saving, etc., during an arbitrarily chosen future *unit period*. These expectations are discounted with respect to the corresponding price formation. All incomes are constructed as *capital incomes*.
>
> $E$ is income.
> $S$ is saving.
> $K_u$ is the gross income of entrepreneurs resulting from sales of consumption goods.
> $K_e$ is the costs of consumers for consumption goods.
> $D$ is depreciation minus appreciation of the existing real capital.
> $C_1$ is the capital value of the existing real capital.
> $C_2$ is the capital value (as discounted expectation) of the real capital one is deciding to construct during the unit period. $C_2$ is calculated gross and, therefore, includes the capital value of both new investment and reinvestment. For simplicity it is assumed that the period of time necessary for the construction of $C_2$ coincides with the chosen unit period.
> $R_1$ is the cost of reproduction of $C_1$.
> $R_2$ is the cost of reproduction of $C_2$ (real investment).
> $i$ is the prevailing money rate of interest.

9a. As Ohlin has pointed out, his critique of Myrdal's conceptual apparatus led to considerable revisions of the German and English versions of the original Swedish text; cf. "Keynesian Economics and the Stockholm School," p. 145.

$i_0$ is the natural rate of interest ($i$ and $i_0$ are calculated as discounted interest for the chosen unit period).

$V$ is free capital disposal [free waiting].

We have the following definitions:

$$S = E - K_e \qquad (8)$$
$$V = S + D \qquad (9)$$
$$i = E/C_1 \qquad (10)$$
$$i_0 = E/R_1 \qquad (11)$$

Furthermore, for the sake of simplicity we assume that the following approximations are permitted:

$$E = K_u + C_2 - D \qquad (12)$$
$$K_u = K_e \qquad (13)$$

We also use our formulation of the equilibrium condition in monetary theory in terms of profitability as a point of departure. The theorem is assumed to be proved generally by the Wicksellian monetary theory (under certain premises, some of which will be examined below). Therefore, in the case of equilibrium

$$i = i_0 \qquad (14)$$

Substituting (14) in (10) and (11) we have

$$C_1 = R_1 \qquad (15)$$

Also since the old and the new real capitals are of the same type then

$$C_2 = R_2$$

or adding (12) and (13) and substituting for $C_2$ we obtain

$$R_2 = E + D - K_e$$

or using (8)

$$R_2 = S + D$$

or (9)

$$R_2 = V \qquad (16)$$

If the equilibrium condition (14) is valid, then equilibrium condition (16) is also valid. In the case of disequilibrium we have

$$i \lesseqgtr i_0 \qquad (17)$$

This results in

$$C_2 \gtreqless R_2$$

which signifies either a positive or negative investment gain. Because of this, $R_2$ increases or decreases, whereby $C_2$ also increases or decreases. The process continues as long as such a difference exists, i.e., as long as (17) is valid. Certain circumstances mentioned earlier in this essay produce the effect that the disequilibrium in (17) is permanent. For present purposes, however, it is sufficient to postulate (17) and to assume that the process indicated above will be realized. This results in

$$R_2 \gtrless V \tag{18}$$

I have to emphasize that these conclusions have been reached on the basis of certain assumptions which are abstract and not always satisfied by reality. Probably the most important result of the hitherto given analysis is indeed the putting into focus of the premises behind the first and second equilibrium equations of Wicksell. . . . [§23, pp. 231–35; cf. the revised version in "Der Gleichgewichtsbegriff," §57, pp. 431–35].

§11. It need not be emphasized in this context that Myrdal clearly understood the fact that the *expected* values of saving and investment would be in equilibrium only by chance and that, on the other hand, the corresponding *realized* values (counted by simple bookkeeping at the end of a period) would always be equal (cf. p. 230 n.2). He succeeded in separating these variables without using the terms *ex ante* and *ex post*, which were introduced first in 1933 in "Der Gleichgewichtsbegriff." It also goes without saying that Myrdal's monetary approach—as stressed above with regard to that of Lindahl—was not limited by the boundaries of the quantity theory as in Keynes' analysis in the *Treatise on Money*. Unlike Lindahl, Myrdal in his 1932 essay, did, however, arrive at the basic notion (Patinkin) of the *General Theory* of the equilibrating role of changes in output. It was in Chapter 5, §§46–47, that he analyzed "the inner mechanics of the depressive process," showing how a reduction in investment demand caused by a fall of "the profit margin" leads initially to a decline in total income and then to a decline in consumption demand, resulting in an increase in unemployment and a restriction of output which, in turn, reduce investment demand, etc. Myrdal was fully aware of the fact that this downward Wicksellian cumulative process could not continue *ad infinitum* if a particular tendency towards a stabilization of total income during a depression was present—his condition for stability being the behavior of "the monetary demand for consumption goods":

> However, it must now be noted that *aggregate purchasing power of the society*, which forms the demand for consumption goods, *shrinks significantly less than does aggregate income. This means*, naturally *that aggregate saving is reduced*, not only because of the reduction in incomes but *also on account of the smaller fraction saved.*[10] The social-psychological, political,

10. Myrdal's assumption means that the *average* propensity to save diminishes as

> and general institutional development of the economy of the countries in an advanced capitalistic stage tends continuously to increase the importance of these shifts in the use of income during a depressive process [p. 271, my italics; no substantive revisions being made in the German and the English version of Myrdal's monetary approach, cf. "Der Gleichgewichtsbegriff," p. 457, and *Monetary Equilibrium*, p. 164]

It becomes clear from this passage that Myrdal, when analyzing changes in level of aggregate *real* income, obtained his insights into the equilibrating or, as he would prefer to call it, the "stabilizing" device of these variations by the application of the Keynesian tool of the propensity to save. Thus, Myrdal clearly anticipated "the distinctive analytical contribution" (Patinkin) of the *General Theory*. The significance of his analysis with regard to Ohlin's monetary approach and its interpretation will be discussed in more detail in Part IV below.

§12. After this detailed account of both Lindahl's and Myrdal's macroeconomic contributions, it is now possible to understand Ohlin's conceptual apparatus and the significance of his approach to monetary theory. Like Lindahl and Myrdal, Ohlin, in his 1933 essay, first and foremost tries to explain changes in the level of prices by analyzing macroeconomic variables, measured in *monetary units*, and without treating the technical monetary details. His approach differs, of course, in several aspects from those of Lindahl and Myrdal; these aspects can be seen as a widening and deepening of the ideas of his predecessors and are listed thus: (i) an aggregate demand/supply approach, as used earlier in his works on international economics, instead of the concentration on *ex ante* disequilibrium between saving and investment for the analysis of macroeconomic processes; (ii) the stressing of the fact that expectations are indeterminate (especially in Lindahl's approach they had the character of probability judgments); (iii) the abandoning of Lindahl's—and Myrdal's—income concept which treated all incomes as capital incomes; (iv) his concern with the explanation of changes not only in the level of prices, but also, although to a minor extent, in the level of physical output and employment.

It is there, especially in §§6–8, that Ohlin is able to present a more precise analysis than Myrdal of the interactions between changes in

total income decreases, which reinforces the equilibrating process, but is not necessary for its existence; cf. Keynes' discussion in the *General Theory*, p. 97, and Part IV, §19, below.

output and the demand for consumption and investment. Such a process is described most clearly in §6, where Ohlin examines the case of a reduction of the propensity to save:

> Imagine that people decide to reduce their saving sharply, so demand for consumers' goods will rise. . . . The decision to reduce savings may not be accompanied by a tightening of credit. If so, investment demand will at first be allowed to go on as usual . . . and the rising investment demand of the consumers' goods industries will eventually bring about an increase in total investment. *Total saving, then, is not reduced but on the contrary increased,* despite the fact that consumption is up. *What makes this possible is expanding output* [p. 61; my italics; as cited in the English translation above, p. 368].

It becomes clear from this passage that Ohlin in his analysis of this case applies the Keynesian tool of the propensity to save in the tradition of Lindahl and Myrdal, i.e., the ratio people *intend* to maintain between saving and *expected* income, an *ex ante* ratio which is entirely different from the ratio *ex post* between saving, equaling new investment, and realized income. But it does not follow immediately from the case above that the application of this tool enabled Ohlin—as Myrdal had demonstrated—to assign the equilibrating forces of the analyzed changes in output by their influence on consumption demand. The anticipation of this "analytical novelty" (Patinkin) of the *General Theory* is, however, carried out decidedly in §8, where Ohlin examines another "type model" of a reduction of the propensity to save:

> Rising consumption demand does not at all mean falling net saving, which equals new real investment. On the contrary, aggregate demand and gross income will be rising *more* rapidly than consumption demand. Consequently, gross saving will be rising while negative incomes are falling. Net saving, then, will be rising for a twofold reason [p. 73; Ohlin's italics; in translation, above, p. 380].

In their contributions on Ohlin's essay to the Symposium and this number of *History of Political Economy*, both Don Patinkin (above) and Hans Brems (below) have paid attention only to Ohlin's case of reduced saving in §6. While Patinkin answers No to the question whether Ohlin's analysis contained "the central innovative feature of the General Theory" of the equilibrating role of changes in output, Brems seems to regard it as unimportant. Their different interpretations of Ohlin's contribution to modern macroeconimics will be discussed in Part IV below.

§13. An aspect which has not yet been considered when comparing Ohlin's monetary approach with the analyses of Lindahl and Myrdal is the different method in which Ohlin, despite the same type of casuistic reasoning, applied his conceptual apparatus to combine elements of the period analysis of Lindahl with those of the "instantaneous analysis" of Myrdal. In his 1937 article in the *Economic Journal* Ohlin characterized his method as "a combination of *ex post* and *ex ante* analysis":

> After a description of actual events during a certain, finished period, and of the differences between these events and the expectations which existed at the beginning of the period follows an account of those expectations for the future which more or less govern actions during the next period. The registration of events during this second period reveals again that expectations do not all come true, a fact which influences expectations and actions during the third period, etc. [p. 59].

It becomes clear from this summary and from §3 of the 1933 essay—"The problem is to describe price changes over time, i.e., *during* a period" (p. 51; my italics; translation, p. 359 above)—that Ohlin's combined *ex post/ex ante* analysis should not be confused with a sequence type of analysis, originally developed by Knut Wicksell (*Geldzins und Güterpreise*, 1898), applied by J. M. Keynes in Volume I of *A Treatise on Money* (1930), and perhaps most commonly defined by D. H. Robertson in *Banking Policy and the Price Level* (1926), where changes of a certain economic variable in one period are related to changes of another one in a preceding (or succeeding) period. In Sweden such sequence models were first of all applied by Dag Hammarskjöld in his article "Utkast till en algebraisk metod för dynamisk prisanalys" (Design for an Algebraic Method for Dynamic Price Analysis), published in the *Ekonomisk Tidskrift*, 34 (1932): 5–6 (printed 1933), which is referred to in Ohlin's essay. Contrary to Ohlin's somewhat cryptic presumption (p. 52 n.2; in English translation, n.8) that Hammarskjöld's method was a mixture between the type of analysis applied in his *Interregional and International Trade* (1933) and that of Lindahl, it has to be emphasized that it relied, first and foremost, on Keynes' sequence analysis in the *Treatise on Money*. This method was extended by Hammarskjöld in his 1933 treatise *Konjunkturspridningen* (The Transmission of Business Cycles) and in the theoretical part of the final report to the

Committee on Unemployment, *Åtgärder mot arbetslöshet* (Measures against Unemployment), in 1935—especially ch. 2 ("The Unemployment of Business Cycles")—which was written by Hammarskjöld when he was the Committee's Secretary. The sequence type of analysis was followed up in Sweden by Alf Johansson in his 1934 treatise *Löneutvecklingen och arbetslösheten* (Wage Trends and Unemployment) and, of course, in Erik Lundberg's famous *Studies in the Theories of Economic Expansion* (1937).

### III. *The Evolution of Ohlin's Monetary Theory 1933–1943*

§14. As has been recorded by Karl-Gustav Landgren (pp. 199–202), Bertil Ohlin did not achieve any significant development of his monetary thought, despite numerous feature articles on economic topics in the newspaper *Stockholms-Tidningen*, between the appearance of his essay in the *Ekonomisk Tidskrift*, July 1933, and the publication of his report to the Committee on Unemployment, April 1934. On the other hand, the 1934 report can be characterized as his most important contribution to monetary theory, his 1933 essay being merely a predecessor. Ohlin's report—*Penningpolitik, offentliga arbeten, subventioner och tullar som medel mot arbetslöshet. Bidrag till expansionens teori* (Monetary Policy, Public Works, Subventions, and Tariffs as Means Against Unemployment: A Contribution to the Theory of Expansion)—is a treatise of 176 pages, arranged in three different parts: (i) "General Theory of Expansion," chs. 1–3, pp. 5–77; (ii) "Certain Measures Against Unemployment . . . ," chs. 4–7, pp. 78–152; (iii) "Expansion, Structural Changes, and Unemployment," ch. 8, pp. 153–76. From a theoretical point of view the following sections deserve attention: (i) the whole of Part I; (ii) Part II, ch. 5, pp. 102–28, on "Public Works"; (iii) Part II, ch. 7, §3, pp. 138–43, on "Further Analysis of Changes in the Direction of Demand." From these sections the following ones are in accordance with the 1933 essay: (i) ch. 1, pp. 5–23, on "Principles of Monetary Theory," which corresponds to §§1–6 in "Penningteoriens uppläggning"; (ii) ch. 2, pp. 24–49, on "The Character of Processes of Expansion and Contraction," which in §§1–3 (pp. 24–42) and §4 (pp. 42–45) corresponds to §§7–9 and §11, respectively, of the 1933 essay. Otherwise §§5 and 6 of ch. 2 (pp. 45–49) and all other sections of the 1934 report are completely new, and §§10 and 12 in "Penningteoriens uppläggning" have been deleted.

§15. A comparison between Ohlin's 1934 treatise and his 1933 essay may show that the sections referred to above are very largely identical, even though revisions and additions were carried out from

1933 to 1934. As Hans Brems in his contribution below has already reviewed the 1934 book, I shall restrict myself to topics which, I think, have been neglected by him or which I would interpret in a somewhat different manner. First and foremost it has to be emphasized that Ohlin's terminology applied in his 1934 Chapter 1 is in greater accordance with that of Lindahl and Myrdal than with that used in his 1933 article. The terms *ex ante* and *ex post* introduced by Myrdal in "Der Gleichgewichtsbegriff" (1933) are applied, and Ohlin explicitly characterizes his method as "*a combination of ex ante and ex post*" (p. 6). The term "propensity to save" is defined in the way shown by Brems, but this is not a new finding, only the application of a tool already developed—as demonstrated above—by Lindahl in his 1929 formula $E(1-s) = PQ$, which, as Ohlin emphasizes, is in *ex ante* terms: " 'Planned saving' is equal to expected income multiplied by the planned saving ratio" (p. 20 n.1; cf. Ohlin, *Economic Journal*, 1937, p. 237 n.1). Furthermore, Ohlin's terminology is supplemented by technical monetary terms (pp. 12–14, 21–23) which, however, do not alter the point of departure for his monetary approach, i.e., to analyze changes in aggregate monetary demand, and not changes in the quantity of money, which he treats as "subsidiary" (p. 14; cf. the more extensive analysis in ch. 2, §5, pp. 45–48, on "The Monetary Mechanism").[11] In this context, interesting observations about "*the cash holdings of the individuals*" (p. 23) are made, which, in my opinion, compare closely with Keynes' analysis in the *Treatise on Money* (ch. 3) and which, according to Ohlin, can be divided in two parts: (i) "the transactions cash" and (ii) "the savings cash." In the language of the *General Theory* (chs. 13 and 15) these forms of cash holdings can be classified under the headings of (i) the transactions motive and (ii) the precautionary motive.[12] In ch. 2, §3 (pp. 36–42), on "The Market for Money and Capital," Ohlin clearly states the case of the Keynesian "liquidity trap" (p. 42), but, contrary to Brems (p. 433), it has to be emphasized that Ohlin never used this finding to elaborate a liquidity-preference theory of the rate of interest; in other words, in

11. It is this emphasis on aggregate monetary demand which, in the 1934 report, leads to a definite rejection of Hammarskjöld's monetary approach. Ohlin characterizes Hammarskjöld's theory as a combination of the approaches of Robertson and Keynes (*Treatise on Money*), where the emphasis is on the monetary mechanism; see p. 23 n.1.

12. Ohlin (p. 23) provides the following definitions: "(1) the transactions cash—its purpose is to bridge the expected differences between receipts and expenditures; (2) the savings cash—it holds savings in liquid form to meet unexpected investment opportunities, inclusive of liabilities"; cf. *General Theory*, pp. 195f.

his approach he did not apply the Keynesian tool of the speculative motive in spite of its being implicit in his reasoning. Instead he develops in this section the fundamentals of what in his 1937 controversy with Keynes in the *Economic Journal* became known as "the loanable funds theory," where the rate of interest is determined by demand and supply for different types of credit.

§16. Brems (pp. 402–4, above) has shown that Ohlin's 1934 treatise, in contrast to his 1933 essay, is concerned to a greater extent and more explicitly with the explanation for changes in the level of physical output. It must, however, be noted that in this analysis changes in the general price level still play a central role. The variations of quantities *and* prices are analyzed first and foremost in ch. 2, especially in §1, pp. 24–32 ("Expansion and Rise in Prices"), §2, pp. 32–36 ("Contraction and Fall in Prices"), and §3 as previously mentioned, where Ohlin develops the fundamentals for a theory of short-term economic expansion and contraction. In ch. 3, pp. 50–77, on "Various Types of Conditions for Expansion," this analysis is extended to a theory of the trade cycle and a theory of the stabilization of economic fluctuations. Contrary to Brems, it has to be emphasized in this context that Ohlin, not only in ch. 3, where he applies the accelerator (pp. 52 f.), but also in ch. 2 where he applies the propensity to save (pp. 32f., 36f.), is able to demonstrate why cumulative processes of expansion and contraction cannot continue *ad infinitum*—an assertion which will be discussed in Part IV below.

Furthermore, in these chapters Ohlin does not confine his analysis of the processes of expansion and contraction to a closed economy, but extends it to an open economy and also to an economy with a public sector. Here he clearly states the expansive effects of a growth in export- and loan-financed public expenditures on the one hand, and the depressive effects of a growth in import and taxes on the other (pp. 73–77; cf. pp. 39, 48f., 55). These aspects are discussed in more detail in Part II of the 1934 book, and particularly in chs. 5 and 7 (§3) which are concerned with the question of "the international margin," i.e., the leakages caused by import for an expansive economic policy. The most important theoretical innovation in this respect is the analysis of the multiplying effects of public works in ch. 5, whereby Ohlin, building on Myrdal's work on the economic effects of fiscal policy (1933, 1934),[13] was able to show the different *expansive* effects

13. See (i) the famous appendix to the Social Democratic Government's 1933 budget, published separately under the title *Konjunktur och offentlig hushållning* (Business Cycles and Public Economics) (Stockholm, 1933), and (ii) *Finanspolitikens ekonomiska verkningar* (The Economic Effects of Fiscal Policy) (Stockholm, 1934),

of loan- *and* tax-financed public expenditures, and thereby anticipated the balanced-budget-multiplier theorem (pp. 110f.).[14] Contrary to Brems (pp. 407–8) it has to be stressed that Ohlin assumed that tax financing would not only reduce consumption but also saving and thus only partially counteract the expansive effects of public works.

§17. In the following decade Ohlin, in his further contributions to monetary theory, was never again able to achieve the richness and depth of the 1934 report. The articles in the *Economic Journal*, 1937, insofar as they represent Ohlin's own contributions, are, with one exception, merely a summary of chs. 1 and 2, §§1–4, of the 1934 book, which corresponds to Section B, §§1–7 (pp. 58–69) and the first half of §8 (pp. 221–24) of the 1937 articles.[15] The exception is the second half of §8 (pp. 224–27), where Ohlin develops his loanable funds theory, to some extent under the influence of Keynes' reasoning on liquidity preference in the *General Theory*, an elaboration of which is continued in the succeeding controversy with Keynes on "Alternative Theories of the Rate of Interest" in the *Economic Journal*, 47 (1937): 423ff. A few years later, in 1941, Ohlin initiated a debate with Lindahl on dynamic theory in the *Ekonomisk Tidskrift*, 43, nos. 2 and 4: 170ff., 327ff.,[16] where he demonstrated that with regard to the method to be applied in monetary theory the gap between his type of analysis and that of Lindahl and Myrdal had widened. In this controversy Ohlin first and foremost questions "*the need for ex ante categories*" (p. 179), especially *aggregate* categories, such as "the concept of aggregate planned saving." Ohlin's, so far as I know, last contribution to monetary theory was his 1943 essay in the *Ekonomisk Tidskrift* on "The Stockholm School versus the Quantity Theory" (cf. *International Economic Papers*, no. 10, 1960, pp. 132 ff.) and the ensuing debate with Jørgen Pedersen on "Likviditet, löner

---

esp. Part IV on "Short-Term Effects of Fiscal Policy in a Business Cycle Perspective," pp. 159–279.

14. This anticipation by Myrdal and Ohlin has not been given full credit in Bent Hansen's contribution to the Symposium on the "Origins of the Balanced-Budget-Multiplier Theorem," *History of Political Economy* 7 (1975): 32–35 ("Introduction to Jørgen Gelting's 'Some Observations on the Financing of Public Activity' ").

15. These sections are almost exactly the contents of the Finlay Lecture, which Ohlin gave at University College, Dublin, in May 1934. They also formed part of his Marshall Lectures given at the University of Cambridge in November 1936. The outlines of the Finlay Lecture and the additions made in this text for the Marshall Lectures have survived; cf. Ohlin, *Letter to Don Patinkin*, Stockholm, 10 October 1977, p. 1.

16. Ohlin's contributions were entitled (i) "Professor Lindahl om dynamisk teori" (Prof. Lindahl on Dynamic Theory) and (ii) "Metodfrågor inom den dynamiska teorien" (Methods in Dynamic Theory).

och penningteori" (Liquidity, Wages and Monetary Theory) in the same journal, 45, no. 3 (1943): 258ff. The 1943 essay is a systematic summary of a book by Ohlin on Swedish wartime monetary problems, published in 1941, *Kapitalmarknad och räntepolitiken* (The Capital Market and Interest Rate Policy), and it is in harmony with the approach to monetary theory as developed in the early thirties by the Stockholm School, especially its emphasizing of the decisive role of expectations for economic processes: *"Of decisive importance for purchasing decisions are the income expectations of households and profit expectations of firms; these expectations are not directly affected by changes in the quantity of means of payments"* (p. 143). The essay ends with a claim that could have been raised by Lindahl, Myrdal, or Ohlin when they attempted to abandon the Wicksellian monetary framework: "Monetary theory, like the rest of economic theory, must be made into an analysis of a process in time where changes in income are taken account of and where a far greater number of monetary concepts are necessary than the formulae entering into the quantity theory" (p. 146).

## IV. *On Interpreting Ohlin's Contributions to Modern Macroeconomics*

§18. The basic question which arises, with respect to Ohlin's 1933 essay and his 1934 report, in Brems' and Patinkin's contributions to the Symposium is as follows: To what extent, if any, did these works anticipate the *General Theory* (Patinkin) and/or go beyond it (Brems)? I would like to discuss this question under the following headings: (i) How relevant are Ohlin's anticipations of Keynesian policy conclusions? (ii) To what extent did his 1933–34 contributions contain "the central innovative feature of the *General Theory*" (Patinkin), i.e., the equilibrating role of changes in output? (iii) How meaningful is the standard presentation of the *General Theory* for an interpretation of Ohlin's approach to monetary theory?

With regard to point (i) Brems (p. 411), in analyzing the 1934 report, emphasizes that Ohlin derived four "strikingly Keynesian policy conclusions," the foremost being "a policy of public works, generating income magnified by the multiplier." Patinkin (p. 417), on the other hand, opposes this claim by demonstrating "Keynes' priority (relative to Ohlin)" with respect to these conclusions, especially in the question of public works as a means against unemployment, where Keynes had influenced Ohlin already in 1929. This argument can be countered with the fact that Ohlin as early as 1927 had discussed "the favorable multiplier effects of credit-financed public works" (see my article in *History of Political Economy* 8: 346f.). However, I fear that such reasoning would lead to a fruitless debate relying too much on "the Walt Disney version of interwar economics" (Mark Blaug),[17] according to which the contemporaries of Keynes were incapable of advocating policies that we today would call Keynesian. This is a version which—as numerous treatises in the last decade have shown[18]—belongs to "the mythology which has come to surround the Keynesian Revolution" (Blaug, ibid.) and which shadows the fact that the crucial point of difference between Keynes and his contemporaries was, as has been emphasized by D. E. Moggridge,[19] not one of policy but one of theory: "Keynes attacked his 'classical' contemporaries, not because most of them disagreed with him on policy proposals in connection with the slump, but because he believed that their policy recommendations were inconsistent with the premises of their theory" (p. 61). Therefore, I conclude that the question whether Ohlin anticipated Keynesian policy conclusions lacks relevance. The question, however, to what extent he anticipated the theoretical underpinning of such a policy—which, as Patinkin emphasizes, is the purpose of the *General Theory*—has still to be discussed.

§19. What, then, did this underpinning consist of? Brems tells us that Ohlin, in his 1933 essay, anticipated the *General Theory* because he treated physical output as a variable and because he saw a feedback mechanism between these variations and consumption demand

17. "Kuhn versus Lakatos, or Paradigms versus Research Programmes in the History of Economics," *History of Political Economy* 7 (1975): 414.

18. Especially in the United States, but also in England, Germany, and Scandinavia, economists as well as politicians, bankers, unionists, and other "cranks" had advocated Keynesian policy conclusions. Cf. the following works: (i) T. W. Hutchison, *Economics and Economic Policy in Britain, 1946–1966* (London, 1968); (ii) D. Winch, *Economics and Policy: A Historical Study* (London, 1972; 1st ed., 1969); (iii) H. Stein, *The Fiscal Revolution in America* (Chicago, 1969); (iv) J. R. Davis, *The New Economics and the Old Economists* (Ames, Iowa, 1971); (v) A. Sweezy, "The Keynesians and Government Policy, 1933–1939," *American Economic Review* 62, no. 2 (1972): 116–24; (vi) S. Beckman et al., "Ekonomisk politik och teori i Norden under mellankrigstiden" (Economic Policy and Theory in Scandinavia during the Interwar Period), in *Kriser och krispolitiken i Norden under mellankrigstiden* (Crises and Crisis Policy in Scandinavia During the Interwar Period) (Uppsala, 1974), pp. 27–70; cf. the English summary by K.-G. Hildebrand, "Economic Policy in Scandinavia During the Interwar Period," *Scandinavian Economic History Review* 23, no. 2 (1975): 99–115; (vii) G. Garvy, "Keynes and the Economics Activities of Pre-Hitler Germany," *Journal of Political Economy* 83 (1975): 391–405; (viii) A. Korsch: "Der Stand der beschäftigungspolitischen Diskussion zur Zeit der Weltwirtschaftskrise in Deutschland," in G. Bombach et al., eds., *Der Keynesianismus, I: Theorie und Praxis keynesianischer Wirtschaftspolitik* (Berlin, 1976), pp. 9–132.

19. "Keynes: The Economist," in D. E. Moggridge, ed., *Keynes: Aspects of the Man and his Work* (London, 1974), p. 61.

via generated income. Patinkin objects to this by maintaining that the *General Theory* was not only concerned with such an analysis of output, but to an even greater extent with the *equilibrating role* of the changes in output:

> In particular, the *General Theory* showed how a (say) initial situation of excess aggregate supply causes a decline in output which (by virtue of a marginal propensity to consume less than unity) is *greater* than the resulting decline in aggregate demand, so that the economy is eventually brought to a position of unemployment equilibrium in which the excess supply has been eliminated [Patinkin, p. 414; my italics].

The crucial point for this analysis is, as Patinkin emphasizes, Keynes' assumption of a marginal propensity to consume less than unity, i.e., that, as output varies, consumption demand will change to a *smaller* extent than income, the gap between them being filled by saving. It is exactly this relation between consumption and income which Ohlin—and Myrdal—assumed in their 1932–34 contributions to macroeconomics.[20] As has been cited (cf. §12 above), Ohlin in §8 of his 1933 essay makes the following assumption when analyzing a process of economic expansion: "Aggregate demand[21] and gross income will be rising more rapidly than consumption demand. Consequently, gross saving will be rising while negative saving will be falling" (p. 73). A few pages earlier in the same section, while analyzing a process of contraction, he states: "The reduced output and declining price of capital goods . . . will reduce net income and with it consumption demand (*K*), but *not necessarily in the same proportion*. The result is a reduced output of consumers' goods and a tendency to falling prices" (p. 70; my italics; in translation, p. 377 above). Furthermore, I would like to refer to Ohlin's polemics against Johan Åkerman in *Det Ekonomiska Läget*, Aug. 1932, on "the paradox of saving," as cited in my article in *History of Political Economy* (8: 351):

> The real savings required for increasing output arise as a result of better utilization of the productive machinery, which causes pro-

20. These insights are most clearly developed in Myrdal's works on the economic effects of fiscal policy, *Konjunktur och offentlig hushållning*, pp. 21–24, and *Finanspolitikens ekonomiska verkningar*, pp. 204–24. For a detailed discussion, see my forthcoming paper "What Was New in Myrdal's 1932–1934 Macroecnomics?" *Diskussionsbeiträge zur Politischen Ökonomie* (Universität Bremen, 1979).

21. Aggregate demand is equal to consumption and investment demand; it grows *more* than consumption demand, because Ohlin assumes income-induced investments; see §20 below.

> duction to grow *faster* than consumption. Åkerman's most fatal error is that he takes into account only the increase in individual savings that take place through reductions in consumption, and neglects the second type, the increase in output which is *stronger* than the increase in consumption [my italics].

As I have emphasized earlier in this article, Ohlin—and Myrdal in the above-cited paragraph of his 1932 essay—achieved these insights by applying the "Keynesian" tool of the propensity to save, which they derived from Lindahl's 1929 equation $E\,(1 - s) = PQ$. This simple formula allows the demonstration of the rule that, when output and hence income ($E$) rises, the increases in income, $\Delta E$, must be *greater* than the increase in consumption, $\Delta PQ$, and vice versa, although the *proportion* between income and consumption is not changed. This is simply so, because the *average* propensity to save ($s$) in Lindahl's equation—and therefore, one may add, even its mirror twin, the *average* propensity to consume $(1 - s)$—is a constant and less than unity.[22] Ohlin was, as was Myrdal, aware of the fact that the existence of the above rule is essential for the stability of the economy in an advanced capitalistic system. This is clearly stated in his 1934 report, ch. 2, §2 on "Contraction and Fall in Prices," where he explains why a downward cumulative process cannot continue *ad infinitum*:

> Every decline in demand diminishes either prices or quantities or both parts and reduces in this way gross incomes, which causes a tendency to further decline in demand. This leads to the question why this deflation spiral, once started, does not proceed to a complete collapse. The explanation of why this does not occur might be found in the fact, among others, that *demand for consumption goods declines only slowly below a certain level, even when net income would decline still more*. Some people live on their savings, while others receive unemployment relief financed out of loans covering a deficit in public finances. First and foremost the constant element in demand consists of people receiving salaries and dividend incomes which during a period of a

22. It follows from this assumption that the average propensity to consume is equal to the *marginal* propensity to consume, which likewise is constant at a value less than unity. In Myrdal's case (cf. n.10 above) where the average propensity to save is assumed to diminish as income declines, we would get a marginal propensity to consume which differs from the average propensity to consume and which is to a greater degree less than unity, i.e., smaller than the marginal propensity to consume in the former case where $(1 - s)$ is assumed to be a constant; cf. Alvin H. Hansen, *A Guide to Keynes* (New York, 1953), pp. 34f., 75f.

> cumulative fall in prices as a rule are partly financed by public or private loans [p. 33; my italics].

In this passage it can be shown that Ohlin heavily relied on Myrdal. In §47 of his 1932 article, Myrdal had explained why during a depression "the total purchasing power of the society . . . shrinks significantly less than does total income" (p. 271; cf. above), with the following considerations:

> The unemployed workers must live, and in view of the ever-growing importance of social ideals, they must not live too badly. The public authority takes its part in several ways. Whether the cost of the care of the unemployed is covered by public loans or by another turn of the tax screw (in so far as this effects saving), in either case there comes about a reduction in total savings [$S$] and thus also in the free capital disposal [$V = S + D$, cf. above] available for real investment [$R_2$] in our second equation of equilibrium ($R_2 = V$), compared to the level this capital disposal would have had if the dole had not been paid. . . . The unemployed also live on their own past savings and those of their relatives, which likewise reduces the quantity $V$.
>
> Corresponding reasoning holds for the other classes of society [p. 271; cf. the unchanged version in "Der Gleichgewichtsbegriff," pp. 457f., and *Monetary Equilibrium*, pp. 164f., which is only slightly revised].

There are striking similarities between these passages of Ohlin and Myrdal and the explanation for the existence of an unemployment equilibrium which Keynes made in ch. 8 of the *General Theory* on "the objective factors" of the propensity to consume:[23]

23. In an earlier version of this note I argued that these similarities *might* be explained by the fact that Myrdal had possibly read Keynes' June 1931 Chicago Lectures on the Harris Foundation "An Economic Analysis of Unemployment," published later that year in Q. Wright, ed., *Unemployment as a World Problem* (Chicago, 1931). In the second of these lectures on "The Abstract Analysis of the Slump," Keynes had hinted for the first time at the possibility of an unemployment equilibrium which he characterized as "a kind of spurious equilibrium": "There is . . . another reason for expecting the decline to reach a stopping-point. . . . As soon as output has declined heavily, strong forces will be brought into play in the direction of reducing the net volume of saving. For one thing the unemployed will, in their effort not to allow too great a decline in their established standard of life, not only cease to save but will probably be responsible for much negative savings and those of their friends and relations. Much more important, however, than this is likely to be the emergence of negative saving on the part of the government, whether by diminished payments to sinking funds or by actual borrowing" (pp. 23f). Myrdal's 1932 essay was written in the spring of that year and sent to the printer of *Ekonomisk Tidskrift* in June. However, as Myrdal has informed me recently, he "never read the book [edited by Wright] then or later, and [has] never heard about it" (Myrdal to Otto Steiger, 5 April 1978).

A decline in income due to a decline in the level of employment, if it goes far, may even cause consumption to exceed income not only by some individuals and institutions using up the financial reserves which they have accumulated in better times, but also by the Government, which will be liable, willingly or unwillingly, to run into a budgetary deficit or will provide unemployment relief, for example, out of borrowed money. Thus, when employment falls to a low level, aggregate consumption will decline by a smaller amount than that by which real income has declined, by reason both of the habitual behavior of individuals and also of the probable policy of governments; which is the explanation why a new position of equilibrium can usually be reached within a modest range of fluctuation. Otherwise a fall in employment and income, once started, might proceed to extreme lengths [p. 98].

Contrary to Patinkin—and to a certain extent even to Brems—I therefore conclude that Ohlin, relying on Lindahl and Myrdal, anticipated the analytical novelty of the *General Theory* of the equilibrating forces of variations in income. It need not be emphasized that this claim does not mean that he was able to present this insight in such a precise and elaborated way as Keynes in the *General Theory*; especially as he did not make any explicit use of the marginal principle when applying the tool of the propensity to save. On the other hand—and in *this* respect, I think, Brems is right—Ohlin did not analyze the changes in income in a *static* Keynesian equilibrium, which is usually illustrated by the diagonal-cross (45°-line) diagram and is central for Patinkin's reasoning.

§20. So far so good. But the question is this: Can the statement that Ohlin was not concerned with a Keynesian static equilibrium be interpreted in the way Brems claims, i.e., that Ohlin went beyond the *General Theory* because he anticipated "Keynesian theory in a dynamic form"? Such an interpretation would imply that the Keynesian theory is essentially static, which is indeed the standard presentation of the *General Theory*, both in the form of the 45°-line diagram and in that of the Hicksian IS-LM diagram. I doubt, however, whether this presentation picks up the full message of the Keynesian theory, and therefore whether it can be considered meaningful for an interpretation of Ohlin's analysis.[24]

In his interpretation of Ohlin, Brems makes the valuable observa-

24. The following passages draw freely on Franz Haslinger and Otto Steiger, "Elemente der allgemeinen Theorie einer Geldwirtschaft, oder Keynes geld- und preistheoretisch auf den Begriff gebracht," *Diskussionsbeiträge zur Politischen Ökonomie* (Universität Regensburg/Universität Bremen, 1979), forthcoming.

tion, that Ohlin not only assumed a partial feedback between changes in output and consumption demand via generated income as did Keynes, but also a more general one by the inclusion in his analysis of a feedback via induced investment. This is a mechanism, however, which, as Ohlin has recently emphasized again in a comment on Patinkin's paper on Keynes and the Stockholm School,[25] "may *take time*" and which means "that *investment will be an endogenous element in the process just as well as savings.*" Such an assumption is only fleetingly considered in the *General Theory*—in the "Notes on the Trade Cycle," ch. 22, pp. 318f. It is *not* in its main body, because, in his efforts to make his theory of the determination of the level of employment as effective as possible, i.e., a theory which determines this level *at any time*, Keynes regarded as "the *causa causans* that factor which is most prone to sudden and wide fluctuation": "the amount of investment" ("The General Theory of Employment," *Quarterly Journal of Economics* (1937): 221). Treated in that way, it was, of course, necessary to look at investment as an exogenous factor and to disregard induced investment. In the Keynesian literature this intended simplification led, however, to an analysis of changes in investment, i.e., the *multiplier theory*, which, usually illustrated by the 45°-line diagram, was treated in complete separation from the other parts of the *General Theory* and not, as Keynes had assumed, as "an *integral* part of our employment theory" (p. 113; my italics). In particular it was not observed that the multiplier holds true only when the future is *fully* foreseen (p. 122).[25a] Thus interpreted, the multiplier became—as in Patinkin's analysis of the equilibrating mechanism of changes in output (which is implicit in the multiplier)—a static theory, or, as John R. Hicks has recently emphasized, a theory "which is out of time."[26]

25. "Keynesian Economics and the Stockholm School," p. 6 of Ohlin's manuscript (omitted from the printed version).

25a. This view has been supported recently by P. Davidson in a postscript to the second edition of his *Money and the Real World* (1978), p. 380.

26. "Some Questions of Time in Economics," in A. M. Tang, F. M. Westfield, J. S. Worley, eds., *Evolution, Welfare and Time in Economics: Essays in Honour of Nicholas Georgescu-Roegen* (Lexington, Mass., 1976), pp. 140f. Contrary to my interpretation, which refers to the *Keynesian* presentation, Hicks complains that the multiplier theory (and the whole theory of production and prices that goes with it) as set out by Keynes himself is "out of time." This has been heavily denied recently by Joan Robinson in her essay "What Are the Questions?" *Journal of Economic Literature* 15 (1977): 1325; but I am of the opinion that her criticism misses the point: namely, the inadmissibility of dividing the *General Theory* into a real sector and a monetary sector which then have to be integrated. It has to be emphasized that in the Keynesian system even the "real" variables are always set out in *monetary terms* and that prices are never assumed to be fixed; see further below, esp. n.29.

The multiplier theory is, however, only one part of the *General Theory*, another one being "that concerned with the *marginal efficiency of capital* and with *liquidity preference*, which is unquestionably *in* time" (Hicks, ibid.). As is well known, the two parts were integrated as early as 1937 by Hicks himself in what was to become the standard presentation of the *General Theory*, the IS-LM diagram; but, as Hicks confesses today, this interpretation "is not really *in* time." Like the 45°-line diagram, it merely "reduces the *General Theory* to equilibrium economics" (p. 141), because it abandons an innovation which Keynes himself had regarded as the most important one of the *General Theory*, i.e., the relationship between *investment and uncertainty*[27] which is unthinkable without taking the factor of time into consideration. In recent years the works of G. L. S. Shackle, Sidney and Roy Weintraub, Paul Davidson, and Hyman P. Minsky, which deal with a reevaluation of Keynes' economics, have shown, in particular by their rediscovery of the monetary and price-theory elements in the "lost" chapters 12, 17, and 19–21 of the *General Theory*, that uncertainty and therefore time are intrinsic parts of Keynes' economic system:[28]

> Keynes' system . . . was dynamic in the traditional sense of involving *time in an essential manner*; so if investment is volatile, because of uncertainty, no one level of output or employment might ever be maintained. It is in this sense that uncertainty can be called a disequilibrium phenomenon, and Keynes can be said to have dealt with disequilibrium problems. At any rate, it should be clear that adjustments to an equilibrium level of employment are meaningless *in a world of uncertainty*, for *there might be no equilibrium in the sense of a maintained state of the system* [E. R. Weintraub, " 'Uncertainty' and the Keynesian Revolution," *History of Political Economy* 7 (1975): 535; my italics].

I therefore conclude that Brems' claim that Ohlin went beyond the Keynesian static equilibrium is lacking in relevance on the grounds that the *General Theory* cannot be reduced to such an equilibrium. The question, however, arises whether and to what extent there were

27. This was Keynes' view when he gave a lecture in Stockholm, autumn 1936, on "Further Reflections on Liquidity Preference" (an early draft of his contribution to the 1937 *Festschrift* for Irving Fisher, "The Theory of the Rate of Interest"), as has been recollected recently by Ohlin, "Some Comments on Keynesianism and the Swedish Theory of Expansion Before 1935", p. 160.

28. For a detailed account of this reevaluation see Haslinger and Steiger, "Elemente der allgemeinen Theorie einer Geldwirtschaft."

differences between Keynes' and Ohlin's treatments of the factor which made their theories dynamic: namely, *uncertainty*. Like Keynes in the *General Theory*, Ohlin, in his monetary approach, not only included expectations about future events but also stressed the fact that these anticipations were uncertain or as he expressed it, "indefinite," i.e., changeable and therefore capable of influencing the present economic outcome (cf. his 1933 essay, esp. pp. 50 n.1, 70 n.1; in the translation, nn.4 and 26).

Keynes incorporated the uncertainty factor in the *General Theory* by means of the concept of *liquidity preference*, where the desire to hold money was regarded as "a barometer of the degree of distrust of our own calculations and conventions concerning the future" (*Quarterly Journal of Economics*, 1937, p. 216), especially with respect to the prospective yield of investment. This analysis enabled Keynes to demonstrate that "*the importance of money essentially flows from its being a link between the present and the future*" (p. 293). This insight into the role of money with regard to uncertainty and thereby time signified that "we cannot even begin to discuss the effects of changing expectations on current activities except in *monetary terms*" (p. 294; my italics). In a world of uncertainty, where output *and* prices[29] are changing and which Keynes characterized as "*a monetary economy*" (Preface, p. vii; my italics), money, he recognized, could not be treated as a veil; and therefore a theory was necessary which would bring the *theory of money* (or absolute prices) back to the *theory of value* (or relative prices). This had to be an approach which "led to a more general theory" (p. vii), i.e., "*the complete theory of a Monetary Economy*" (p. 293; my italics)—an approach which the *General Theory* in fact was intended to represent.

In his treatment of the uncertainty factor, Ohlin did not use

29. Brems claims that Ohlin also went beyond Keynes, because, with regard to Ohlin's approach, "prices did not come in as an afterthought" (p. ). It is true that Keynes paid much less attention to variations in prices than to changes in physical output, but, in spite of this, it must be emphasized that *from the very outset* of the *General Theory*—and not first in ch. 21 as Brems asserts—prices are always assumed to change *along with* employment; see, e.g., pp. 119, 173. In this context, Keynes carefully distinguished between a rise in prices in a state of full employment, which he called "true inflation," and a rise in prices in a state of unemployment preceded by heavy deflation, which should be characterized as "reflation." This means a rise in the general price-level to generate higher income and employment, which was already worked out by Keynes in *The Means to Prosperity* (London, 1933), esp. in ch. 3 on "The Raising of Prices," and which Ohlin also had in mind; see the 1933 article, pp. 66f. (in the translation, pp. f.), and the 1934 report, pp. 94, 96. Brems, therefore, gives too much credit to Ohlin in claiming that this analysis "points to a present-day inflation-unemployment tradeoff" (ibid.).

a conception like Keynes' liquidity preference,[29a] but it can be shown that even into his economic framework money enters in an essential manner. Ohlin incorporated uncertainty directly in the *ex ante* calculations of economic individuals with regard to consumption and investment demand, emphasizing that particularly the investors' expectations are subject to sudden changes, i.e., that their plans and actual decisions often diverge. Ohlin analyzed the effects of these changes and explicitly pointed out that they must be discussed in *monetary terms* (1933 article, p. 49—in translation, p. 357 above; 1934 report, p. 5), but unlike Keynes he did not see something perculiar in this procedure.[30] Its necessity had, however, already been explained by Myrdal, upon whose analysis Ohlin heavily relied in his treatment of the uncertainty factor. In his 1932 essay Myrdal had achieved the insight (which was already implicit in Lindahl's 1929 book) that as soon as *time* is essential in an economic process, e.g., production, changes may occur which affect the value of money and which cannot be fully foreseen. Therefore, one has to consider uncertain expectations with regard to *absolute* future prices; i.e., as soon as we include time and thereby uncertainty in our analysis, money can no longer be regarded as a *veil*. This was made clear in Myrdal's attack on Wicksell's conception of a physically, technically determined "natural" rate of interest:

> Wicksell says: "If now money is actually *lent at this interest rate* by moneylenders, then the use of money serves only as *clothing* for a process which *in abstracto* could happen as well without money, and the conditions of economic equilibrium are fulfilled in exactly the same manner" . . . [Myrdal's italics]. This assertion is correct only under absolutely stationary conditions where all *relative* prices, including the value of money, are not changing; it is therefore *not* correct under more realistic assumptions which Wicksell treats immediately afterwards, namely, when various primary changes occur which cannot be foreseen completely and with certainty. For the exchange value of money is then necessarily changed in different ways with respect to *different* commodities, and credit has therefore at each interest rate a different significance for the profitability of different kinds of en-

29a. It has to be emphasized, however, that Ohlin had clearly stated the case of the Keynesian liquidity trap; cf. §15 above. Myrdal had also hinted at this idea; cf. *Finanspolitikens ekonomiska verkningar*, p. 165.

30. Cf. the following statement in his 1937 article in the *Economic Journal*: "A reasoning in monetary terms does not prevent any amount of considerations of the 'real' implications, whenever such considerations may be desirable" (p. 230).

trepreneurs' activity and consequently for the exchange relations. Money is no longer only a "clothing" for the process of price formation ["Penningteoretisk jämvikt," p. 199; cf. "Der Gleichgewichtsbegriff," p. 393, and *Monetary Equilibrium*, p. 52].

Shackle has observed that Myrdal, in this critique of Wicksell, "dimly foreshadowed the notion and influence of liquidity" (*The Years of High Theory*, 1969, p. 101). He did not hint directly at Keynes' concept of the speculative demand for money, but he did come very close to Keynes' insight into the role of money in that he concentrated on money in the form of *credit contracts* (and money interest rates) and stressed their importance as being a *link between two different points of time*. For Myrdal it was impossible to think of changes in "real" values, "which . . . are independent of the *absolute money units* in which credit contracts are included" (p. 200; my italics; cf. "Der Gleichgewichtsbegriff," p. 394, and *Monetary Equilibrium*, p. 53). Therefore, Myrdal, in his 1932 approach, discussed the effects of changing expectations on macroeconomic *ex ante* variables in monetary terms. In this analysis he was merely concerned with *price changes*, which result in investment gains and losses. Ohlin, in his 1933 essay, made clear that such a monetary reasoning could be extended to an analysis of *quantity changes*.

## V. *Conclusions*

§21. To summarize: In their 1932–34 macroeconomics both Ohlin and Myrdal (and to a certain extent also Lindahl as early as 1929) anticipated what Keynes himself had regarded as the two essentials of the *General Theory*:[31] (i) the significance of uncertainty for investment decisons, and (ii) the equilibrating device of changes in aggregate output. This claim does not mean that the monetary approaches of the Stockholm economists were worked out as clearly as the *General Theory*, which, furthermore, formed a coherent system which they never achieved. On the other hand, it must be emphasized that Ohlin's and Myrdal's 1932–34 macroeconomic theories should be viewed as forming an important part of an innovation in the history of economic thought which has been lost in the Keynesian literature and which, from the point of view of the current reevaluation of Keynes' monetary thought, I think, is most interesting—the development of *the theory of a monetary economy*.

31. Cf. his 1937 article in the *Quarterly Journal of Economics*, pp. 222f. In point (ii) the aggregate demand/supply approach is incorporated in which Ohlin was a forerunner; cf. my article in *History of Political Economy* 8: 348 ff., 364.

# [7]

*History of Political Economy 10:3*


# Ohlin's 1933 reformation of monetary theory

*William P. Yohe*

> I tried [in the 1933 article] to make a contribution to a systematic treatment of the role of variations in "total demand" (aggregate spending) in monetary theory, as a background for an analysis of processes of expansion and contraction.—BERTIL OHLIN[1]

I still have painful memories of struggling with the 1933 Ohlin paper twenty years ago in connection with my doctoral dissertation.[2] The pain arose from the facts that the article was so long and my translating so slow (and there were no graphs, which are much easier to figure out). I finally gave up and concluded that "the 1933 article . . . is an enigmatic combination of destructive criticisms of the simplifying assumptions . . . used by Wicksell, Myrdal, and Lindahl, among others, and the attempts to formulate a whole bevy of strange, empirically-oriented concepts."[3]

The original publication of the article apparently elicited little response. It was eclipsed the following year by the appearance of Ohlin's long report for the Unemployment Committee.[4] The first detailed discussion of the paper appeared in an entire chapter of Karl-Gustav Landgren's book, *Den 'nya ekonomien' i Sverige* (The "New Economics" in Sweden), Stockholm, 1960. Landgren argued: "Ohlin's characteristic place in the history of doctrine is precisely that he developed, with the aid of ideas in 'The Means to Prosperity,' a preliminary Keynesian theory before Keynes himself" (p. 166). In an excellent 1976 paper, which is indispensable to anyone interested in

WILLIAM P. YOHE *is Professor of Economics at Duke University.*

1. "On the Slow Development of the 'Total Demand' Idea in Economic Theory: Reflections in Connection with Dr. Oppenheimer's Note," *Journal of Economic Literature*, 1974, p. 893.

2. "The Wicksellian Tradition in Swedish Macroeconomic Theory" (Univ. of Michigan, 1958).

3. Ibid., p. 204, n.59.

4. *Penningpolitik, offentliga arbeten, subventioner och tullar som medel mot arbetslöshet* (Monetary Policy, Public Works, Subsidies, and Tariffs as Remedies for Unemployment) (Stockholm, 1934).

origins and development of Ohlin's ideas, Otto Steiger has compared an early draft of the 1933 Ohlin paper, completed in the fall of 1932 (six months before "The Means to Prosperity"), and the published version and found them virtually identical.[5] This provides strong support for the independent development of the "new economics" in Sweden.

Landgren and Steiger have both traced Ohlin's earlier use of the aggregate demand (or, as he continues to call it, "total demand") approach to macroeconomic problems, an obvious legacy from Wicksell.[6] For example, in an address before a meeting of Scandinavian economists in June 1931, Ohlin asserted:

> It is quite obvious . . . that underlying the cyclical contraction we have had the phenomenon which, in technical terms, is customarily called underinvestment or excess saving, i.e., a part of saving has not been used for business investment. The corresponding purchasing power has thus been lost, and prices have tended to fall.[7]
>
> . . . why, then, has the rate of interest, the price of capital, not fallen enough to stimulate the demand for capital? If this had occurred to a sufficient extent, no purchasing power would have been lost, and a general fall in prices could have been avoided.[8]

The latter, of course, suggests a floor to a fall in interest rates, which was discussed in more detail in Ohlin's 1934 book.[9]

One of the more striking features of Ohlin's 1933 paper is its harshly polemical style, with most of the barbs directed toward the

5. "Bertil Ohlin and the Origins of the Keynesian Revolution," *History of Political Economy*, 1976, pp. 341–66. Unfortunately, Kark-Gustav Landgren died in October 1977, before he could prepare a paper for the present discussion.

6. In my dissertation, pp. 162–63, I argued that the "Wicksellian tradition" had three pillars: an aggregate demand explanation of price level changes, a quantity theory with an endogenous money supply, and the analysis of price level movements as a discrete (discontinuous) process in time. Much of the work of the Stockholm School may be related to this tradition.

7. *Forhandlingar vid Nordiska nationalekonomisk mötet i Stockholm 15–17 juni 1931* (Proceedings of the Nordic Economic Meeting in Stockholm, 15–17 June 1931), p. 22 (quoted in Swedish in Landgren, p. 152).

8. Ohlin, quoted in Landgren, p. 152 (no page reference is given for the original).

9. See Hans Brems, in this issue, "What Was New in Ohlin's 1933–34 Macroeconomics?" Landgren, pp. 152–53, also cites another provocative statement in Ohlin's 1931 address: "Were it good times and bond prices fall, they [capitalists] lose. Therefore they prefer to hold their money in bank accounts at 1% interest rather than buy bonds yielding 4%. They are pessimistic and save for worse times and therefore they purchase no stocks, and they are optimistic and save for better times and therefore they purchase no bonds."

works of the very colleagues Ohlin was to include in his 1937 portrait of a homogeneous "Stockholm School."[10] According to Landgren,

> When Ohlin gave the [Stockholm] school its name in two articles in the *Economic Journal* in 1937, he gave readers a condensed version of the train of thought in the essay "Till frågan om penningteoriens uppläggning" (On the Formulation of Monetary Theory) from the year 1933 and in the supplement to the unemployment report from the year 1934. In addition, extremely brief account was given of the theories of some of the other Stockholm economists. . . . [Alf Johansson] related in an interview that the Stockholm School was, in his words, an *ex post* construction. He believed that Ohlin chose the name of the school because of the fact that Swedish economics in the early 1930's was known abroad and needed to be given a name which supported the common interests.[11]

Thus, in Landgren's view, Ohlin alone broke from the Wicksellian tradition and later tried to attribute his views to an entire "school." This, too, has been seriously questioned by Steiger, who has carefully traced the influence of Lindahl's and Myrdal's writings on Ohlin and documented the resolution of differences between Ohlin and Lindahl.[12]

Ohlin, in a commemorative article on Lindahl in 1960, attributed influence on the early Stockholm School to Robertson and Hawtrey, although he despaired over the complicated terminology of the former.[13] Tor Fernholm, who served as the faculty opponent of Landgren at his dissertation defense, has stated, regarding the 1933 paper: "Ohlin's investment concept was . . . not net, neither gross as in OEEC statistics nor 'gross-gross-' as in Sweden, but 'gross-gross-gross': it even embraced all kinds of reinvestment in circulating real

10. "Some Notes on the Stockholm Theory of Savings and Investment," *Economic Journal*, 1937, pp. 53–69 and 221–40.

11. Landgren, p. 223. Johansson was the author of one of the reports for the Unemployment Committee and held an appointment at the University of Stockholm.

12. Steiger, pp. 354–64. Interestingly, Erik Lundberg had more sympathy for Landgren's thesis; in "Om att begripa Keynes och att förstå andra" (To Comprehend Keynes and to Understand Others), a paper in a symposium on Landgren's book in the *Ekonomisk Tidskrift*, 1960, he declared (p. 204): "The real tragedy—although Landgren does not say so—was perhaps that we [i.e., all the economists mentioned except possibly Ohlin himself] evidently were so hardened by the Wicksell-Lindahl influence that we did not notice the revolution, much less allow ourselves to be shaken out of our ruts."

13. "Erik Lindahl—några minnesord" (Erik Lindahl—In Commemoration), *Ekonomisk Tidskrift*, 1960, pp. 2–3. This section appears in translation in Steiger, p. 358 n.

capital."[14] Ohlin's detailed treatment of both the sources of saving and types of investment is reminiscent of Robertson's careful delineation of various kinds of "lacking" and their application in real and "imaginary" capital formation.[15] Similarly, Ohlin's aggregate demand (literally "total demand") approach is clearly related not only to Wicksell but also to Hawtrey's simple designation of consumers', traders', and total income and outlay.[16]

Reading the 1933 paper in an *ex post* Keynes perspective tempts one to read into many of the passages profundities that may or may not be there. The most striking example, perhaps, is in §6, where Ohlin supposed that a decision to reduce saving might stimulate consumption and investment, so that saving ended up being actually larger than initially, suggesting the "paradox of thrift." Landgren interpreted this as the virtual discovery of the paradox and embellished Ohlin's words with the standard graph showing saving and investment as positive functions of income and the effect of a shift in the saving function on the equilibrium levels of income, saving, and investment.[17] Fernholm soundly attacked this use of late 1940's constructs to explain Ohlin's meaning:

> But has the author [Landgren] . . . really *shown* that this is not a dubious ex post construction? Did Ohlin really think as mechanically as the Keynesian scheme of thought assumes? On the contrary, was it not true that the whole exercise sought to make it "*sufficiently clear* that the effects of a given primary change will differ widely if the secondary reactions occur *in one time sequence rather than another*" [italics added]. Did the statement concern an equilibrium position, which Landgren believes, or, more likely, what may be stated at the end of a time period, after the statistics have been collected? Cannot Ohlin have thought, quite simply: *If* the new investment recorded during a period must be equal to the net new saving recorded and *if* an increased consumption demand has also led to increased demand for new investment, "*thus*" (p. 175 in Landgren, last Ohlin quotation) net new saving must have increased?[18]

14. "Idéutveckling, ekonomisk politik och ekonomisk teori—Commentarer till Karl-Gustav Landgren: Den 'nya ekonomien' i Sverige" (The Development of Ideas, Economic Policy and Economic Theory: Comments on Karl-Gustav Landgren, *The "New Economics" in Sweden*), *Ekonomisk Tidskrift*, 1960, pp. 175–76.

15. D. H. Robertson, *Banking Policy and the Price Level* (London, 1926), ch. 5.

16. Ohlin, quoted in Steiger, p. 358 n.

17. Landgren, pp. 175–77.

18. Fernholm, pp. 176–77. He adds in a footnote (p. 177 n.9): "That he [Ohlin] still

The Fernholm criterion needs also to be applied to Ohlin's passages in §7 apparently suggesting Kahn-Keynes multiplier phenomena:

> The tendency to increasing output of capital goods will generate increasing income in the capital-goods industries, which, in turn, will increase the demand for consumers' goods, as well as the income generated in the consumers' goods industries. . . .[19]
>
> In this situation demand will rise for durable capital goods and indirectly for other capital goods, their prices will tend to rise, capacity will be better utilized, and incomes are shooting upwards. This will, in turn, generate expanded consumption demand, which feeds new investment demand, etc. . . .[20]

Ohlin made no explicit reference to the 1931 Kahn paper until his 1934 report to the Unemployment Committee, in which he presented a hypothetical, numerical multiplier sequence extending over four time periods.[21]

It is in the broad sense of the term that Ohlin's 1933 paper may be classed at all as "monetary theory," i.e., a synonym for business-cycle theory.[22] Any special significance of monetary disturbances and interest rate disequilibrium for changes in output and prices was subject to serious question. Ohlin's own formal monetary theory in the narrow sense was developed later, notably in his 1937 *Economic Journal* articles, in a 1941 book, and in two papers in the *Ekonomisk Tidskrift* in 1943.[23] In the 1933 paper there are several themes which not only characterize his later work[24] but also suggest affinities with

---

reasoned along these lines eight years later is quite obvious in the essay 'Professor Lindahl om ekonomisk teori' (Professor Lindahl on Economic Theory), *Ekonomisk Tidskrift*, 1941, p. 178."

19. "On the Formulation of Monetary Theory," p. 373 above.

20. Ibid., p. 375.

21. See Landgren, pp. 214–15. The Kahn reference is to "The Relation of Home Investment to Unemployment," *Economic Journal*, 1931, pp. 173–98. Interestingly, R. F. Kahn translated (from German) Wicksell's *Interest and Prices* (London, 1936).

22. For a discussion of broad and narrow definitions of what constitutes monetary theory see Henry H. Villard, "Monetary Theory," in Howard S. Ellis, ed., *A Survey of Contemporary Economics*, I (Homewood, Ill., 1948): 314–15.

23. "Some Notes"; *Kapitalmarknad och räntepolitik* (The Capital Market and Interest Rate Policy) (Stockholm, 1941); "Stockholmsskolan kontra kvantitetsteorien" (The Stockholm School Versus the Quantity Theory), *Ekonomisk Tidskrift*, 1943, pp. 27–46 (translated in *International Economic Papers*, no. 10, 1960, pp. 132–46); and "Likviditet, löner och penningteori" (Liquidity, Wages, and Monetary Theory), *Ekonomisk Tidskrift*, 1943, pp. 258–67. A useful summary of the book may be found in Karl-Gustav Landgren, *Economics in Modern Sweden* (Washington, 1957), pp. 51–55.

24. Björn Hansson of the University of Lund, who is writing a dissertation, "The

certain Keynesian and post-Keynesian beliefs (e.g., Gurley and Shaw, the Radcliffe Committee, and the "New View"):

1. The central role of interest rates ("as a summary expression for the terms of credit supply") in transmitting central bank actions and other monetary disturbances to the real sectors of the economy. In §9 ("The Rate of Interest") he outlined a loanable funds (flow) theory for the determination of single-period "equilibrium" rates of interest in the course of a dynamic disequilibrium adjustment process, which was elaborated in the 1937 *Economic Journal* articles and the 1941 book.[25]
2. The possibility that changes in money and credit may be endogenous (see §11, the first part of "A Critique of Neo-Wicksellian Monetary Theory"). It is, of course, a major Wicksellian theme that changes in aggregate demand may induce changes in money and credit, but Ohlin questioned whether the latter were necessary and sufficient for changes in spending to occur.
3. The non-uniqueness of conventional "money" and, related thereto, the nature of "velocity" as a statistical artifact. In short, "many problems will completely elude such schematic treatment [as given with the simply quantity-theoretical formulae]."[26] The most extensive discussion of these views appeared in §6, where the time sequence of price changes was considered, but throughout Ohlin generally talked about "means of payment" and rarely mentioned currency or deposits.

Subject to the qualifications noted above, the 1933 Ohlin paper was a revolutionary piece of work. It was not only the precursor to his own later writings, many of which because of language and timing went largely unnoticed outside Swedish-speaking circles, but also clearly anticipated much of the Keynesian Revolution. The article is so comprehensive in its scope and so eclectic in its method that, had an English translation of it or Ohlin's 1934 book (which incorporates the text of the 1933 article) quickly appeared,[27] the reception given to

Stockholm School in Reference to the Keynesian Revolution," affirms (in a letter dated 11 Nov. 1977): "There is no significant change in Ohlin's monetary thought from the [1933] article translated here and up to his article . . . published in *Ekonomisk Tidskrift* in 1943."

25. On the role of interest rates, see also §7 of the 1933 paper.

26. "On the Formulation of Monetary Theory," p. 370 above.

27. Curiously, Ohlin, in his introduction to the English translation of Wicksell's *Interest and Prices*, stated that "a revised English version [of his 1934 book] will appear in 1936 under the title *The Theory of Expansion*" (p. xv n.).

Keynes' *General Theory* might have been very different. However, the Ohlin paper did not have the appeal of a simple, more-or-less explicit (static) model. As with much of the Swedish writings of the 1930's, its primary concern was with what I called "dynamatics" in my dissertation, rather than with dynamic theory, i.e., with cataloging all of the factors that should constitute the analysis of a dynamic disequilibrium process, and specific attention was directed only at what might occur in one or a few periods in the course of such a process.[28]

28. The bitter methodological dispute between Lindahl and Ohlin on the feasibility of constructing a truly general dynamic theory (Ohlin was a nonbeliever) is discussed in my article, "The Lesser Known Works of Professor Lindahl," *Canadian Journal of Economics and Political Science*, 1962, pp. 274–80.

# [8]

## Bertil Ohlin, 1899–1979

Bertil Ohlin died suddenly on Friday, August 3, 1979, at the high age of eighty, but still very active in scientific and political writings.[1] Along with Gunnar Myrdal, he was the most influential economist in Sweden

1. A working plan by Ohlin which has survived and which covers the period June 8 to November 1979 is engaged with five topics: (i) "The Swedish Model," June 8–11, in Swedish; (ii) "What Are the [Wage-Earner] Fund's Problems for Wage Earners and Others?" June 12–20, in Swedish; (iii) "Comments on Comments in Monetary Theory," June 21 to July 1; (iv) "Cambridge and Stockholm—Some Aspects of Monetary and Output Variations," July 1 to Aug. 6; (v) "Autobiography 1952–1960," Aug. to Nov. 1979.

since the days of Knut Wicksell and Gustav Cassel, one of those rare political economists who are able to achieve prominence in both their academic discipline and political affairs. Ohlin had already become a professor of economics at the age of twenty-five and did pathbreaking work in two fields: *international economics* (which earned him the 1977 Nobel Memorial Prize in Economics) and *macroeconomics* (remarkably at a time when this revolutionary branch of our discipline was far away from being established). Of no less importance was his role as leader of the Liberal Party in twenty-three years (two as Minister of Trade): he became one of the architects of the Swedish model of "social Liberalism," combining positive attitudes to both social reforms and individual liberty.

*Education as an economist*

Bertil Ohlin was born in Klippan, a village in southern Sweden, on April 23, 1899, the son of a district attorney. At the age of sixteen he left school for studies at Lund University in mathematics, statistics, and economics, which he finished after only two years, in 1917, with the degree of candidatus philosophiae (B.A.). His teacher in economics was Emil Sommarin, a great admirer of Knut Wicksell and editor of the later Swedish editions of Wicksell's *Lectures on Political Economy*.

Having seen in a Swedish daily a review of a book on the economic aspects of the First World War by Eli F. Heckscher, at that time the most prominent political economist at Handelshögskolan (the School of Business Economics) in Stockholm, Ohlin decided to continue his studies there. This step soon proved to be of far-reaching importance for his work in international economics, although his contact with Heckscher, in the latter's seminar, 1917, started with a cleavage of opinion about the correct principles for the right time to cut trees in forestry. As has been demonstrated recently by Paul A. Samuelson (*Economic Inquiry*, 1976), Ohlin in this important contribution to capital theory, published as "Till frågan om skogarnas omloppstid" (On the Question of Forestry Rotation Time) in the Knut Wicksell festschrift (*Ekonomisk Tidskrift*, 1921), solved what is now called the Faustmann-Ohlin theorem.

Having finished the two-year course at Handelshögskolan with the degree of civil economist in 1919, Ohlin moved to Stockholm University, where Gustav Cassel and Gösta Bagge became his teachers in his postgraduate studies in economics. At that time he had already become a member of Nationalekonomiska Klubben (the Political Economy Club), a small elite of about twenty trained economists (four of them graduate students), with his three main teachers and Sven Brisman, David Davidson, and Knut Wicksell as the most prominent members.

In this gathering he was most stimulated by Wicksell, who provided him with a deeper insight into monetary theory—not without importance for his work on macroeconomics in the 1930s.

*The Heckscher-Ohlin theorem*

At that time Ohlin's field of interest was above all international economics, and here Heckscher gave him the decisive impulse. In the David Davidson festschrift in *Ekonomisk Tidskrift*, 1919, Heckscher had written his later celebrated paper on "Utrikeshandelns verkan på inkomstfördelningen. Några teoretiska grundlinjer" (The Effects of Foreign Trade on the Distribution of Income. Some Theoretical Foundations; translated in *Readings in the Theory of International Trade*, 1949) in which he had analyzed facts behind the differences in comparative costs, the first decisive break with Ricardo's law of comparative costs. Heckscher's approach (which he himself had regarded only as a kind of supplement to Ricardo's analysis) inspired Ohlin, while walking along Unter den Linden in Berlin in 1920 (as recalled in his memoirs), to formulate the theorem of differences in productive factor endowment as the cause of *trade in general*, the famous Heckscher-Ohlin theorem which brought him recognition as founder of the modern theory of international trade: a nation (region) tends to export (sell) commodities requiring large quantities of its relatively abundant factors, and import (buy) those requiring—if produced at home—relatively large quantities of its scarce factors. By the generality of his approach, Ohlin, furthermore, dissolved the traditional split between the theories of international trade, interregional trade, and location.

The Heckscher-Ohlin theorem had already been developed by Ohlin in the spring of 1922, in his unpublished thesis on international trade theory, which he presented to Cassel to obtain the degree of licentiatus philosophiae (at that time a prerequisite for a Swedish Ph.D.). It followed the same lines as his doctor's thesis in 1924, *Handelns teori* (Theory of Trade), and his later book *International and Interregional Trade* (1933, revised edition, 1967; sent earlier to Harvard in 1928 in the competition for the David Wells prize) which made his ideas known to an international public. With his doctoral thesis Ohlin had earned the title *docent* (associate professor) after its public defense at Stockholm University on May 28, 1924. This was a most remarkable event, not only for its length (about five and a half hours) but also because—besides the official 'challengers' (Gösta Bagge and Curt Rohtlieb)—Sweden's most prominent economists at that time, Gustav Cassel and Knut Wicksell, intervened as extraordinary critics.

A presentation of the Heckscher-Ohlin theorem for the English-speaking world could have been given, however, a decade earlier. At Cassel's suggestion, Ohlin in the late spring of 1922 sent a brief version of his licentiatus thesis to Francis Edgeworth as editor of the *Economic Journal*, which presented systems of equations for an analysis of the causes and effects of international trade similar to the essence of Chapters 1–3 and the mathematical appendix in *International and Interregional Trade*. Edgeworth sent Ohlin's paper to his co-editor John Maynard Keynes and asked for the latter's opinion. Keynes wrote on a sheet of notepaper with his printed address (46, Gordon Square, Bloomsbury) and dated "30/8" [1922]: "This amounts to nothing, I think, and should be refused. J.M. Keynes." Probably by mistake, this note followed the manuscript back to Ohlin via Edgeworth. The note has survived.[2]

Ohlin's and Keynes' paths crossed again, however, in their famous controversy on "The German Reparation Problem," *Economic Journal*, 1929, where Ohlin not only succeeded in presenting a major contribution to the theory of capital transfers but also made—building on Wicksell's aggregate demand/supply approach—the pioneering distinction between national income and aggregate spending—a major innovation in Keynes' *General Theory* (1936), but a distinction which Keynes at that time quite failed to grasp, as pointed out some years ago by P. M. Oppenheimer (*Journal of Economic Literature*, 1974).

*Contacts with Britain and America*

Ohlin's personal contacts with leading Anglo-Saxon economists were close. Already in the summer of 1922 he had spent a few months at Cambridge, where he met Austin Robinson. In the academic year 1922–23 he visited Harvard, studying international economics (Frank W. Taussig and John H. Williams), agricultural economics (Thomas Nixon Carver), and the history of political economy (Allyn A. Young) and graduating as M.A. On his return to Sweden he spent another two months at Cambridge, visiting A. C. Pigou and following D. H. Robertson's lectures.

With regard to Ohlin's numerous meetings with Keynes in London and at Cambridge in 1929, 1930, 1932, and 1936—where he also had talks with Lionel Robbins, Theodore Gregory, Friedrich A. Hayek (in London) and D. H. Robertson, Joan Robinson, R. F. Kahn (at

2. "I still have the note, and regard it as a valuable document": see B. Ohlin, "Appendix III: Some Comments on Keynesianism and the Swedish Theory of Expansion Before 1935," in D. Patinkin and J. C. Leith, eds., *Keynes, Cambridge and the General Theory* (London, 1977), p. 161. It was, therefore, "not without a broad smile" that Ohlin in 1934 accepted Keynes' request to review the latter's *Essays in Persuasion* in the *Economic Journal*, but as Ohlin expressed it: "Even Jupiter may shut his eyes sometimes"; see *Bertil Ohlins memoarer 1940–1951*, p. 107.

Cambridge)—as well as in Brussels in 1935, I refer to his detailed comments in his Appendix III in *Keynes, Cambridge and the General Theory* (1977). In addition to these meetings I want to mention also Keynes' visit to Stockholm in the early autumn of 1936, where he lectured at Nationalekonomiska Klubben on "Liquidity Preference" (an early draft of his contribution to the Irving Fisher festschrift, 1937) and where he had discussions with Ohlin and other members of the Stockholm School.

Important for both his personal contacts and publications were also numerous lectures which Ohlin gave in the English-speaking world. The most important were (i) the Finlay Lecture at University College, Dublin, in May 1934, and (ii) the Marshall Lectures at Cambridge University, in November 1936. Both these lectures were identical with the outlines[3] of Ohlin's celebrated articles on the 'Stockholm theory' in the *Economic Journal*, 1937, which he finished at the University of California, Berkeley, where he had spent the first half of 1937 as a guest professor.[4]

*J. M. Keynes and Bertil Ohlin in Antwerp, Belgium, 1935*

3. These outlines have survived; see further Ohlin's main paper below in this issue of *HOPE*, esp. n. 52.

4. Furthermore, Ohlin's following lectures and their publications should be named. (i) In May 1932 he delivered the Newmarch Lectures at the University of London,

*Five years in Copenhagen*

Back to the 1920s. In autumn 1924 Ohlin won a 'competition' for the chair in economics at the University of Copenhagen which had been held by the famous statistician Harald Westergaard. At that time the Danish universities had a system of arranging a competition when there were different applicants and no one clearly superior. In the competition for the chair in economics in 1924 the applicants were given three months to write a thesis on "The Economic Effects of the Eight-Hour Workday."[5] They also had to give a lecture on Guild Socialism after 48 hours of preparation and two lectures on a freely chosen subject, which in Ohlin's case was Monetary Stabilization. The outcome was that five of the seven judges voted for Ohlin and two for Erik Lindahl, later his colleague in the Stockholm School (see below).

Ohlin was appointed in Copenhagen in January 1925 and stayed there for five years. During that time the Danish economist L. V. Birck had the greatest influence on him, but he also learned from Carl Iversen, Thorkel Christensen, Jørgen Dich and Jørgen Pedersen, all of whom later made important contributions to economics. Of special importance for Ohlin's development were, however, contributions on employment policy which discussed the multiplier effects of public works by Fr. Johannsen, an engineer and director of the Copenhagen Telephone Company, in 1925 and 1927, as well as by the statistician Jens Warming (known for his discussion on the multiplier with Kahn in the *Economic Journal*, 1932) in 1928. Ohlin also participated in the public discussion on employment and published a pamphlet in 1927 entitled *Saet Produktionen i Gang* (Start Up Production Again), in which he was fully aware of the subsequent and multiplying effects of some initial outlays. The Danish writings on the multiplier may also have influenced Ohlin to follow the contemporary discussion in England, es-

which resulted in two articles on how to fight the Great Depression, in *Weltwirtschaftliches Archiv* ("Ungelöste Probleme der gegenwärtigen Krise") and *Svenska Handelsbankens Index* ("Now or Never"). (ii) In January 1947 Ohlin gave the Julius Beer Foundation Lectures at Columbia University, repeated in a somewhat modified form as the Chichele Lectures at Oxford University later in the autumn and published as *The Problem of Employment Stabilization* (1949). (iii) In March and April 1979, a few months before his death, Ohlin gave two lectures which are related to his most outstanding contributions to economics: (a) "On Keynesian and Stockholm Theories of Employment in 1930 and 1936" at the University of California, Berkeley, and at the Jacob Marschak Colloquium, University of California, Los Angeles (published as Appendix II below in this issue of *HOPE*) and (b) "Some Insufficiencies in the Theories of International Economic Relations," the Frank D. Graham Memorial Lecture at Princeton University, published as *Essays in International Finance*, no. 134, Princeton, September 1979.

5. Ohlin's thesis was published as "Åttatimmarsdagens ekonomiska problem" (The Economic Effects of the Eight-Hour Workday), *Ekonomisk Tidskrift*, 1924, pp. 193–218, and ibid., 1925, pp. 65–94.

pecially Keynes' and H. D. Henderson's proposals for public works as a remedy for unemployment in 1928–29, which he reviewed extensively in Swedish newspapers.

*The 1930s and the Stockholm School*

In January 1930 Ohlin moved to the chair in political economy at Handelshögskolan in Stockholm as successor of Heckscher—a chair which he held until 1965. From that time on he became again very active in Nationalekonomiska Klubben, which now consisted of colleagues of his own generation, especially Erik Lindahl and Gunnar Myrdal, but also younger economists such as Dag Hammarskjöld, Alf Johansson, and Erik Lundberg, all of whom made important contributions to what Ohlin in 1937 called the Stockholm School.

From the early 1930s onwards, Ohlin concentrated his attention chiefly on monetary theory and economic expansion or what was later to be called macroeconomics. From January to the end of August 1931 he stayed in Geneva to write a League of Nations report, *The Course and Phases of the World Economic Depression* (1931), in which he recommended loan-financed public works against unemployment and also noted the deficiency of monetary policy when hinting at the idea of what later became known as the liquidity trap. His theoretical breakthrough came, however, first in 1933 with his paper in *Ekonomisk Tidskrift*, "Till frågan om penningteoriens uppläggning" (translated as "On the Formulation of Monetary Theory," *HOPE*, 1978). Utilizing earlier achievements by Wicksell and—more important—the criticism of Wicksell by Erik Lindahl in *Penningpolitikens medel* (The Means of Monetary Policy, 1930) and Gunnar Myrdal in "Om penningteoretisk jämvikt" (On Monetary Equilibrium), *Ekonomisk Tidskrift*, 1931 (printed in 1932), Ohlin tried to construct a model for an analysis of a process of expansion in a state of large unused resources, in which he heavily emphasized the role of uncertain expectations analyzed earlier by Lindahl (1924) and Myrdal (1927). The 1933 model was further developed in his report to the Swedish Committee on Unemployment, *Penningpolitik, offentliga arbeten, subventioner och tullar som medel mot arbetslöshet* (Monetary Policy, Public Works, Subsidies and Tariffs as Remedies for Unemployment), published in April 1934 and summarized in the Finlay and Marshall lectures (see above) in 1934 and 1936, respectively. The outlines of these lectures formed considerable parts of Ohlin's articles in the *Economic Journal*, 1937, on "The Stockholm theory of Savings and Investment I–II" (most of part III is published below in this issue as Appendix III to "Stockholm and Cambridge"). These led to a debate with Keynes, D. H. Robertson, and R. G. Hawtrey in the *Economic Journal*, September 1937, mainly on the theory of interest.

While Ohlin's pioneering contribution in international economics has been clearly recognized, the question to what extent his achievements, as well as those of Lindahl and Myrdal (Ohlin never forgot to stress that he could not have developed his macroeconomic theory without the previous results of his two Swedish colleagues), moved parallel to and in some respects preceded Keynes' *General Theory* is a matter which has been subject of intensive discussions in recent years, particularly in *History of Political Economy* (see "A Bertil Ohlin Symposium," 1978, and this issue of *HOPE*) and in earlier books by Karl-Gustav Landgren (1960) and Otto Steiger (1971).[6]

*Three decades of political activities*

At the dawn of the Second World War Ohlin shifted the emphasis of his activities from academic economics to national affairs. In 1938 he became a member of the Riksdag, the Swedish Parliament, and by 1944 he had risen to the post of leader of the Liberal Party, a position he retained until 1967. He was Minister of Trade in the Swedish wartime government from 1944 to 1945, and thereafter—as leader of the main opposition party—he came close to attaining the position of Prime Minister.

As emphasized above, Ohlin's political goals were in favor of both social and liberal ideas. At the time of the Great Depression he strongly supported the New Economic Policy of the Social Democrats in Sweden, based on credit-financed public works as a remedy for unemployment. He was positive toward social reforms and stabilization policy, but negative toward nationalization of industry or unnecessarily detailed central state control of economic life. He worked for a society in which the economic system is built on the freedom of individuals to take their own initiative, but where the state at the same time guarantees that this freedom is not reduced, as Ohlin expressed it, to "the freedom of the bosses." With this attitude Ohlin influenced the politics both of his main opponents, the Social Democrats, and of his potential partners for a coalition, the Conservatives. The high degree of consent to the Swedish model of 'social liberalism' in the four major Swedish parties probably would never have been a reality without the convincing ideological struggle of Bertil Ohlin, the political economist.

6. I would like to mention the important recent study by Björn Hansson, "The Stockholm School and the Development of Dynamic Method: A Reconstruction of the Origin of Dynamic Method and Macroeconomic Theory Within the Stockholm School 1927–1937 and Its Relation to the Keynesian Revolution" (Ph.D. diss., Cambridge, May 1980).

*Back to economics in the 1970s*

After he left the Riksdag in 1970, Ohlin returned to research in the two fields in which he had achieved his most outstanding results, in international trade theory and in macroeconomics, with an emphasis—particularly with regard to the latter—on the history of political economy. He had also time to write his autobiography, published in two volumes (unfortunately in Swedish only) in 1972 and 1975, which has fascinating chapters on the leading Swedish economists of the 1920s and 1930s and of his meetings with Keynes.

In Ohlin's contributions to international economics in the 1970s, reflections on contemporary theories from the view of his 1922 approach played a prominent role—e.g., in his papers (i) "On Model Construction in International Trade Theory" (in the Roy Harrod festschrift, 1971) and (ii) "Some Aspects of the Relations Between International Movements of Commodities, Factors of Production, and Technology" (in *The International Allocation of Economic Activity*, edited by Ohlin himself and others, 1977). His last contribution in international economics was the published version of his Frank D. Graham Memorial Lecture, which he gave at Princeton in April 1979 (see note 4 above).

In comparison with his reflections on international economics, Ohlin's writings on the origins and significance of the macroeconomic theories in Cambridge and Stockholm were of a highly controversial nature, e.g., his comments (i) in his article "On the Slow Development of the 'Total Demand' Idea in Economics" (*Journal of Economic Literature*, 1974); (ii) in his already cited Appendix III "On Keynesianism and the Swedish Theory of Expansion Before 1935" (in *Keynes, Cambridge and the General Theory*, edited by Don Patinkin and J. C. Leith, 1977); (iii) in his controversy with Patinkin on "Keynesianism and the 'Stockholm School' " (*Scandinavian Journal of Economics*, 1978); (iv) in his Nobel Memorial Lecture, delivered on December 8, 1977, when he was awarded the Nobel Memorial Prize in Economics, on "1933 and 1977" (printed in *Scandinavian Journal of Economics*, 1978, and containing an important section on "Keynesian and Stockholm Models for Expansion"); (v) in his reflections and comments on "A Bertil Ohlin Symposium" (*HOPE*, 1978), published as his main paper below in this issue of *HOPE*; and (vi) in his unfinished paper "Cambridge and Stockholm—Some Aspects of Monetary and Output Variations," together with (vii) Ohlin's last contribution to our discipline (published also in this number of *HOPE*; see Appendices I and II to "Stockholm and Cambridge," below).

It is a great privilege to have known Bertil Ohlin. Personally, not only was I much stimulated by the interest and vitality with which he was still engaged in the controversy over the origins of what has been called the Keynesian Revolution, but I was also impressed as much by his warmth a ıd the modest attitude with which he, already a classical scholar in the history of political economy, met an economist of a much younger generation.

*Universität Bremen* OTTO STEIGER

This memorial is based on Bertil Ohlin's autobiography, published in two volumes as (i) *Bertil Ohlins memoarer. Ung man blir politiker* (B. Ohlin's Memoirs: A Young Man Becomes a Politician), Stockholm, 1972 (esp. chs. 4–10, 13–16, 18–19), and (ii) *Bertil Ohlins memoarer 1940–1951. Socialistisk skördetid kom bort* (B. Ohlin's Memoirs 1940–1951: How Socialism's Harvest Time Vanished), Stockholm, 1975 (esp. chs. 7, 17, 32). I rely further on my paper "Bertil Ohlin and the Origins of the Keynesian Revolution," *History of Political Economy*, 1976; and on information left by Ohlin in personal communication with me since 1963, but particularly during 1977–79. For a detailed bibliography of Ohlin's writings, 1919–77, see *Scandinavian Journal of Economics*, 1978, pp. 93–99.

# [9]

*History of Political Economy* 13:2


# Stockholm and Cambridge: four papers on the monetary and employment theory of the 1930s

By the late *Bertil Ohlin*

Edited with introductions and comments by *Otto Steiger*, Universität Bremen

*Introduction by the editor*

*On January 9, 1979, after receiving a copy of* History of Political Economy *10, no. 3 (1978), which contained the symposium on Bertil Ohlin's paper on monetary theory published more than forty-five years ago, Ohlin wrote in a letter to the editor of this journal, Craufurd D. Goodwin: "Last year you were kind enough to invite me to make comments. I shall be happy to do so. However, I hope you don't object if I send you a manuscript towards the end of this year." On June 21, 1979, Ohlin started to work on these comments (the information is from Mrs. Evy Ohlin to Otto Steiger, August 21, 1979), and in a letter of July 25, 1979, he invited me to discuss the results with him at his place in Stockholm on August 23 or 24. Only one week after this invitation, however, on August 3, 1979, Bertil Ohlin died, leaving on his desk a manuscript entitled "Some Observations on the Monetary Theory of the [Period] 1930–[19]36," now printed below.*

*About half of the material of this manuscript consisted of handwritten notes (23 pages, of which 15 were numbered successively as pages 1–15), the other half (i) of a cassette recording, (ii) of excerpts of three letters, (iii) of excerpts from his printed memoirs, and (iv) of a typewritten page (with handwritten additions). Furthermore, there were references to two typewritten papers entitled "On Prewar Keynesian and Stockholm Theories of Employment—Chiefly through Demand Management" and "A Comparison of the Development of Monetary Theory at Cambridge and in Sweden in 1928–[19]36." Both papers are published below in this issue of* HOPE *as Appendix I and Appendix II, respectively, together with the hitherto unpublished parts of Ohlin's famous 1937 articles "Some Notes on the Stockholm Theory of Savings and Investment, III," reproduced here as Appendix III and illuminating in a most interesting way from an additional point of view the relations between the theories in Stockholm and Cambridge in the 1930s.*

*The edited text of Ohlin's main manuscript is—when not otherwise indicated—from his handwritten notes. A few obvious errors of minor importance have been corrected; additions, alterations, etc. by myself have been marked by square brackets, [ ], and editorial comments by the addition of* Ed.

*I am very much indebted to Mrs. Evy Ohlin, widow of the late Professor Ohlin, for her kindness in giving me access to the literary remains of her husband. Her assistance and generosity is greatly appreciated. I would like to dedicate my edited version, which I have entitled "Stockholm and Cambridge," and which I present with pride and pleasure, to her and to the memory of Bertil Ohlin.*

# Some Observations on the Monetary Theory of the [Period] 1930–[19]36—Comments on Comments on [My] Monetary Theory

*[Introduction]*

I am deeply grateful to the Editor of the *History of Political Economy*, Professor C. D. W. Goodwin, and his Associate Editor, Professor N. de Marchi, for the more than generous attitude they have taken to the publication of a translation of a paper of mine on monetary theory, originally written in 1932 and published in the *Ekonomisk Tidskrift* in 1933.[1] Very great is also my gratitude to Professors W. P. Yohe and Hans Brems for their skillful translation, originally made by the former and thereafter considerably revised by Brems and him with some useful observations by Moshe Apelblat, Carl G. Uhr, Björn Hansson, Don Patinkin, Otto Steiger, and Royall Brandis.

Furthermore I express sincere thanks to Otto Steiger, who has made important research about the development of the Stockholm monetary theory and has published a penetrating analysis in 1976[2] as well as comments in 1978 in the company of Hans Brems, Don Patinkin and W[illiam] Yohe.[3] All these contributions will, I hope, make the development of the Swedish Theory of money, employment and employment policy and its relation to the corresponding Cambridge Theory in some respects clearer and more accessible. In spite of some not very

1. [B. Ohlin, "On the Formulation of Monetary Theory," *History of Political Economy*, 10 (1978): 353–88; translated from the Swedish "Till frågan om penningteoriens uppläggning," *Ekonomisk Tidskrift*, 1933, pp. 45–81.]

2. [O. Steiger, "Bertil Ohlin and the Origins of the Keynesian Revolution"], *History of Political Economy*, 1976 (Vol. 8, No. 3, [pp. 341–66]).

3. ["A Bertil Ohlin Symposium," *History of Political Economy*], 1978 (Vol. 10, No. 3), [pp. 389–453].

serious mistakes and a few cleavages of opinion I feel confident that they have made very useful contributions to the theoretical development in the 1930s.

I confine myself below to some comments on the papers presented by Brems, Patinkin, Steiger, and Yohe in 1978 with some reference also to Steiger's penetrating paper in the 1976 issue of this journal.

There has been in many places some exaggeration of the priority rights to innovations in monetary theory. The difficulty for the establishment of such priorities is partly due to the fact that the discussion has moved from employment policy—chiefly public works to basic monetary theory and back again to policy—without much explicit theoretical argument⟨s⟩ as a justification of the policy. However, how can one draw a line between common-sense arguments for public works in times of surplus capacity, on the one hand, and a theoretical reasoning based on a simplified model, on the other hand?

## I. *Comments on the Development of the Stockholm Monetary Theory in the 1930s*

### §1. *Public works against unemployment—an old story*

Recommendations of public works to reduce unemployment—in times of depression or 'underdevelopment'—were presented by Sidney and Beatrice Webb already in 1909.[4] Similar proposals were made in Sweden in the following three years, e.g. in a municipal body with conservative majority in the university town Lund[4a] and in the *riksdag* [the Swedish parliament] by representatives of the Labour party.[4b] It was assumed that the financing could be arranged to a large extent or wholly with the aid of borrowing.

After the first world war several economists and technicians presented similar proposals and reasoning, e.g. in Germany Prof. [N.] Johannsen[5] who gave reasons for expecting increased employment as a result of new or raised import tariffs and in Denmark a civil engineer with protectionistic leanings, [Fr.] Johannsen.[6] Similar reasonings

4. S. and B. Webb, *The Minority Report [Reports of the Royal Commission on the Poor Laws and Relief of Distress*. Vol. III: *Separate Report*, London, 1909].

4a. [Cf. the autobiography of the Swedish Prime Minister 1946–1969, the Social Democrat Tage Erlander, *Tage Erlander 1901–1939* (in Swedish), Stockholm, 1972, p. 175].

4b. [Cf. O. Steiger, *Studien zur Entstehung der Neuen Wirtschaftslehre in Schweden. Eine Anti-Kritik*, Berlin, 1971, pp. 99–118.]

5. [N.A.F.L. Johannsen's works had appeared even before the First World War: (i) *Der Kreislauf des Geldes und der Mechanismus des Soziallebens*, Berlin, 1903 (published under the pseudonym J. J. O. Lahn), (ii) *A Neglected Point in Connection with Crises*, New York, 1908, and (iii) *Die Steuer der Zukunft*, Berlin, 1913.—*Ed.*]

6. [Fr. Johannsen, "Arbejdsstandsningen og Landets Økonomi" (Employment Cre-

about the expansion effects of public initiatives were published by myself in Copenhagen 1927[7] and the following year by my colleague in the University of Copenhagen, Jens Warming,[8] who also presented comments on Kahn's well-known paper on the consumption multiplier.[9]

But already in 1925 the Swedish economist and labour market specialist Gösta Bagge had argued in favour of a contracyclical variation of public investment to smoothen the employment curve.[10] Similar viewpoints appeared elsewhere. More well-known were the British *Yellow Book* [*Britain's Industrial Future*], which dealt with measures against long-time underemployment in Great Britain rather than business depressions. A little more 'theory' was contained in *Can Lloyd George Do It?* in 1929, written by Keynes and [Hubert] Henderson, followed by a second pamphlet in 1930.[11] In the 1929 pamphlet and in a paper by Keynes in a volume edited by [Arthur] Salter [et al.] in the spring of 1932[12] the arguments were presented forcefully, evidently in a feeling that the depreciation of the pound sterling in September 1931 had eliminated the risk for serious monetary imbalances.

## §2. *Emphasis on budget deficits as independent expansionist measure*

I suspect that several other publications could be found in the decade before 1933. The Swedish *The Means of Monetary Policy* [*Penningpolitikens medel*] by [Erik] Lindahl in 1930[13] dealt also with budget deficits as 'stimulants' to employment. So did a lecture by myself at a Nordic meeting of economists in June 1931.[14]

---

ation and the Country's Economy), *Ingeniøren*, 1925, pp. 397–401, and "Tidens Krav" (The Demand of Time), *Berlingske Tidende*, March 23–25, 1927.]

7. [B. Ohlin, *Saet Produktionen i Gang* (Start Up Production Again), Copenhagen, 1927).]

8. [J. Warming, "Beskaeftigelseproblemet" (The Employment Problem), *Gads Danie Magasin*, 1927, pp. 609–21]

9. [R. F. Kahn], "The Relation of Home Investment to Unemployment," *Economic Journal*, June 1931, [pp. 173–98]. It contained a more detailed analysis than its predecessors. [Warming's comments were published as "International Difficulties Arising out of the Financing of Public Works During Depression," *Economic Journal*, 1932, pp. 211–24.]

10. [G. Bagge, "Produktionens reglering som medel mot arbeslöshet" (The Regulation of Production as Remedy Against Unemployment), *Svensk Tidskrift*, 1925, pp. 513–23.]

11. [*We Can Conquer Unemployment. We Mobilized for War—Let Us Mobilize for Prosperity. Mr. Lloyd George's Pledge*; already published in 1929—*Ed*.]

12. [J. M. Keynes, Contribution "III," in A. Salter, J. Stamp, J. M. Keynes, A. Clay, and W. H. Beveridge, *The World's Economic Crisis and the Way of Escape*, Halley Stuart Lectures 1931 (London, 1932), pp. 71–88.]

13. Lindahl's book was distributed in proofs in the summer of 1929.

14. [B.] Ohlin, ["Den internationella penningpolitiken och dess inverkan på konjunkturutvecklingen" (International Monetary Policy and Its Influence on the De-

How is one to decide in which period an expansionist theory of employment was created and by whom? More is required than a recommendation to fight unemployment through public works or tax measures in order to lift the volume of aggregate demand. But the latter was a good beginning. Many prominent economists—e.g. in the United States before 1934—were against such a policy.

Strangely enough many economists have accepted the opinion that there was no essential part of a theory of employment available before *General Theory* in 1936. In my opinion this is to do less than justice to a group of economists—among them several British, Danish, German and Swedish—who presented fragments of such a theory in the years 1925–1934. One of the merits of comments by Steiger, Brems and Yohe is that this impression of progress cannot be avoided by any careful reader. The comment of Patinkin does not, it seems to me, convincingly contradict this conclusion, even though he is right in claiming that Keynes' contributions were highly stimulating and important from 1929.

Looking upon the development of monetary theory in a wide sense—including an analysis of employment and output variations—one cannot avoid some surprise that the innovations in the period between the two wars dealt with rather simple matters. Some work was done on business cycle theory in continuation of the analysis in this field in preceding decades. But it was to a considerable extent 'a separate compartment.' There were exceptions, e.g. contributions by Hayek, Hicks and Haberler,[15] who combined viewpoints from both the above-mentioned fields.

The dominating question for scientific debate in the 1930s was, however, undoubtedly then the possibility of raising the average level of employment with the aid of '*demand management*.' The chief initiators of this direction of scientific effort and concentration on employment policy were a few prominent British economists—above all J. M. Keynes with his unique ability to make people listen to simplified theories of economic policy.

But as to the core of the theory of economic expansion and the distribution of the innovations Keynes shared the merit with several other economists.[16]

---

velopment of the Business Cycle), *Förhandlingar vid Nordiska nationalekonomiska mötet i Stockholm 15–17 juni 1931*, Stockholm, 1931, pp. 11–31, 63–68, and 208–10, esp. pp. 28f., 64, 67].

15. [F.] Hayek, *Prices and Production*, 1931.—[G.] Haberler, *Prosperity and Depression*, 1936, rev. ed. 1937.—[J. R.] Hicks, ["A Suggestion for Simplifying the Theory of Money," *Economica*, 1935, pp. 1–19].

16. Above all, several British and Swedish economists and a German engineer, [Carl] Föhl, [*Geldschöpfung und Wirtschaftskreislauf*, München, 1937].

The relation of Swedish contributions to 'The Keynesian Revolution' has been taken up chiefly by two theses by Landgren and Steiger,[17] in a collection of papers in the *Ekonomisk Tidskrift*, 1960,[17a] and in Steiger's paper in *HOPE*, 1976, as well as the symposium volume of *HOPE* in nr. 3, 1978 [cf. above, nn.2 and 3].

As I have been offered the opportunity to explain how I look upon the friendly comments made by my four distinguished colleagues, I am happy to make some observations on this matter with some reference to their characterization of my own contributions. I also add some words about the timing of the development in Sweden and Great Britain.

## §3. *Some aspects of the development of expansion theory. Wicksell a pioneer*

Let me begin with the basic theory of an expansion of output and employment.

As far as I can see, Knut Wicksell's cumulative process of *price development* can be regarded as a beginning, although he failed to illuminate the changes in output and employment.[18] He regarded the variation of GNP as a central variable and the consequent changes in consumers' demand and investment demand. In other words, he introduced relations of savings and investment decisions as an essential *addition* to the theory. Strangely enough, saving and investment decisions attracted so much attention that the relation of aggregate demand and supply were rather neglected in the development of monetary theory in the first three decades of the 20th century, e.g. by [Gustav] Cassel and Keynes as well as by the post-Wicksellians Lindahl and [Gunnar] Myrdal. One cannot, however, say that the relation of the aggregates was forgotten or completely overlooked. But, when in 1932 I wrote my paper on monetary theory[19] and in 1933 completed it for the

17. [K.-G. Landgren, *Den 'nya ekonomien' i Sverige. J. M. Keynes, E. Wigforss, B. Ohlin och utvecklingen 1927–39* (The 'New Economics' in Sweden. J. M. Keynes, E. Wigforss, B. Ohlin, and the Development 1927–39), Stockholm and Uppsala, 1960.—O. Steiger, *Studien zur Entstehung der Neuen Wirtschaftslehre in Schweden. Eine Anti-Kritik*, Berlin, 1971)].

17a. ["Stockholmsskolan: Idéer, tillkomst och utveckling. Ett symposium" (The Stockholm School: Ideas, Origin and Development: A Symposium), *Ekonomisk Tidskrift*, 1960, pp. 159–205, 296–300 (with contributions by T. Fernholm, E. Wigforss, E. Lundberg, and G. Lindahl).]

18. K. Wicksell, *Geldzins und Güterpreise*, [Jena], 1898, [trans. R. F. Kahn, as *Interest and Prices*, London, 1936]. He discussed changes in output separately—in connection with business cycle theory. This fact is often overlooked.

19. [An earlier draft of Ohlin's paper in *Ekonomisk Tidskrift*, 1933, entitled *Till penningteoriens centralproblem* (On the Central Problems of Monetary Theory) was circulated among Swedish economists in late autumn 1932; cf. O. Steiger, *History of Political Economy* 8 (1976): 353.—*Ed.*]

volume of 1934,[20] I regarded it as an improvement compared with Myrdal's concentration on the balance between saving and investment in his monetary equilibrium analysis of 1932.[21] It is also worth noting that Keynes after finishing *General Theory* regarded the aggregate analysis as one of his own important innovations in this book. In a letter to me [of January 27, 1937] he wanted assistance in finding where Wicksell had pointed out the mistake of J. B. Say.[22] Landgren and Steiger stressed the importance of this aspect of my monetary theory compared to Lindahl's and Myrdal's in the years 1930–33. I had used a similar construction in writings about international capital movements in 1928 and 1929.[23] The addition or subtraction of such capital transfers to and from GNP seemed to me self-evident in a simple model. But, secondary changes in the national income should also be considered.[24]

I regarded it as a special innovation that a rise in the price level could occur even during a period of equilibrium between saving and investment. E.g. wages and national income could be lifted through a collective agreement, and consumption could be raised by the whole amount of the wage increase. The value of investment could rise as much as the prices of capital goods.

Later I found that in *Treatise [on Money]* (1930) Keynes had observed this possibility, although he used somewhat different income concepts, which may explain why I did not straight away check the possibility of an indication already in this book which I knew well.

Some of my commentators have touched upon the relations be-

20. [B. Ohlin, *Penningpolitik, offentliga arbeten, subventioner och tullar som medel mot arbetslöshet. Bidrag till expansionens teori* (Monetary Policy, Public Works, Subsidies and Tariffs as Remedies for Unemployment: A Contribution to the Theory of Expansion), Stockholm, 1934.]

21. [G. Myrdal, "Om penningteoretisk jämvikt. En studie över den 'normala räntan' i Wicksells penninglära" (On Monetary Equilibrium. A Study of the 'Normal Rate of Interest' in Wicksell's Monetary Economics), *Ekonomisk Tidskrift*, 1931, pp. 191–302; printed 1932.]

22. See J. M. K[eynes], *Collected Writings [of John Maynard Keynes]*, Vol. XIV: [*The General Theory and After. Part II: Defence and Development*, ed. D. E. Moggridge, London, 1973, p. 184].

23. [(i) B. Ohlin, "The Reparations Problem," *Svenska Handelsbankens Index*, March 1928, pp. 2–13, and April 1928, pp. 2–33; (ii) B. Ohlin, "The Reparations Problem: A Discussion: I. Transfer Difficulties, Real and Imagined," *Economic Journal*, 1929, pp. 172–78; (iii) B. Ohlin, "Mr. Keynes' Views on the Transfer Problem: II. A Rejoinder," *Economic Journal*, 1929, pp. 400–404.]

24. As a matter of fact this reasoning was used also in my thesis in 1924 [*Handelns teori* (The Theory of Trade), Stockholm, 1924, pp. 41 ff., 114 ff.], and on other occasions in the 1920s. The pioneer paper was written by Wicksell ["International Freights and Prices"] in *Quarterly Journal of Economics*, [Feb. 1918, pp. 404–10]. See my paper: "On the Slow Development of the 'Total Demand' Idea in Economic Theory: [Reflections in Connection with Dr. Oppenheimer's Note"], *Journal of Economic Literature*, 1974, [pp. 888–96].

tween the theoretical constructions which [were used by] Lindahl, Myrdal and myself. On the whole, I want to leave to them and others the task of clearing up this matter. It is much less important than the relation between the development of the Keynesian theory and the Swedish theory.[25] Some aspects of this question will be briefly touched upon below with special reference not to Wicksell but rather to his Swedish followers. However, I begin with some indications as to the birth history of the Stockholm Theory.[26]

§4. *The new phase of the Swedish development. Lindahl and Myrdal*

First of all, Lindahl in 1930 took the initiative in following up Wicksell's monetary theory. In a period analysis he considered not only price changes but on a few pages also variations in employment. His interest even in the latter section was directed to the price level variations. On the whole he followed Wicksell in not analysing employment and output volume variations, but paying a great deal of attention to changes in the direction of production—capital goods and consumers' goods.

Before the appearance of this book Myrdal's thesis about *Pricing and Variability*[27] had appeared in 1927. He did not have monetary theory in mind but revised price theory fundamentally. Acting individuals, firms and organisations base their action largely on expectation about the future. But the future is uncertain. Evidently, this book brought two important innovations: the importance of ideas about the future and the uncertainty of the future, although previous events helped in the forming of an opinion.

Lindahl saw the importance of Myrdal's innovation to pay attention to ideas about the future.[28] He used [this innovation] in a simple period

25. A part of such a comparison—with special reference to Wicksell's possible influence on Keynes' theory—is to be found in my "Appendix III: Some Comments on Keynesianism and the Swedish Theory of Expansion Before 1935," in *Keynes, Cambridge and the General Theory*, ed. by Don Patinkin and J. Clark Leith, [London], 1977, [pp. 149–65]. See also pp. 53–55 and 72–79 [in this volume].

26. This account adds some observations about the 'division of labour' between Lindahl, Myrdal and myself to the description in the *Economic Journal* in 1937 [in my paper "Some Notes on the Stockholm Theory of Savings and Investment I–II"] without changing the picture in a very essential way.

27. [G. Myrdal, *Prisbildningsproblemet och föränderligheten* (The Problem of Price Formation and Changeability), Uppsala and Stockholm, 1927.]

28. [A point which has not been recognized up to now in debate on the genesis of the Stockholm School has to be stressed here against Ohlin. It can be shown that Myrdal in his thesis of 1927, was decisively influenced by Lindahl's reasonings on calculations of the entrepreneur about the future and uncertainty, in *Penningpolitikens mål and medel. Del I* (Ends and Means of Monetary Policy. Part I), Lund, 1924, the original edition, distributed in proofs, of Lindahl's *Penningpolitikens mål* (The Ends of

analysis in his 1930 volume.

§5. *Myrdal's equilibrium analysis of Wicksell*

Next came Myrdal's pioneer Swedish paper about *Monetary Equilibrium* ["Om penningteoretisk jämvikt," 1932; cf. n. 21 above] which analysed Wicksell's different definitions of equilibria for the rate of interest. It was an analysis of tendencies from a point of equilibrium —*not a sequence analysis like Lindahl's*. Myrdal's opinion was very negative to period analysis.[29] His emphasis was on expectations about the future. There was some but not much retrospective observations.[30]

The income concept used by Lindahl was as follows. The expected future revenues from the activity under consideration are discounted with the expected future rates of interest. These revenues when added together are the estimated present capital value of future incomes. The computed interest on this estimated capital in a certain period is the income during that period, which is at the disposal of the firm or the individual for consumption or saving. Myrdal employed a similar 'capitalization' of future expected revenues. On the whole, one can say that Myrdal paid even more attention to capital gains and losses than Lindahl.

I found it necessary to use a simpler and more realistic backward looking method with standardized income ideas similar to those governing business accounts and the income ideas of business firms and individuals. A rise in the value of real estate during a period does not normally convince a house owner that his income has been increased with this 'capital gain.' Nor does he regard the interest on expected

---

Monetary Policy), Lund, 1929; cf. Lindahl, 1924, ch. 3 (pp. 25–40), with Myrdal, 1927, ch. 9 (pp. 145–80), esp. p. 180 n. 1, where Myrdal explicitly refers to Lindahl's book of 1924.—*Ed.*]

29. Myrdal wrote the following in "Om penningteoretisk jämvikt," 1932, §23, p. 231: "All quantities refer to a particular *instantaneous state of price formation*. This means that quantities which cannot be directly classed as instantaneous capital values are sums of individual expectations of income, saving, etc., during an arbitrarily chosen future *unit period*. These expectations are discounted with respect to the corresponding price formation. All incomes are constructed as *capital incomes*." As motivation for the latter, Myrdal refers to Lindahl's *Penningpolitikens medel*, p. 15. [Translation of this note from the Swedish by Ed.]

30. Steiger who is otherwise so well informed has made the mistake of attributing to Myrdal in this paper a sequence analysis. Steiger correctly points out that the distinction between anticipated and realized macroeconomic values worked out for Myrdal's German paper [see n. 37, below] in the following year (1933), where he had added a dozen pages, [was] largely based on period analysis. [Ohlin's criticism refers to my paper in *History of Political Economy* 8 (1976): 357. In my contribution to the "Bertil Ohlin Symposium," however, I made clear that Myrdal in 1932 vehemently opposed Lindahl's sequence analysis; cf. my "Prelude to the Theory of a Monetary Economy: Origins and Significance of Ohlin's 1933 Approach," *History of Political Economy* 10 (1978): 425.—*Ed.*]

future capital gains added together and discounted to a higher capital value as his disposable income. In brief, I regarded Lindahl's and Myrdal's concepts as unsuitable for an explanation of the actions of individuals and firms.

I came also to the conclusion that the many equilibria with which Myrdal worked in his interpretation and revision of Wicksell made the reasoning highly complicated and unrealistic. I chose the accounting method as an alternative.

§6. *An alternative approach to sequence analysis. Ohlin's conceptual apparatus*

In the spring of 1932—after eight months' eye disease—I again started work on my [Swedish] report on *Monetary Policy, Public Works, Subsidies and Tariffs as Remedies for Unemployment* [*Penningpolitik* etc., 1934; cf. n. 20 above], the first part of which was sent to the editor of *Ekonomisk Tidskrift* in February 1933 and published there a few months later after some not very essential revisions.[31] The income concepts of my two colleagues I found unrealistic and unsuitable for an analysis of the actions of businessmen and consumers. A much more realistic account of the cumulative process could be obtained if the basic concepts referred to a finished period. In other words they should tell what actually happened with regard to the quantity and value of consumption, investment, depreciation and income. As a former student of business economics and accounting and professor in a business school I found this quite natural.—The expectations explained the motivation for the actions. But this is something different from the actual events, which should be described in their relations. Both estimates of expectations and accounting of quantities during preceding periods was necessary, as explained in §2 of my paper already, in the form it had towards the end of 1932.

Strangely enough the other participants in the discussion in the *Economic Club* [Nationalekonomiska Klubben in Stockholm]—above all Lindahl, [Dag] Hammarskjöld, [Erik] Lundberg and Myrdal—were very critical towards my terminology. Above all they insisted on a fundamental income concept: the interest on the expected present capital value of all future expected income streams. So capital values played a great role in their account. As indicated in my 1933 paper[32] I found this income concept—although logically consistent with some of the capital

31. See Steiger's account in *History of Political Economy*, No. 3, (1978) ["Substantive Changes in the Final Version of Ohlin's 1933 Paper," pp. 389–97].

32. [As translated in] *History of Political Economy*, 10, No. 3, 1978, §2, pp. 354–59. The essential parts of the paper were written in the autumn of 1932 [cf. n. 19, above].

value concepts—very unsuitable for an explanation how much the acting individuals would spend on consumption and how much they would regard as saving. The bookkeeping definitions of income and depreciation were in my opinion fundamental for the opinions of individuals and firms in the measurement of their income during a passed period. This also influenced the size of their expected income during future periods. "Let us stick to the way businessmen and others actually think," was my attitude, "even if the consistency of capital value concepts and income concepts suffers."[33]

I sent Myrdal some suggestions and critical observations[33a]—as margin[al] notes in the print of his [Swedish] *Monetary Equilibrium* paper (printed early in the summer 1932). Lindahl and Myrdal had talks many times in the summer, he told me in a letter in August.[34] Both L[indahl] and I were advocating the use of period analysis which could be added to Myrdal's equilibrium start analysis in his printed paper. Whether our remarks help[ed] to convince Myrdal that he ought to add a new section with period analysis to the German translation, is not for me to say. Anyhow he did so, writing three brilliant chapters giving an account of [the] development.[35] It was natural that a comparison of forward looking and backward looking (*ex ante* and *ex post*) was characteristic of this section.

## §7. *The mutual interdependence in the scientific work in Stockholm in the second half of 1932*

I have always stressed how much I learned from Myrdal's Swedish paper. When returning from Norway—and no reading during seven

33. I have naturally been gratified to find some similarity between my attitude and the one Prof. Henry Simon developed and applied to a great part of price theory. The decisive aspect is to explain the actions of individuals and firms and of course—as a separate matter—the actions of public bodies.

33a. In a letter to Ohlin of June 22, 1932, Myrdal acknowledged Ohlin's helpful suggestions and comments on the final draft of the Swedish version of *Monetary Equilibrium*, which he immediately afterwards sen. to the printers of *Ekonomisk Tidskrift*.

34. [This letter has not survived. I have checked without result both the collections of Ohlin's and Myrdal's papers which are deposited in Stockholm at the Kungliga Biblioteket (Royal Library) and the Arbetarrörelsens Arkiv (Records of the Swedish Labour Movement), respectively.—*Ed.*]

35. [About this influence on Myrdal cf. the following quotation from a letter by Myrdal to Ohlin, Aug. 29, 1932: "Thank you for your letters and your kind remarks on my [Swedish] essay. The German text has been altered completely. The analysis of profitability [has been made] more full-length. Over and above that, I am discussing more detailed changes in saving and business cycles. Moreover, three introductory chapters [have been added] which I think fill the gap with regard to your criticism on the question of the price level. The whole of this chapter [is] written much more purely negative, which is more in accordance with your intentions. I shall send you the rubbish when I get it ready from the printers."—Translation from the Swedish by Ed.].

months—I started working gradually in April and read his paper in MS. or proof, when it was practically finished for printing. I do not remember having made more than one suggestion of changes. But after reading the printed version I made numerous suggestions, for which Myrdal thanks in a letter in August, where he also refers to a number of discussions with Lindahl.[36] Myrdal had started revising and adding a new section and was interested in our suggestions. He promised to send a proof of his new German version, when it was ready, but delay seems to have prevented this before the printing in the early spring of 1933. Hence, the *German* paper[37] was not available to me in manuscript or proof in 1932. It could not influence my own paper, which was distributed to some colleagues in the *Economic Club* towards the end of 1932 and accepted for publishing by Prof. [David] Davidson [on 26] February 1933. This paper of mine was rather critical of Myrdal's Swedish paper—as pointed out by Yohe—but for obvious reasons did not mention his German [at that time] unfinished paper.

To what extent my paper possibly influenced my colleagues is not for me to say. What is quite clear about the development of monetary theory in Sweden in the 1930s is that Lindahl started the ball rolling in the late 1920s by taking up the old Wicksell cumulative process and transforming it with a more precise period analysis. Myrdal drew the attention to the importance of expectations and the uncertainty of the future[38] and—possibly under some stimulus from colleagues—developed the *ex ante/ex post* concepts. My own role I leave to others to judge. The fact that my system of concepts was rather similar to those used by Keynes is in this connection a matter of limited interest. My stressing of the importance of 'backward looking' and the use of 'bookkeeping' concepts probably helped to finish the overemphasis in the system of concepts in Stockholm. However, Myrdal was no doubt the originator of the basic distinction which his translator and pupil G[erhard] Mackenroth gave the name *ex ante* and *ex post*.[39]

36. [Cf. the letter quoted in n. 35 above. However, in this letter there is no reference to Myrdal's discussions with Lindahl; cf. also n. 34 above.—*Ed.*].

37. [G. Myrdal, "Der Gleichgewichtsbegriff als Instrument der geldtheoretischen Analyse," in F. A. Hayek (ed.), *Beiträge zur Geldtheorie*, Vienna, 1933, pp. 361–487.]

38. [Cf., however, n. 28 above on the priority of Lindahl in recognizing the importance of an uncertain future.—*Ed.*]

39. [The term *ex post*, however, had already been used in 1924 by Lindahl in his *Penningpolitikens mål och medel*, p. 33, where he discussed a "negative investment recognized only *ex post*." The term was deleted in the final version of this book, *Penningpolitikens mål* (1929), but "the closest and most intimate relations" between Lindahl and Myrdal in the 1920s and the early '30s which had them "feeling almost as one family" and where they "discussed all the time and showed each other our manuscripts" (Myrdal in a letter to O. Steiger, April 5, 1978), make it probable that the concept of *ex post*, instead of being lost, was saved and developed by Myrdal.—*Ed.*]

An interesting question, which I hope someone will take up, is Myrdal's development. It speaks to his credit that he was able to add three chapters on sequence analysis in 1933 and to revise two chapters radically for the 1939 edition.[40] In my opinion this little volume can be regarded as two works. One half is a translation of the 1932 equilibrium analysis of Wicksell's interest theory; the other half consists of a sequence analysis he wrote 1932–33 and 1938–39. Both sections are important.

I should add that the report on *Wage Development and Unemployment* [*Löneutvecklingen och arbetslösheten*], 1934, by Dr. Alf Johansson is a highly qualified product, far above the old static wage theory. It would carry me too far to comment upon it. The same is true of the important dynamic analysis with the aid of time using models, called *Studies in the Theory of Expansion*, published by Erik Lundberg in 1937. While it has probably obtained inspiration from both Wicksell and the contributions of his followers, it deviates from the methods of the early 1930s, as it goes much further in the development of simple dynamic and precise models. Lundberg's thesis belongs to the important pioneer works in its fields, but also to another stage of monetary theory.

§8. [*Comments on Steiger's papers*]

[(i)] *A comment on Steiger's paper in HOPE* [*1976*]. As to the many friendly observations by my colleagues I should perhaps report that in some respects I hold a different opinion. [In his paper in *HOPE*, 1976, pp. 358 f.,] Steiger has misunderstood my statement in the [article "Some Notes on the Stockholm Theory of Savings and Investment I,"] *Economic Journal*, 1937, p. 57. It indicates my debt to Myrdal's Swedish paper. It also emphasizes similarities between the terminology in Myrdal's new section in his German paper and the terms I used at an early stage, before the text to the German paper was available. I left open the question whether there had been any influence. I used fundamentally the same approach in my paper in 1933, book in 1934 and paper in 1937. As a matter of fact, the basic text in my report of 1934 is virtually identical with my paper of 1933—as far as the basic theory is concerned. So it cannot have been adapted to manuscripts or texts that appeared after the distribution of the former towards the end of 1932. The source of Steiger's misunderstanding is justifiably that he did not know that the bookkeeping approach was presented by me in the *Economic Club* under much criticism from others.

40. [G. Myrdal, *Monetary Equilibrium*, London, 1939.]

Myrdal's note [in] the summer of 1932 [on the inner mechanics of a depressive process in "Om penningteoretisk jämvikt"], (§47, p. 271)[41] contains a natural conclusion if the *ex post* income is defined in the way I did. But this conclusion is doubtful in the setting of the terms used by Myrdal in the 1932 paper, where all concepts were prospective (later called *ex ante*).[42] I had already at that time presented the backward looking concepts as fundamental and borrowed the forward looking approach from Myrdal and Lindahl. The extremely complicated system of expected return on expected capital values seemed to me unpractical. I could not see that it lent itself well to bookkeeping approach which I was convinced to use—under criticism from the other discussants in the *Economic Club*.[43]

Some time in the spring or summer of 1933 I sent to Myrdal a first draft of the first third of the MS. for my report [*Penningpolitik* etc.] (printed spring 1934). He suggested a concentration of the theoretical reasonings to the first part and less theory in the later policy aspects, but suggested no revision of the theory. Such a regrouping would make [the] task for the reader less difficult. I followed this advice. The main body of theory remained unchanged as seen from the two versions of my 1933 paper, which appear also practically unchanged in my report in the spring of 1934. Myrdal was in the summer and autumn of 1933 very busy with two tasks: [(i)] His "appendix-report on financial policy"[44] which he sent me a week or two before the printing [in January 1933]. I made no suggestions worth mentioning. [(ii)] He also worked on his 'big' report on financial policy which was finished late in 1933 and printed early in 1934.[45] I was at that time exceedingly busy with the finishing of my own report and since November 1931 [with] the contribution of four leading articles [editorials] and two 'comments'

41. [Quoted in full in my paper "Prelude" etc., in *History of Political Economy* 10 (1978): 428.—*Ed.*]

42. Myrdal's *depressive process* [. . .] is an analysis (*without the concept of anticipation*) of how a reduction in saving leads to equilibrium with reduced investment. This is similar to Kahn and not to Myrdal et al. later on. [There is] no pair of contrasts [like] *ex ante/ex post*. (This is developed in a certain way in [his] German text of spring 1933.) [Translated from the Swedish by Ed.]

43. The brief footnote in Myrdal's paper of 1932 ["Om penningteoretisk jämvikt," § 47, pp. 230 f., n. 2] fits in better with the backward looking income concept and may have been added at a late stage before the manuscript was sent to *Ekonomisk Tidskrift* in the spring of 1932. [It should be emphasized that Myrdal's footnote is not "brief"—21 lines or about half a page—but that Ohlin nevertheless is right: the note is not integrated with the main text; it seems in fact to have been added at a later stage.—*Ed.*]

44. [G. Myrdal's famous Appendix No. III to the Social Democratic Government's budget in 1933, also published separately under the title *Konjunktur och offentlig hushållning* (Business Cycles and Public Finance), Stockholm, 1933.]

45. [G. Myrdal, *Finanspolitikens ekonomiska verkningar* (The Economic Effects of Fiscal Policy), Stockholm, 1934.].

[commentaries] in [the daily] *Stockholms-Tidningen* every month. There is no letter or other indication of mutual criticism after the summer of 1933.

In the spring of 1934 I was invited to deliver a double lecture in the Catholic University (?) of Dublin, which were delivered in June.[46] My impression was that something rather precise and concentrated was expected from me. I, therefore, developed a system of equations which is practically the same as the one[s] I used in my paper in the *Economic Journal* in 1937 [Section B, §§1–2 (pp. 58–60)].—So the dismay of the majority of the audience which expected a more 'cultural lecture.' At one time I became doubtful if there was much use for the aggregate of all expected incomes. What one above all needs as far as expectations go are all the *individual* expected incomes, planned sums of consumption and planned sums of investment. These planned and expected individual amounts can be added together into planned sums for consumption and planned investment sums. The casual element is the conglomerate of plans and expectations, not the sums. However, a parallel treatment of *ex ante* and *ex post* offers many advantages and is to be preferred.[47]

[(ii) *A comment on Steiger's paper in HOPE, 1978*].[48] Your article in HOPE, 1978, entitled "Prelude etc." contains an interesting presentation of Lindahl and Myrdal. It is excellent that such a completion has been done so far. But some matters seem to me to be hasty. From spring 1932 onwards I 'struggled'—in opposition to L[indahl] and M[yrdal]—for a more *systematical* role of the idea of *ex post* and the *comparison* with *ex ante*. Both Lindahl and Myrdal as well as Lundberg and Hammarskjöld criticized me in the *Economic Club* in 1932—maybe also in 1933—for not letting dominate the *ex ante* terms. (The 'terms' themselves came into existence for the first time in early 1933 in Mackenroth's [German] translation [of Myrdal's "Om penningteoretisk jämvikt" of 1932]). I myself concentrated more on the *comparisons*.[49]

Let me add some criticism and comments to your "Prelude," p.

46. [Ohlin means the second Finlay Lecture, which he had already delivered, however, on *May* 16, 1934, at *University College*, Dublin; cf. his "Some Notes on the Stockholm Theory . . ." I., p. 58 n. 2, and a letter to Ohlin from George O'Brien, University College, Dublin, March 14, 1934.—*Ed.*]

47. Steiger makes a mistake when he attributes to me some doubt whether one needs *ex ante* categories. They are required to explain the actions of firms and individuals. What I [questioned] was the need for *aggregates* of *ex ante* categories. See my paper in *Scandinavian Journal of Economics*, 1978 ["Keynesian Economics and the Stockholm School. A Comment on Patinkin's Paper", pp. 144–47, esp. p. 145] and Steiger's paper ["Prelude" etc.], p. 435, in *History of Political Economy*, fall 1978.

48. *Addendum* to a letter [from Bertil Ohlin] to Otto Steiger, January 9, 1979.

49. [This paragraph of the addendum is written in Swedish and translated by Ed.]

439. I want to stress Lindahl's pioneer achievement through a Wicksellian period analysis with some consideration of the opinions about the future. Very important! So is Myrdal's consistent distinction *ex post* and *ex ante* and his stress of uncertainty. My emphasis on both *ex post* and *ex ante* meant that I utilized Myrdal's idea. The 'feedback' was clear to me—and to Myrdal also—before my writing of the dialogue with Johan Åkerman (printed in the summer 1932).[50] Both G. M[yrdal] and I may have been influenced by Kahn's paper in June 1931! My own impression was that the Stockholm group saw these matters clearly in the summer of 1932, when Lindahl and I recommended Myrdal to include a period analysis in his German paper. This is very well done by G. M[yrdal], even if he was helped by discussion with L[indahl] and B. O[hlin]. When I saw his and my own paper, I felt that we had worked in a parallel fashion. But, considerable differences remained, although not so great as 12 months earlier, when his 'instantaneous . . .' [analysis] dominated his paper.

*p. 431, line 6–8*: This is a surprising and unfounded suggestion. My combination of *ex post/ex ante* had nothing at all to do with Myrdal's 'instantaneous' analysis. To look forward and backward has nothing to do with 'instantaneous' equilibrium of tendencies, which latter interested me only as an implicit criticism of Wicksell.

*p. 433, line 4–11*: A combination of *ex post/ex ante* was used already in my 1933 paper, which was written in 1932, and in my outline for the lecture in the autumn 1932.[51] The *ex post/ex ante* was no new idea in 1933, but we all took *the name* from Myrdal's German paper. I had the same conceptual apparatus in *1934* as in 1933 and autumn of 1932, but the former was more complete. (You have seen the original 'stolparna' [outlines] from 1934—Dublin—).[52] Lindahl's survey of concepts from

50. [B. Ohlin, "Prisstegringens problem. I. Replik till fil. d:r Johan Åkerman" (The Problems Relating to the Rise of Prices. I. Rejoinder to Dr. Johan Åkerman), *Det Ekonomiska Läget*, No. 3, Aug. 1932, pp. 21–32.]

51. [B. Ohlin, *Ett konjunkturuppsvings förutsättningar och möjligheter. Föredrag vid 1932 års ordinarie bankmöte* (Conditions of and Possibilities for a Business Upswing. Lecture at the Annual Meeting of the Swedish Banker's Association in 1932), *Svenska Bankföreningens Skrifter*, No. 55, Stockholm, 1933, 21 pp.]

52. [Ohlin refers to the Finlay Lecture of 1934; cf. n. 46, above. The outlines of this lecture, entitled "The Mechanism of Expansion," have survived. They consist of a manuscript of 21 pages, all of them handwritten notes, which also contain "some *minor* new additions without importance" (Ohlin, spring 1977, see below) for the Marshall Lectures. These lectures were entitled "Recent Swedish Contributions to the Economics of Unused Resources" and given by Ohlin at the University of Cambridge, November 16, 18, and 20, 1936; cf. a letter of M. H. Dobb to Ohlin, Cambridge, October 17, 1936. The surviving parts of the outlines of the Marshall Lectures consist of a manuscript of 58 pages, where pp. 52–55 have been lost and pp. 23–43 (i.e. Lecture II and the first part of Lecture III) are identical with the outlines of the Finlay Lecture.—At the request of University College, Dublin (cf. letter from Moore McDowell to Ohlin,

November 1934[53] was *a development*, which brought it to agree with my 1934 report—except the income concept. Myrdal changed his emphasis in the Lindahl-Ohlin direction during and after the summer 1932 away from 'instantaneous equilibrium.'

*p. 434, last lines*: Neither Lindahl nor I built on any theory of fiscal policy, which came from Myrdal. Lindahl was a pioneer in his University lectures in Lund on price policy in the years after 1926.[54] If I learned from anybody about financial policy, it was from Bagge in 1925 and perhaps the British [see §1, above]. When I gave my "Municipal lecture" in 1926[55]—not included in my bibliography in *The Scandinavian Economic Journal*, 1978, [pp. 93–99]—and in 1931 (June) [cf. above, n. 14]. Myrdal had not published anything important on these matters.—What is your evidence, Otto?[56]

*p. 435, line 8*: My *Economic Journal* paper in 1937 built on the Marshall lectures in 1936. The latter were an expansion of the Dublin

---

March 24, 1977), Ohlin in the spring of 1977 prepared a typescript of the amended manuscript of the Finlay Lecture, (from which his above-quoted statement is taken) entitled "Aspects of a Theory of Expansion" and consisting of 12 typewritten pages. Ohlin was never informed by University College whether they had published his typescript, which in any case has survived.—*Ed.*]

53. [E. Lindahl, "A Note on the Dynamic Pricing Problem," Handelshögskolan i Göteborg, Oct. 23, 1934, 4 pp., mimeo., reproduced in (i) O. Steiger, *Studien zur Entstehung der Neuen Wirtschaftslehre in Schweden*, pp. 204–11 (corr. version), and (ii) D. E. Moggridge (ed.), *The Collected Writings of John Maynard Keynes. Vol. XXIX: The General Theory and After—A Supplement*, London, 1979, pp. 123–31 (uncorr. version),]—[In an additional note with regard to Lindahl's 1934 paper, Ohlin makes the following correction to my paper in *HOPE* 10 (1978): 439 (Ed.):] Lindahl's equation $E(1-s) = PQ$, [i.e.] $E(1-s) = C$, is not used by B. O[hlin]. Lindahl had the impression that his system of $Es = I$ concepts ([Oct.] 1934) gave a more complete and logical account. He did not realize that they were identical with B. O[hlin's], except that the definition of income was different, but the relation between the concepts otherwise [was] illustrated by equal equations.

54. [Cf. Lindahl's discussion of the possibility of a systematic use of changes in the budget balance as a means to stabilize economic fluctuations as early as 1925 in his "Penningpolitikens mål och medel. Föreläsningar vårterminen 1925 vid Uppsala Universitet" (Ends and Means of Monetary Policy. Lectures at the University of Uppsala, Spring Term 1925), ms., esp. §6 (pp. 35–37) on "Den monetära köpkraftens reglering" (The Regulation of the Monetary Purchasing Power); quoted in O. Steiger, *Studien* etc., pp. 174 f.]

55. [It has not been possible to identify this lecture. As far as I know, Ohlin gave only one "Municipal lecture": "Kommunala finansproblem under kristider" (Fiscal Problems of Local Governments in Times of Crisis), *Svenska Stadsförbundets Tidskrift*, 1932, pp. 395–400.—*Ed.*]

56. [Myrdal discussed the necessity of public expenditure as a remedy for unemployment for the first time in the autumn of 1931, in various papers and his pamphlet *Sveriges väg genom penningkrisen* (Sweden's Way through the Monetary Crisis), Stockholm, 1931, esp. pp. 126 ff., but not yet at a theoretically advanced level; cf. my *Studien* etc., pp. 182 ff. I withhold, however, that Ohlin in his *analysis of the multiplying effects of public works* was decisively influenced by Myrdal's works on the economic effects of fiscal policy of 1933 and 1934 (cf. n. 43 and n. 44, resp., above).—*Ed.*]

lectures in 1934, which came close to the skeleton of my 1934 report, part I.[57]

*p. 429 ff. (§12 etc.)*: Should not Otto Steiger explain that more optimistic expectations without physical changes can cause expansion etc.? Output and employment variations have the centre of attention in 1934 report.

*p. 433–34*: The liquidity trap affects the demand for credit and is part of loanable fund theory.

## II. *Relations to the Cambridge Theory and Policy of Expansion*

### §9. *Theories of interest*

I return now to the not very important question of the possible influences of the different economists on the work of the group which I later called the Stockholm School.

With regard to the theory of interest I confine myself to a brief remark. The importance of liquidity and the liquidity trap which I touched upon in 1931[58] is not incompatible with a theory of demand and supply for credit as the determinant of the interest level. The normal rate of interest is the level that is compatible with an economic development, which is regarded as normal. This is a more illuminative statement[59]—in my opinion—than the indication of any 'equilibrium' level of the Wicksell-Myrdal type, which is described in Myrdal's brilliant paper in 1932. But it is obviously a quite different theory of interest than the one theory or the two theories which Keynes developed. On the other hand it has a certain similarity with the interest theory of D. H. Robertson, which may have exercised a considerable influence on my thinking in this matter.

### §10. [*Comments on Patinkin's paper*]

[(i)] *Answer to Patinkin*. The Stockholm Theory—as Brems and Steiger rightly emphasize in polemics with Patinkin—uses physical output as a variable in writings that were published in 1933–34. To some extent it is true also of earlier texts which in most cases were primarily aiming at an analysis of price level development and control over such a development. Of course, prices and price levels were also

57. [This has already been recognized in my "Prelude" etc., *History of Political Economy* 10 (1978): 435 n. 15.—*Ed.*]

58. [Cf. the following works of Ohlin: (i) "Den internationella penningpolitiken" etc., p. 23, and (ii) *The Course and Phases of the World Economic Depression. Report Presented to the Assembly of the League of Nations*, Geneva, 1931, p. 225.]

59. See the doctrine I presented in [*Penningpolitik* etc.] 1934, pp. [43–44].

regarded as variables. This cannot be wrong. The 'feedback' mechanism depends on *variations in the value of output*, due to a varying quantity of output, varying price level or both. It may be a pedagogical advantage—or disadvantage—to separate the quantity changes in case A from the price level change in another similar case [B] and then combine the two. But it does not become a different theory through this simplification. I cannot follow Don Patinkin when he makes it an essential part of a new theory to deal at first *only* with quantity changes in a separate section. After all, it is a very unrealistic assumption. Keynes took up price level variations late in his analysis (Chapter 21) and combined it with consideration of the quantity variations. Why not take both into account at the first stage? Or start with price level changes alone and add the influence of quantity changes?[60]

The construction of an underemployment *equilibrium* is superfluous. The 'financing' e.g. of increased public works without any previous increase in the disposition to save follows from the definitions used by Keynes as well as by myself. For ex definitione the value of savings is equal to the value of new investment when we look back on events in a finished period.

[(ii) *A comment on*] *Patinkin's paper in History of Political Economy, No. 3, 1978.*[61] The paper deals with my paper of 1933 [in *Ekonomisk Tidskrift*].

As indicated in other brief papers by myself in the last two years,[62] my paper emphasizes the importance of the 'feedback' from changes in aggregate income towards changes in saving and investment—aggregate income variations taking into account quantitative changes as well as price changes. It is clearly indicated that a change in the volume of income may have such a feedback. Nowhere is it said that a feedback is dependent on the simultaneous occurrence of changes in prices. But in many cases both prices and volume vary. This is actually so in the real world in most cases. It is therefore more realistic to study cases where both prices and volume change.

60. [Ohlin is right that Keynes in fact in the *General Theory* paid much less attention to variations in prices than to changes in physical output, but in spite of this, it must be emphasized that *from the very outset* of the *General Theory*—and not first in ch. 21 as Ohlin reasons—prices are always assumed to change *along with* employment; cf., e.g., J. M. Keynes, *The General Theory of Employment, Interest and Money*, London, 1936, pp. 119, 173. What Ohlin, therefore, attacks is not Keynes, but an interpretation of Keynes which even Patinkin does not hold; cf. D. Patinkin (i) *Keynes' Monetary Thought: A Study of Its Development*, Durham, North Carolina, 1976, p. 91 n. 13, and (ii) "A Study of Keynes' Theory of Effective Demand," *Economic Inquiry*, 1979, p. 168, n. 14.—*Ed.*]

61. [From a cassette recorded by Ohlin and dated January 9, 1979.]

62. [Cf. B. Ohlin, (i) "Some Comments on Keynesianism and the Swedish Theory" etc., 1977, p. 159, and—more explicitly—(ii) "Keynesian Economics and the Stockholm School" etc., 1978, pp. 145 f.]

Keynes first deals with a very simplified case where only a change in the volume of output occurs as a result of a change in investment—the price level remaining constant—and then considers the feedback without any consideration of secondary reactions of investment. It is the same reasoning as Kahn's consumption multiplier. Later on Keynes takes price level variations into account and in that way combines the two aspects. In that way he arrives at the more realistic picture which was presented in Stockholm. Patinkin points out that Keynes in *A Treatise on Money* (1930) concentrates attention on "the determination of the prices of consumption and investment goods as contrasted with their respective cost of production and the effects of the resulting profits (or losses) in these industries in increasing (or decreasing) their respective outputs."[63] Evidently these variations in profits will in most cases lead to changes in investment.

I fail to see that there is anything wrong in pointing out this kind of interdependence. It is taken into account in the Stockholm model which considers secondary reactions not only of the volume and value of consumption but also [of . . .] investment [. . .] expressed in value, which means either in quantity alone or in prices alone or, most likely, changes in both quantity and prices.

The *important* thing is that the feedback mechanism works through changes in output in terms of money, whether this change is due only to a quantity variation or only to a price variation or, which is most likely, is due to both.

Patinkin has obviously fixed his attention on the assumption that to convey the important knowledge it is absolutely necessary first to use a very simple model where only the quantity of output varies and not at all prices. But he gives no reason for this opinion. The change in aggregate income may, as already mentioned, be due to quantity changes alone, price changes alone or to both.

Secondly, it is no special advantage to leave the secondary reactions of investment out of account in the first presentation.

Later in his paper Patinkin makes a comment based on Brems' summary of my book published 1934, the object of which was to analyze and explain changes in output and employment and discuss different methods to bring about desirable effects in this regard. Patinkin mentions that there is no indication in Brems' summary of the book that it "contained the central innovative feature of the *General Theory* whose absence in the 1933 paper I have already noted: namely, the fact that variations in output per se affect the extent of excess demand in the

63. [D. Patinkin, "Some Observations on Ohlin's 1933 Article," *History of Political Economy* 10 (1978): 414.]

commodity market" [p. 416]. This must mean that in Patinkin's opinion it is a decisive deficiency that—what he assumes—I do not deal with the possibility that a variation in output "per se" will have an equilibrating influence and eliminate the "excess demand" even if there is no price change. However, the Stockholm reasoning, as expressed by myself both [in] 1933 and, still more, in 1934, is valid when the change in income and total employment is due to quantitative changes alone or price changes alone or to both these types of variations.

The obviously unrealistic case is that on which Patinkin concentrates his interest: namely, the variation in the quantity of output alone.

Patinkin does not seem to realize that one can use different roads of simplification in the construction of models and yet arrive at the same insight.

As to the use of public works to increase employment in times of surplus capacity of labour and machinery, it is well-known that, with a more or less explicit motivation, this was recommended a quarter of a century before the 1930s. I refer to the Webbs' *Minority Report* and to various political proposals in Sweden before the first world war [see above, §1]. I also refer to a paper by a well-known conservative Swedish economist, Gösta Bagge, who in the middle of the 'twenties argued in favour of an equalization of the total volume of investment during good and bad times through the use of public investments which vary inversely with the private investments [cf. above, n. 10]. It was no innovation that, during otherwise equal circumstances, financing by borrowing would have a greater effect on employment in depressions and that the public investments must consider in which places and which industries the surplus capacity existed. But before the 'thirties there was no coherent picture of the mechanism which one would put into effect through the public works in depression times. Relatively little attention was also given to the method of financing these investments.

I may also add that I published a paper in Swedish in 1926 in the Swedish periodical for municipal economics [cf. n. 55, above].

A much discussed problem which Patinkin touches upon is the following. Will the finance that is necessary for an increased public works come forward automatically if there is no previous increase in the disposition to save? I have a couple of years ago pointed out that Keynes and Henderson in their pamphlet *Can Lloyd George Do It?* (1929) indicated that the increase in savings would be sufficient.[64] One may add,

64. [B. Ohlin, "Keynesian Economics and the Stockholm School" etc., 1978, p. 147; for an earlier reference to Keynes' and Henderson's pamphlet, but without an explicit indication of the sufficiency of savings, cf. B. Ohlin, *Bertil Ohlins memoarer*.

however, that they used such an expression that it could be interpreted as meaning that only part of the increased savings would be called forward by the increase in national income. Patinkin adds: "Indeed, one of the major contributions of Richard Kahn's subsequent multiplier article was the rigorous demonstration of this proposition (Kahn 1931, pp. 16–19; see also Warming 1932, pp. 215–16, and Kahn 1932, pp. 494–95)" [p. 415]. These papers were in the *Economic Journal*.[65] Patinkin also refers to "Kahn's recent statement that this is the way he himself regards his article (Patinkin and Leith 1977, p. 147)"[66] [p. 415 n. 5].

If one uses the backward looking income concept which Keynes used in *General Theory*—I did the same in my writings from 1932—this sufficiency of finance for the new investment is self-evident. As far I can see, the same is true of Kahn's paper in this respect. The question is not *if* savings will come to equalize investment, because this follows from the terminology used. The problem is which process [. . .] brings about this result, if we start with the position that the investment plans are larger than the expected and planned savings. Myrdal's pathbreaking initiative in making a consistent distinction between forward looking and backward looking helps very much to arrive at an account of this process. I refer to my paper in the *Economic Journal*, March 1937, which in this respect agrees with my book of 1934 and my lecture in Dublin the same year as well as my lecture in Cambridge in 1936 [the Finaly and Marshall lectures, respectively; cf. my paper "Prelude etc.," *HOPE*, 1978, p. 435 n. 15—*Ed*.]. It is necessary to study the difference that will arise between realized income and expected income as well as between realized investment and planned investment and realized savings and expected savings. It is also necessary to remember that expected income in one period may exceed the realized income during the preceding period. The fact that real events may differ from expectations will complicate the account.

I want to stress that this account is a more realistic picture than Keynes' underemployment equilibrium. The former does pay attention to changes in the quantity of output and the price of output and thus the value of output and the changes of consumption as well as the changes in investment.

*Ung man blir politiker* (B. Ohlin's Memoirs. A Young Man Becomes a Politician), Stockholm, 1972, p. 198.—*Ed*.]

65. [Concerning Kahn's (1931) and Warming's (1932) papers cf. n. 9, above; Kahn's comment on Warming (1932) was entitled "The Financing of Public Works—A Note," pp. 492–95.]

66. [R. F. Kahn, letter to D. Patinkin, March 19, 1974, in "Appendix II: Correspondence Between R. F. Kahn and D. Patinkin on the 1931 Multiplier Article and the 'Cambridge Circus,' " in *Keynes, Cambridge and the General Theory*; cf. n. 25, above.]

Kahn's paper which uses "Mr. Meade's Relation" pays attention to savings in doles when employment goes up, and why not to other matters?—he mentions the secondary investment reactions in passing —and is therefore more realistic than Keynes' model. I am convinced that Keynes was well aware of this fact. For pedagogical reasons he emphasized only certain matters in a complicated system of mutual interdependence, but he left to Patinkin the role to regard it as a *deathly sin* to give a more complicated picture than his own exceedingly simplified one.

On this last question I refer to a forthcoming paper which I hope to publish very soon in—[67]

The important thing[67a] is to give an account of the mutual interdependence of the changes in the quantities in total income, savings and investments. It is possible to do so only if one takes into account both the expectations and the real outcome. Without a description of the differences between the *ex ante* quantities and the results much in the process remains unexplained. It is not sufficient to use one *ex ante* element, i.e., the propensity to consume. Anyone who wants to compare the two theoretical constructions must, of course, ask which of them ⟨that⟩ gives the more realistic account of the process.

In each concrete case one has to consider the following facts: How is the surplus capacity distributed between different industries, and how large is it? How large is the original increase in investment demand, and how is it spread between different markets? How much of their expected new income will consumers decide to spend, and how will this demand be spread between the markets? How much will the secondary investment rise, and in which industries will the rise in production take place? To what extent can commodity stocks make the expansion easier and keep the rise in wages and prices on a lower level than would otherwise be the case?

The important question is not to demonstrate that there would be enough finance to take care of the increased investment. The question is rather to find out how much of the originally planned investment increase ⟨that⟩ will be realized and how large the following growth in investment and in output of consumers' goods will be. It is self-evident that there will be enough saving to take care of this investment, as *ex post* total savings and total investment are ex definitione equal. The real task is to describe how the relative size of the different relevant

67. Bertil Ohlin, ["Cambridge and Stockholm—Some Aspects of Monetary and Output Variations." Ohlin planned to finish this article, which is outlined in his papers published as Appendix I and Appendix II, below, immediately after his comments for *HOPE* and considered sending it to the *Economic Journal*; cf. a letter from B. Ohlin to H. Brems, Feb. 20, 1979. — *Ed.*]

67a. [Cf. Appendix II, below, n. 36. — *Ed.*]

circumstances will affect the process and limit the size of different parts of the process. Then the variations in employment up and down can only be explained if the whole process and the circumstances which keep it still or change the direction of its movements are analyzed and explained.

§11. *Comments on Brems*[68]

[. . .]

The very essence [of your comment] was your clear demonstration that I regarded variations in the total value of output as one of the fundamental variables and that these variations could be due to quantity changes or price changes or to both. How Pantinkin can continue denying this is a puzzle to me. His reasoning in *HOPE* [1978], p. 416, §2, is a good joke indeed! By the way, it is difficult to see what he means with "per se."

Maybe on some point of minor consequence one can say that you in your friendly frame of mind have attributed to me a little more priority than wholly justified. Keynes, e.g., had hinted at the idea of liquidity preference in *Treatise*.

You are right that for a long time many [economists] opposed the idea of public works financed by borrowing as means against unemployment, but this had been discussed already in the 'twenties by Bagge with regard to a policy to smooth business cycles. This idea had also been accepted in general in Stockholm in a more exclusive form from 1932 onwards (see Myrdal's promemoria of 1933 [cf. n. 44, above]). Therefore, it was no news in 1934. On the other hand, one can say that my heavy emphasis on a budgetary deficit as a method to create employment, in my lecture of 1931 [cf. n. 14 above], appeared at the same time as Keynes discussed such ideas which he had hinted at in 1929.

One may also insist on that Keynes' articles early in 1933, [*The Means to Prosperity*], went no further than my exposition in this respect.

I do not know where Patinkin [p. 417] has got the view that "open market operations" had long-since been a central part of the Wicksellian tradition. On the other hand, he is right in arguing that Keynes was well acquainted with these operations. The same is true of the economists of the Treasury. Even though I touched upon the idea in one or a few articles in *Stockholms-Tidningen*—as far as I remember already in the 'twenties—I cannot, therefore, claim any priority.

68. [Excerpts from Ohlin's above-quoted letter to Brems, referring to H. Brems, "What Was New in Ohlin's 1933–34 Macroeconomics?" *History of Political Economy* 10 (1978): 398–412.]

I am not quite certain if I wrote something about the capability of tariffs to raise the scope for an expansive policy in the 1920['s]. I am much inclined to think that Keynes' plan in 1931 was the first one which was well considered, but this is evidently a question of minor importance. You have placed in perspective the question of the important role of physical output among the variables, and you have shown that there is no need for simplified equilibrium constructions, which are quite unrealistic, in elucidating the interdependence of different macroeconomic variables in processes of expansion and contraction. In this respect, my exposition does seem more dynamic and comprehensive than Keynes' equilibrium reasoning.

[. . .]

§12. *Comments on Yohe*[69]

[. . .]

You may be interested in knowing that I do not at all agree with Dr. Fernholm's observation in *Ekonomisk Tidskrift*, 1960, which you quote.[70] I discuss a case where a decision is made to reduce savings, which under given circumstances must mean a decision to increase consumption. This will be the consequence as no assumption is made about any change in the expected income in the original situation. Fernholm evidently makes some other tacit assumption as he does not use the word 'will' but instead the word 'might'.—The investment reactions—on the other hand—are of course somewhat uncertain. But an increase in the aggregate demand will probably at the second stage lead to increased investment.

In this case, like in others, there may be special circumstances which affect the order of events. I am glad you pay attention tc this aspect.

Let me add that I think that you are quite right in what you say on page 443. In Stockholm we used an account of a development, which is less precise than a truly dynamic theory and of course is something quite different from a static theory. Lindahl and I stuck to this method. In his first paper, printed in 1932 ["Om penningteoretisk jämvikt," cf. above], Gunnar Myrdal chiefly talked about *tendencies in an instantaneous equilibrium* to demonstrate the weakness of Wicksell's theory.

69. [Excerpts from a letter from B. Ohlin to W. P. Yohe, Jan. 9, 1979, referring to the latter's "Ohlin's 1933 Reformation of Monetary Theory," *History of Political Economy* 10 (1978): 446–53.]

70. [T. Fernholm, "Idéutveckling, ekonomisk politik och ekonomisk teori. Kommentarer till Karl-Gustav Landgren: *Den 'nya ekonomien' i Sverige*" (The Development of Ideas, Economic Policy and Economic Theory. Comments on K.-G. Landgren, *The 'New Economics' in Sweden*), *Ekonomisk Tidskrift*, 1960, pp. 176f.; as quoted by Yohe, p. 450.]

There was very little of process analysis in this important paper, which building on his Doctor's Thesis [of 1927, cf. §4, above], laid the foundation for a consistent use of the distinction between forward looking and backward looking. I regard this as the most essential conceptual innovation of the whole decade and therefore a very important contribution by Myrdal. It is interesting that he in his Swedish publication of 1931 [printed 1932] and his book of 1939 [*Monetary Equilibrium*] really had two different theoretical constructions, which he did not combine. He maintained an instantaneous equilibrium, which dominated his Swedish paper in 1932. But under some influence from Lindahl and myself, he expanded the little embryo to a process analysis, which was similar to the method used by Lindahl and myself. The first three chapters in the German paper ["Der Gleichgewichtsbegriff etc.," 1933; cf. n. 37 above], which are quite newly written, are very important and his revision in the proofs of the English text in some other chapters of his book (1939) is also valuable. I did not see the manuscript to the first three chapters of the proofs until after the writing of my Swedish paper [in *Ekonomisk Tidskrift*, 1933]. To a certain extent we must have written similar things independently of one another. However, to some extent we might both have been a little influenced by discussion with Lindahl.

I am making some more far-reaching critical comments about some aspects of Steiger's paper in *HOPE*, [1978], No. 3. [. . .]

## §13. *Comments on Landgren*[71]

A Swedish critic questioning the claims of priority of the Stockholm School [vis-à-vis Keynes . . .] is Dr. K.-G. Landgren who wrote a—in some respects—valuable treatise in the history of economic thought, entitled *Den 'nya ekonomien' i Sverige. J. M. Keynes, E. Wigforss, B. Ohlin och utvecklingen 1927–39* [1960; cf. n. 17 above]. According to him, the definite turning point in economic theory, in spring 1933, is marked by Keynes' pamphlet *Means to Prosperity*, which was published in April. [. . .] Landgren heavily emphasizes that in this work, Keynes in his analysis of changes in the volume of employment used the approach of aggregate supply and aggregate demand. In this point my detailed paper "Till frågan om penningteoriens uppläggning" [*Ekonomisk Tidskrift*, 1933; cf. n. 1 above] applied the same approach; it was published one or a few months after my very positive review of Keynes in *Stockholms-Tidningen* which, according to Landgren, makes it probable that I borrowed this important methodological idea

71. [Excerpts from B. Ohlin, *Bertil Ohlins memoarer*, 1972, ch. 13 ("The Stockholm School of Economics and Keynes"), pp. 165–67.]

from him. It was Keynes, therefore, who initiated this useful, important theoretical approach in Stockholm, Landgren concludes.

[. . .]

To be sure, Landgren takes note of the fact that I referred to Wicksell, but believes that it was Keynes' new work rather than Wicksell's old one which influenced me. Myrdal and Lindahl did not apply this approach much, but on the whole concentrated on the more limited relation between savings and investment. Contrary to Wicksell—but in accordance with Keynes—I regarded not only the price level but also real national income as an obviously variable magnitude. Landgren writes: "Ohlin was acquainted with Wicksell's idea to work with the relation between aggregate demand and aggregate supply, when he read *Means to Prosperity*, but it was through the reading of this pamphlet that he realized the possibilities of arriving at a better knowledge of macroeconomics, which was later elaborated by Keynes in a systematic form in *General Theory*" [p. 166]. [. . .].

With respect to the theoretical method I was inspired by Wicksell, Lindahl and Myrdal, probably also Hawtrey even if I did not realize this at that time. In a letter to me in February, 1933, Professor Davidson accepted my paper for printing [in *Ekonomisk Tidskrift*]—one month before Keynes' articles [first published in *The Times*]. Following Wicksell I had applied the approach of aggregate supply and aggregate demand earlier in a more cursory way but in a more consistent manner only in works on variations in foreign trade and international capital movements. More important is the fact that my paper, entitled "Till penningteoriens centralproblem" [On the Central Problems of Monetary Theory] which was circulated among some colleagues in late autumn, 1932,[72] was practically identical with the version accepted by Davidson in February[73] which Landgren thinks was inspired by Keynes. It was printed in May [June], 1933, with a modified title. This has been proved by Otto Steiger in his thesis *Studien zur Entstehung der Neuen Wirtschaftslehre in Schweden* (1971) which contains a careful and very illuminating analysis of the new economics in Sweden. Steiger found a copy of the paper among Lindahl's literary remains. Also other contributions—especially Myrdal's appendix to the [Swedish] Government's budget which he gave in December, 1932 [cf. above, n. 44]—demonstrated that our decisive theoretical debate happened earlier than the publication of Keynes' pamphlet.

72. [Cf. O. Steiger, "Bertil Ohlin and the Origins of the Keynesian Revolution," 1976, pp. 353 f.]

73. [On February 26, 1933, Davidson accepted *not* the later printed version, but the original draft, "Till penningteoriens centralproblem"; on the similarities of the two versions cf. O. Steiger, "Substantive Changes" etc., 1978, pp. 389–97.—*Ed.*]

My second comment is that Landgren heavily underestimates Myrdal's and Lindahl's role. Even if in a mere formal sense my theoretical approach was closer to Keynes' in *General Theory*, 1936, than theirs, nevertheless, the similarities between us three were great—maybe that we, as Steiger demonstrates, mutually criticized to a certain extent each other's approach. The thesis that Keynes' articles in March and his book in April, 1933, decisively inspired the 'Stockholm School' obviously is groundless. We did not need to mobilize a higher form of originality to recognize that the volume of employment is necessary as a central theoretical variable for an analysis of measures against unemployment.

§14. *Survey of similarities between the scientific conclusions in Stockholm and Cambridge*[74]

[(a)] *Differences from the 'old theory.'* i. Demand management is characteristic both of the Swedish theory based on Wicksell and of the Keynesian theory—which was influenced by Wicksell. The former was developed in 1930–34 in a less simplistic manner, particularly through a sequence analysis with different cases as far as the 'spread of surplus capacity,' the flexibility of different prices and wages and the 'spread of the increase in demand' is concerned. The use of aggregate demand and aggregate supply as fundamental constructions. Aggregate supply variations as equilibrating force. Criticism of Say's law. Wicksell. Later stressed by B. O[hlin] (1933, 34) as the main approach, including the concepts which make the value of new savings equal to the value of new investment. See Keynes' letter to B. O[hlin, Jan. 27, 1937; cf. n. 22 above].

ii. The analysis in (i) gives a theoretical foundation for the use of public finance-expansion and deficit—[especially] public works, subsidies, tariffs as remedies for unemployment.

iii. The great influence of the uncertainty of the future. Cf. Keynes in *QJE* 1937.[75] Myrdal 1927. Later Lindahl also. L. saw its importance.

iv. No automatic change from low employment to full employment. Equilibrium constructions are not essential. Early writings both in England and Sweden.

v. In general wage reductions in depressions in an isolated country will not lead to greater employment. May do so under special circumstances.

74. [Parts (a) and (b) are from a typewritten page (with handwritten additions); part (c) is from the handwritten notes.]

75. [J. M. Keynes, "The General Theory of Employment," *Quarterly Journal of Economics*, 1937, pp. 209–23.]

vi. A decline in the disposition to save in a depression will ceteris paribus lead to greater investment and greater volume of savings.

vii. Backward looking concepts which make the quantity of savings always equal to the quantity of new investment make⟨s⟩ it obvious that there is always sufficient 'finance' for the investment which can be carried out with the aid of unused resources. Such concepts used as fundamental by B. O[hlin] and J. M. K[eyne]s. Kahn and Meade.

[(b)] *Other merits of the Stockholm Theory*. viii. The stressing of the importance of the order of events in processes of expansion and contraction as well as the speed of reactions.

ix. Contribution to the theory of interest. Some affinity to the interest theory of D. H. Robertson.

[(c) *More detailed comments on the similarities between Cambridge and Stockholm*.] The consumption multiplier and the accelerator were analyzed in greater detail at Cambridge and Oxford than in Stockholm. But Wicksell's cumulative process took both into account with regard to *price development*. The quantitative expansion and contraction was added to price level variations in the Swedish Theory.[76] This greater precision may have been due to stimulus from Kahn's well-known paper,[77] although Myrdal does not remember having read it in time for such an influence[78] being possible.

The time sequence of reactions in a process is important for the outcome. This was not taken much into account by Keynes but it was stressed in the Stockholm Theory.

The disposition to save—and thus also to consume—was considered in both Cambridge and Stockholm. In a more fruitful way in the former place.

Neither of the two schools retained the old theory of automatic restoration of full employment equilibrium on the labour market.[79]

Financial policy as a stimulus to expansion was like credit policy recommended in both places: Wicksell was a pioneer in the latter respect. Borrowing and budget deficits were discussed by Lindahl in the 1920s (finally in his 1930 volume [*Penningpolitikens medel*, esp. ch. 2, §8 on "The Influence on the Price Level by Means of Public Finance,"

76. See Myrdal's paper ["Om penningteoretisk jämvikt"], 1932, [§47, p. 271]. His reasoning in this paper has no use of his later *ex post/ex ante* terminology.

77. *The Economic Journal*, June 1931 [cf. n. 9, above].

78. Information from G. M[yrdal] to Steiger [in a letter of April 5, 1978; quoted by Steiger in *History of Political Economy* 10 (1978): 440 n. 23—In this letter, however, there is no reference to Kahn, but to Keynes' Chicago Lectures on the Harris Foundation, June 1931, "An Economic Analysis of Unemployment," published in Q. Wright, ed., *Unemployment as a World Problem*, Chicago, 1931, pp. 3–42. Myrdal only informed me that he never had read or heard about *this* book.—*Ed*.]

79. See Alf Johansson, [*Löneutvecklingen och arbetslösheten*, 1934.]

pp. 63–68]), by B. O[hlin] in a lecture in 1931 ["Den internationella penningpolitiken etc.," esp. pp. 28–30] and later on much more thoroughly by Myrdal.[80] The use of price level expectations as a method of credit policy was advocated by Wicksell and a number of [following] prominent Swedish economists. This matter was not given much attention at Cambridge.

There can be no doubt that the attention in Stockholm was drawn to policies of expansion by British writings in 1927–29. But the Sw[edish] Com[mittee on Unemployment] was appointed in 1928 and the questions about employment policy were asked. What would have happened if Keynes had turned his attention to other problems in 1930? Would no policy of expansion have been accepted in the following years?

## *Appendix I:* On Pre-War Keynesian and Stockholm Theories of Employment—Chiefly Through Demand Management

*Introduction by Otto Steiger*

*In his letter to Hans Brems of February 20, 1979, quoted above (cf. main text, n. 67), Ohlin wrote as follows: "Next summer I shall probably write (i) a comment on the four comments in* HOPE *and (ii) a comparison of Cambridge and Stockholm—not aimed to discussing questions of priorities, but meant to contribute to a better analysis of economic sequences and employment policy. The latter paper must not be referred to before it is finished because I have not yet decided to which journal it will be offered. There are strong reasons in favour of the* Economic Journal, *because this would put pressure on the British economists to take a stand toward it" (translated from the Swedish by Ed.). A working plan of Ohlin's for the summer and autumn of 1979 which has survived shows that this paper was to be entitled "Cambridge and Stockholm—Some Aspects of Monetary and Output Variations."*

*There exist two different, only partly overlapping outlines of Ohlin's unfinished paper on Cambridge and Stockholm, reproduced in this issue of* HOPE *as Appendix I and II, respectively. The text published as Appendix I is based on (i) a typescript of nine pages—correlated in two different versions—dated February 27–28, 1979, and entitled "On Pre-War Keynesian and Stockholm Theories of*

80. [Cf. his] reports [on fiscal policy], 1933 and 1934; [cf. n. 44 and n. 45, above].

*Employment—Chiefly Through Demand Management," as well as (ii) a revised and abridged version of this paper, a typescript (with handwritten insertions) of four pages, dated March 8, 1979, and entitled "On Keynesian and Stockholm Theories of Employment in 1930 to 1936." In the preparation of Appendix I, I have followed versions (i) but considered all corrections, revisions and additions made in (ii) (which comprehended only sections I–V of the published text).*

*Ohlin had prepared both versions of the paper for two lectures which he gave during his visit to the United States in the spring of 1979: (i) at the University of California, Berkeley, on March 30, and (ii) at the Jacob Marschak Colloquium, University of California, Los Angeles, on April 6. The latter lecture had the same title as version (ii).*

To discuss priorities in the development of employment theory in the 1930s is not the primary goal of this analysis. It is rather my intention to compare two alternative approaches to the employment problem in the hope that this may facilitate a merger of somewhat revised theories. Furthermore, the contradictions and differences of opinion between the 'Keynesians' and 'the Monetarists' with regard to policies of economic expansion through demand management in times of unemployment may be modified in the future. However, I am also interested in the history of doctrine in this field before the Second World War.

### I. *Wicksell as a Pioneer in Aggregate Demand Analysis*

Wicksell saw that Say's law was untenable. He also realized the importance of investment management and above all *the necessity of a distinction between savings and investment*. His attention was concentrated on price development, but his cumulative process included scanty comments on variations in output. The reasoning could easily be extended to cover simultaneous changes in real national income and in commodity price levels and wage levels.

Wicksell also saw the importance of aggregate demand analysis for understanding changes in the international economic relations. In this respect I followed him in my thesis of 1924[1] and in different papers a few years later, e.g., the discussion with Keynes in 1929.[2] Keynes re-

1. [B. Ohlin, *Handelns teori* (The Theory of Trade), Stockholm, 1924. (In the following, no translation of titles will be given which have already been quoted in Ohlin's main text.—*Ed.*)]

2. [B. Ohlin, (i) "The Reparation Problem: A Discussion. I. Transfer Difficulties, Real and Imagined," *Economic Journal*, 1929, pp. 172–78, and (ii) "Mr. Keynes' Views on the Transfer Problem: II. A Rejoinder," *Economic Journal*, 1929, pp. 400–404.]

fused to accept the relation of aggregate demand to aggregate supply as important for international economic adjustments, at least in the case of capital movements. He made a concession in 1931. But in *General Theory*, 1936, Keynes gave to this relation a central role, although in the strange form of the equation of effective demand. As a matter of fact the idea was presented already in *The Means to Prosperity*, 1933.

## II. [*Earlier Ideas on Public Works as Remedy for Unemployment*]

The low employment in Great Britain in the 1920s made British economists put the *employment problem* in the focus of their attention, particularly after the return to the gold standard in 1925, in spite of a relatively high British cost level.

Keynes and Henderson in 1929[3] discussed the possibility that increased investment—without any previous increase in the disposition to save—would be possible and lead to larger employment, if at the outset a considerable surplus capacity existed.

In the middle of the '20s Swedish economists, particularly Professor Bagge in 1925,[4] took up the idea of smoothing out the business cycle and creating a more even curve of employment through demand management. Aggregate demand should be restricted in boom periods and expanded in recessions. The idea of increasing public works in times of unemployment was an old one. But there was only little coherent economic theory behind this reasoning. Voluntary large deficits in the public budget [were] recommended by me in a lecture in the summer of 1931.[5] It would be a supplement to active credit policy to stimulate employment.

## III. *The Stockholm Period Analysis*

The impetus was given by Erik Lindahl,[6] who followed up Wicksell's analysis of methods to counteract large movements in price levels. He did not take up counter-action of employment changes as a goal in itself. But he analysed carefully both credit policy and financial policy and the importance of influencing public expectation of future price movements. Myrdal's paper "Monetary Equilibrium" in Swed-

3. [J. M Keynes and H. D. Henderson, *Can Lloyd George Do It?: An Examination of the Liberal Pledge*, London, 1929.]

4. [G. Bagge, "Produktionens reglering som medel mot arbetslöshet," *Svensk Tidskrift*, 1925, pp. 513–23.]

5. [B. Ohlin, "Den internationella penningpolitiken och dess inverkan på konjunkturutvecklingen," *Förhandlingar vid Nordiska nationalekonomiska mötet i Stockholm 15–17 juni 1931*, Stockholm, 1931, pp. 28f., 64, 67.]

6. [E. Lindahl, *Penningpolitikens medel* (1929), Lund, 1930.]

ish in the summer of 1932[7] was the second important step. There followed a long paper by myself—translated in *History of Political Economy* last autumn[8] and besides further papers and books by the three of us and by Alf Johansson on wage development.[9]

In my opinion the most important step—since Lindahl had set the ball rolling in 1930—was Myrdal's distinction between 'forward looking' and 'backward looking.' (It was utilized by Stockholm economists consistently in 1933 and 1934 in Swedish publications dealing with employment and price policy.)[10] A natural conclusion was that practically all the macroeconomic variables would exist in two forms: The *plans*, which people try to realize, and the *real outcome*, which would more or less differ from the plans.—The future is always uncertain and to some extent unpredictable.

*Ex post*, savings would always equal *ex post* investment. The task was to demonstrate which process had brought this about during the finished period in spite of differences between the sum of planned savings and the sum of planned investments. Naturally, *supply reactions* influenced the process. How important is the flexibility of the wage rates? Under what conditions will the process stop or price rises continue [once] full employment has been reached? The sequence analysis becomes more easily understandable when the number of concepts is increased in this way. It would obviously be necessary to study the changes in aggregate demand and in investment demand and consumption demand etc. There is a mutual interdependence between all these variables. One cannot say that changes in investments have a role that is causally different from the role of changes in consumption or changes in the total aggregate demand. See below.

A special part of the Swedish theory of economic expansion considered how much *the order of events and the speeds of reactions* could influence the development. If wages rise rapidly while the prices are relatively stable, the consequence will be quite different from the case when wages are rather stable, but prices rise rapidly. In the latter case

7. ["Om penningteoretisk jämvikt" etc., *Ekonomisk Tidskrift*, 1931, pp. 191–302 (printed 1932).]

8. [B. Ohlin, "On the Formulation of Monetary Theory" (1933), *HOPE* 10 (1978): 353–88.]

9. [A. Johansson, *Löneutvecklingen och arbetslösheten*, Stockholm, 1934.]

10. [See esp. B. Ohlin, (i) "On the Formulation of Monetary Theory" (1933), and (ii) *Penningpolitik, offentliga arbeten, subventioner and tullar som medel mot arbetslöshet etc.*, Stockholm, 1934, part I; G. Myrdal, "Der Gleichgewichtsbegriff als Instrument der geldtheoretischen Analyse," in F. A. Hayek (ed.), *Beiträge zur Geldtheorie*, Vienna, 1933, pp. 361–487; E. Lindahl, "A Note on the Dynamic Pricing Problem" (1934), as originally reproduced in O. Steiger, *Studien zur Entstehung der Neuen Wirtschaftslehre in Schweden* etc., Berlin, 1971, pp. 204–11.]

an expansion of profit comes early. Besides, the changes in expectations about the future as well as the uncertainty of the future will exercise a considerable role on the investment and saving plans and, thereby, on the whole process of expansion.

This is a brief outline of parts of the Stockholm theory around 1933–34, with some emphasis on my own method of presentation.

## IV. *The Keynesian Simplification*

My thesis is that the Keynesian reasoning about underemployment equilibrium is formally different but, as far as insight goes, chiefly a simplified demonstration of some of the results of the sequence analysis in Stockholm. In *General Theory*, 1936, Keynes explained how an increase in investment works under highly simplified assumptions and demonstrated that employment can remain low during long periods. To make this into an equilibrium analysis one has to make all sorts of unrealistic assumptions. Keynes assumed that the increased output of consumers' goods will not lead to any endogenous increase in the volume of investment. His assumptions about wage development are also highly special. He maintains that increased employment will necessarily lead to a lower real wage. It is not surprising that the man who probably helped Keynes more than anyone else, Lord Kahn, in his Keynes Lecture in 1974[11] explains why he thinks that Keynes wage reasoning is unsatisfactory.

In Stockholm the effects of an increase in investment was analyzed with the more many-sided model I touched upon above. It was self-evident that the increase of the volume of output and national income and the further effect on aggregate demand and on consumption and investment would be considered. If one makes unrealistic assumptions about a stable price level, the Stockholm model would demonstrate the mutual interdependence of the *quantitative* variables alone. But this is unnecessarily unrealistic. It is better to take into account that both quantities and prices vary. I cannot understand Patinkin's[12] insistence on the necessity of first using a model, which assumes stable prices and illustrates the feedback from changes in aggregate output to changes in savings and brings the [latter to agree] with the expanded investment. Certainly, a reasoning in terms of money is natural. Furthermore, changes in relative prices play a role for the development, also for the

11. [R. F. Kahn, *On Re-reading Keynes. Fourth Keynes Lecture in Economics*, London 1975, pp. 18–24.]

12. [Cf. D. Patinkin, (i) "On the Relation between Keynesian Economics and the 'Stockholm School,'" *Scandinavian Journal of Economics*, 1978, pp. 135–43, and (ii) "Some Observations on Ohlin's 1933 Article," *History of Political Economy* 10 (1978): 413–18.]

changes in quantities. Why insist on studying quantities, e.g., of savings, on the basis of unrealistic assumptions about price stability?

An expansive economic policy, which brings about some recovery, would probably lead to a speedy increase in at least some raw material prices, which will affect the prices of some finished commodities. Evidently, the structure and the distribution of inventories has an influence on the effects of an increase in aggregate demand. This was emphasized in Stockholm in the early [19]30s, quite as the importance of the degree of flexibility of wage rates. We denied that wage reductions would be certain to lead to a greater employment in an isolated country. Prices might fall and profits decline, which could lead to lower employment.

Stagflation is simply a parallel case to those, which were analyzed during the depression in the 1930s. In some periods in the 1970s wages have gone up quicker than prices. Hence, profits became unsatisfactory and employment fell. Under such circumstances cost inflation can go hand in hand with rising unemployment.

## V. *Some Questions*

Keynes' special theory of interest plays no vital role for the theory of employment. One may just as well use an interest theory which is based on the supply of and demand for different kinds of credit instruments. The different types of interest rates are determined on the market. If some important rates are kept on a low level, the willingness to invest—planned investment—may exceed the willingness to save—planned saving. The outcome when the first period is finished may demonstrate that the equality between the ex-post concepts has been achieved, e.g., through unexpected inflation and reduction of inventories. The equilibrium rate of interest has to be such that it is compatible with an economic development which is regarded as natural or stable. To define a general economic situation by means of very simplified assumptions in order to arrive at one equilibrium rate of interest is hardly illuminating.

## VI. *Is the Stockholm Theory Operational?*

This theory assumes that individuals and corporations have an opinion about future income and let this opinion affect their plans and purchases. Compare with this construction the Marshall demand and supply curves based on the aggregate income and output in the whole country. Keynes' theory of effective demand is based on such supply and demand curves, where only labour and consumer's goods and capital goods are considered apart from entrepreneurs. Will each entrepreneur have a clear opinion about how many workers he would employ in the future *under each conceivable assumption about different wage rates and different market conditions*? The idea that there is a basis for such a curve seems to me to be more unrealisitc than the Stockholm idea that individuals and corporations have employment plans and budgets for the future. They are based on assumed prices and on wages, that are fixed for the first coming brief period. Some prices on finished goods are fixed by the producers when the period begins.

Secondly, the concept [of] planned aggregate demand compared to the planned aggregate supply during a period has proved usable for prognoses about the inflationary forces, e.g., under the influence of recently accepted general wage contracts. It is sometimes obvious that the aggregate demand will be increased much more than the aggregate supply would be, if prices rose only as much as costs. If so, there will be a demand inflation over and above cost inflation: an inflationary 'gap.'

*Demand management* is characteristic both of the Swedish theory based on Wicksell and of the Keynesian theory—which was influenced by Wicksell. The former was developed in 1930–34 in a less simplistic manner, particularly through a sequence analysis with different cases as far as the 'spread of surplus capacity,' the flexibility of different prices and wages and the 'spread of the increase in demand' are concerned.[13] The Keynesian theory is more 'special' and more open to criticism from members of the 'Monetarist school,' who emphasize the difficulty in adapting the increased demand to the more or less adaptable increase in the supply of different products. [. . .]

## VII. *A Question of Methodology*

Is the advantage of having a *closed* model paid too dearly by the necessity of violent simplifications?

The more casuistic Stockholm theory considered many different cases with regard to the order of events and the speed of reaction. I am referring to wage rates, prices of raw materials, prices of finished goods, employment in different industries etc. An increase in investment demand will bring about different processes during different conditions in these respects. Did not the Keynesian equilibrium theory predispose for a simplistic theory of the effects of a policy of expansion? Above all rather little attention was given to the effect which the beginning of the process and the gaining of some experiences would have on wage policy and furthermore also on the expected profits and the willingness to increase investment.

13. [The first two sentences in this paragraph ("Demand . . . concerned") were used by Ohlin in his main paper, §14, sect. a (i); cf. p. 216 above.—*Ed.*]

The reactions of savings in the course of the process cannot be well explained if we think about the individual income earners. Large changes in the volume of the savings may come as a result of the reduced profits in corporations. During a recovery phase a businessman may expect still larger profits in the future and may increase the share of the present income which goes to consumption so that it reaches a higher percentage than in the preceding period when income was lower.

Is not Keynes' feedback analysis oversimplified, if we want to know the effects of an increased investment on the economic system in a state of surplus capacity?

Above all, is there any other method of analysing a development than to take into account the order of events and the speed of reactions in a system with many elements grouped together as macro-economic variables and with a careful consideration of the role of the expectations about the future?

### VIII. *The Determination of the Real National Income in an Isolated Country*

It depends on productivity and employment. Aggregate demand determines how much of aggregate supply of commodities can be sold.

In an existing starting situation $Da = 0{,}9\ Sa$. E.g. Great Britain in the 1920s. What will determine a rise in employment? Of course, an increase in aggregate demand. Full employment will be established if planned consumption ($Ca$) is equal to $Sa$' planned supply of consumer's goods, and planned investment ($I_a$) is equal to planned saving, when employment is full.

Investment volume must be large enough in a full employment state to agree with the amount people want to save in that situation.

A more illuminating approach is: What process determines *changes* in the G.N.P. and in employment? The answer is The Stockholm Sequence analysis and the Keynesian more simplified underemployment equilibrium analysis. When Keynes adds consideration of price changes, the result is a vague (see ch. XXI, *G[eneral] T[heory]*) reasoning about the relation between employment, growth and price growth.

### [IX.] *An Open Country*

If the country is open for international trade, factor investments and other contacts, the aggregate demand analysis—including exports, imports and capital movements—indicated the relative position of different countries, Walras-Cassel-Ohlin Productivity Consideration. Due regard to foreign exchange rates and Taussig-Viner's productivity effects.

[X.] *Practical Conclusions*

i. A positive attitude to active employment policy. The relation of aggregate demand to aggregate supply is vital.

ii. *Demand Management* emphasis. Easier to use credit and financial policy.

| | | |
|---|---|---|
| *Differences*: | STOCKHOLM | More attention to supply conditions in different industries. (Keynes a little in ch. XXI.) |
| | STOCKHOLM | More attention to different *order of events and speed of reactions*. Risk of inflation is greater than assumed by the Keynesians. The cleavage between them and the Monetarists depends partly on this Keynesian simplification. Stockholm lies 'in between.' (Micro analysis is the most important thing at the second stage of macro analysis.) |

iii. Wage reductions in an isolated country will as a rule not increase employment.

| | |
|---|---|
| *Difference*: | Wage theory difference. Stockholm does not accept marginal productivity. |

iv. *The propensity to save* (or will to save):

| | |
|---|---|
| STOCKHOLM THEORY | more realistic in the case of corporations' savings variations. This affects the 'feedback' reaction.—How much increase in investment can be financed without a primary decision to increase savings! The Stockholm 'mutual interdependence' is more realistic than the Keynesian simple causation from aggregate output change to increased savings. |

v. *The endogenous investment reaction*: Stockholm easily on Harrod's lines.

vi. *The Money market reactions*: More obvious for different types of credit in the Stockholm theory.

## *Appendix II:* A Comparison of the Development of Monetary Theory at Cambridge and in Sweden in 1928–[19]36

*Introduction by Otto Steiger*

*This is the second outline which Ohlin wrote for his planned paper, "Cambridge and Stockholm—Some Aspects of Monetary and Output Variations"; cf. my introduction to Appendix I, above. This outline consists of (i) a typescript of eight pages containing the introduction and part I, (ii) a typescript (with handwritten insertions) of six pages containing part II, and (iii) a typescript (with handwritten insertions) of three pages which is a revised and abridged version of typescript (ii). In the preparation of Appendix II, I have reproduced (i), followed (ii) and, thereby, considered all corrections, revisions and additions made in (iii) (which comprehended only paragraphs 2–8 of part II). The outline can be dated between January 12, 1979, when Ohlin sent an uncorrected version of (i) and (ii) to Don Patinkin, and February 8, 1979, which is the date of (iii).*

### *Introduction*

Keynes was well aware of the imbalance of the external value of the pound sterling. He wanted a lower sterling quotation in 1925–31. When the depreciation came in the autumn of 1931 he was very happy. (See his letter to B.O.)[1] Until then the insufficient competitive power of British industry kept the volume of investment on too low a level and made the balance of payments weak, i.e. limited "the external room" for an internal expansionary policy. Hence, "permanent" unemployment followed, Keynes regarded this kind of insufficient employment as often due to other causes and as a rather common trait of the capitalistic system. But it was a fault that could be remedied. He saw it as his task to do it.

However, he pushed the *international* imbalance question—from which he had started—almost completely aside and developed a theory for expansionist policy to increase employment in a closed society. It seems probable that the *world wide depression* and large unemployment in industrialized nations in the 1930s was the chief cause of his attitude. His reasoning became a kind of general theory for different degrees of employment and a recipe for stabilization policy. But, the knowledge about variations in investment and consumption, which had

1. [In this letter of Sept. 24, 1931, Keynes wrote to Ohlin: "We in Great Britain are feeling in a state of boisterous cheerfulness over the events of the last week!"]

been assembled in the theories of business cycles *during several decades*, was left aside, at least the larger part of it.

The approach used at Cambridge in the years 1933–35, when the General Theory was worked out, naturally was much affected by the British economic development from 1924 as well as by the kind of theory Keynes, as well as Kahn and other young Cambridge and Oxford economists (Joan Robinson, Meade, Harrod) were working on during the changing development in this decade. It seems almost certain that D. H. Robertson, H. D. Henderson and Hawtrey made essential contributions to the theoretical development as well as some Treasury economists—partly through their presentation of alternative approaches. (About the influence of Wicksell, see below.)

The *General Theory* brought several 'innovations.' To some extent they were started by Keynes, Henderson and Hawtrey in the late 1920s. An *essential innovation*—although a tautology—in this line was made *by Kahn*—with the aid of "Mr. Meade's Relation"—in 1931. (See p[oint] 4 below.) However, other essential parts were created by Keynes in the two years 1933–34.

A comparison between the insight brought by this Cambridge theory and that brought by the Stockholm theory, which was published in the period 1930–34, is naturally more concerned with the knowledge transmitted than with the formal theoretical constructions. Even if a great deal of agreement between the two schools of thought and their economic policy conclusions can be found, it would be absurd to expect identical theoretical constructions.

Let me add that my 'survey' below makes no claim to cover more than parts of the two theories. My time has not permitted a renewed study of all books and papers to which a reference might well have been made.

As I have mentioned several times the expansionistic measures advocated by Keynes and some other Cambridge economists from 1926 to 1930 probably exercised an influence on the general expansionistic attitude among Swedish economists. Before that period the emphasis by Professor Bagge and others had been on a reduction of public investment in boom periods and expansion in recessions. Professor Lindahl—at that time in Lund—took up the problem of public borrowing for investment as a stimulus to employment in his lectures for the students, but as far as I know, did not print anything before 1930. (*The Means of Monetary Policy*, printed in Swedish. Proofs were circulated in 1929.[2]) The emphasis was, however, on the effects on price

2. [E. Lindahl, *Penningpolitikens medel* (1929), Lund, 1930. (In this and the following footnotes no translation of titles will be given which have already been quoted in Ohlin's main text.—*Ed.*]

levels and on *the maintenance of price stability*.—I published a pamphlet on some measures to increase investment, employment and output in Denmark in 1927.[3] Another relatively early publication, which touched upon price development, expansion of output and the liquidity trap, was my lecture at the Nordic Economic Meeting in June 1931.[4]

[Part I. *Survey of the Theoretical Insights in Cambridge and Stockholm*]

1. *Underemployment equilibrium*. One of the partly new ideas, which Keynes developed in *General Theory* (1936)—about its earlier history see point 4 below—was the following: A state of unemployment can exist during long periods. There is no automatic tendency to bring about full employment. The degree of unemployment will, of course, rise and fall under the influence of endogenous changes in essential variables. To convince economists of this fact Keynes developed a theory of underemployment equilibrium in a very simple form.

2. *Comparison with the Stockholm theory*. One important theory problem is the following: Is there any need of an *equilibrium* construction? The chief task is to demonstrate the character of different processes of expansion and contraction, i.e. the mutual interdependence of different variables. In Sweden this was done through ⟨the⟩ following up Wicksell's *cumulative process*, where changes in interest rates, investment and savings [had been] discussed since several decades, chiefly to explain price level changes, but with some reference to output variations. From 1932 the writings in Stockholm took *the changes in output* into account more fully than they had done before. One difference from Keynes' reasoning was that we did not use an equilibrium construction in this sequence analysis. In my opinion Keynes' underemployment theory gets the character of an equilibrium only because he rules out secondary investment reactions. When Kahn talked about secondary investment reactions—he did it briefly already in his 1931 paper—he had to leave the equilibrium method of Keynes or make artificial assumptions.[5]

3. One essential aspect of the process is "*the speed of reactions*" of prices, wages, output as well as conclusions about future incomes, when earlier incomes have been established etc. The *differences* in speed will affect the outcome. To this I gave lot of attention in the Em-

3. [B. Ohlin, *Saet Produktionen i Gang*, Copenhagen, 1927.]

4. [B. Ohlin, "Den internationella penningpolitiken och dess inverkan på konjunkturutvecklingen," *Förhandlingar vid Nordiska nationalekonomiska mötet i Stockholm 15–17 juni 1931*, Stockholm, 1931, pp. 21f., 28ff. (on price and output variations), p. 23 (on liquidity trap).]

5. See [R. F. Kahn, "The Relation of Home Investment to Unemployment"], *Economic Journal*, 1931, June, p. [197].

ployment policy report of 1934[6] and in the League of Nations report in 1931.[7] Many of Keynes' surprising conclusions were based on assumptions of a low and slow flexibility of wages and commodity prices and swift reactions of production—the expansion of output—by entrepreneurs.

"Stagflation" in the [19]70's is partly due to a greater speed of reaction of wages to expansion policies than in earlier depressions. It is surprising that Keynes thought his account of the process was part of a "*general* theory." The Stockholm Theory was also special, but probably a little less so than Keynes' account of the process. In any case there is no need of assuming that an equilibrium position is reached. The use of equilibrium constructions has pedagogical merits but gives no greater insight into the outcome than the Swedish process theory. The thinking in equilibrium terms has a tendency to take attention away from the speed of reactions!

4. *Will there be enough savings* [italics added] when people decide to increase investment in a state of unused resources, if no preceding decision to increase savings is taken? The investment is possible only to the extent it is compatible with equality between saving and investment. Not all planned investment is carried out—or it is partly offset by an unintentional negative investment, e.g. through unintentional reduction of inventories. A positive answer was given in 1929 by Keynes and Henderson: See *Can Lloyd George Do It?* But it was not a quite satisfactory reasoning. It was improved by Kahn—who in his famous paper about "The Relation of Home Investment to Unemployment" in *Economic Journal*, June 1931, made use of and referred to an unpublished theory of Meade. In the latter paper it was demonstrated that in a state of unused resources of labour and capital, it was possible to increase investment without any *previous* decision to increase the volume of savings in the whole economy.

The Stockholm economists acted on the same assumption but gave no theoretical foundation in printing until early in 1932, when Myrdal sent his manuscript to the editor of the *Ekonomisk Tidskrift* (printed in the early summer of 1932 as the last issue of [the] 1931 volume).[8] Hence, one can not rule out the possibility that Myrdal and his Swedish colleagues were influenced by Kahn's paper, although we were not

6. [B. Ohlin, *Penningpolitik, offentliga arbeten, subventioner och tullar som medel mot arbetslöshet etc.*, Stockholm, 1934, ch. I, §5, pp. 19–23.]

7. [B. Ohlin, *The Course and Phases of the World Economic Depression*, Geneva, 1931, pp. 156 ff. There are, however, no explicit statements in this treatise about "the speed of reactions."—*Ed.*]

8. [G. Myrdal, "Om penningteoretisk jämvikt" etc., *Ekonomisk Tidskrift*, 1931, pp. 191–302 (printed 1932).]

aware of such an influence.[9] The papers by Myrdal and myself in 1933[10] gave a more exact picture through the reference to unintentional changes.

Keynes presented a separate, very simple model, which illuminates the mutual interdependence of changes in the volume of output and employment, in savings, consumption and investment but not changes in price levels. This brought pedagogical advantages, particularly as it was presented by some 'post Keynesians' like Paul Samuelson in his textbook.

5. In the Stockholm theory variations in quantities and *price levels* were dealt with *simultaneously* with aid of the same interdependencies: total income, savings, consumption, investment. All these concepts were used both in their *ex ante* and their *ex post* form. Endogenous investment changes were also considered. There was no equilibrium construction in this part of the Swedish theory. Hence, the picture was more realistic. Keynes' "equilibrium" was only his way of explaining (1) why expansion and contraction of employment could occur [and] (2) why the classical mechanism of automatic creation of full employment did not work. This was also explained in Stockholm in 1933–34.

6. Mydral's concepts *ex ante* and *ex post* made the accounts of the processes much clearer than had been done in the description of Wicksell and also clearer than it was in Keynes' terminology. (See e.g. the comparison in my paper in the *Economic Journal* in 1937 and in my book on *Employment Stabilization* in 19[49]).[11] Lerner did not in the [19]'40s and later (conversation with Samuelson) understand the importance. (See [pp. 77, 159], Canada-Israel symposium 1977).[12] The use of consistent *ex post* and *ex ante* concepts explained together more about the process than Keynes' single *ex ante* concept "propensity to consume" did. It was also more realistic to explain how and why corporations made "unintentional" savings, than it was to concentrate attention wholly on the relation of the planned savings of individuals to their incomes.

7. The problem about the sufficiency of savings when investment is

9. See my paper ["On the Slow Development of the 'Total Demand' Idea in Economic Theory"] in the *Journal of Economic Literature*, 1974, [p. 893].

10. [Cf. G. Myrdal, "Der Gleichgewichtsbegriff als Instrument der geldtheoretischen Analyse," in F. A. Hayek (ed.), *Beiträge zur Geldtheorie*, Vienna, 1933, pp. 361–487; B. Ohlin, "On the Formulation of Monetary Theory" (1933), *History of Political Economy* 10 (1978): 353–88.]

11. [Cf. B. Ohlin, (i) "Some Notes on the Stockholm Theory of Savings and Investment," *Economic Journal*, 1937, pp. 64f., 235–40, and (ii) *The Problem of Employment Stabilization*, New York, 1949, pp. 113–15, 143–45.]

12. [D. Patinkin and J. C. Leith (eds.), *Keynes, Cambridge and the General Theory*, London, 1977.]

expanded—see point 4 above—is *not* to demonstrate *that* savings will be equal to investment. That is always the case *ex definitione*. The task is to explain *how* it is done. Through which process of changes in the variables. If the surplus capacity at the outset is smaller than the increase in investment—or badly distributed—unintentional negative investment and inflation will come. A first class economist like Joan Robinson did not understand this a year or two after 1936. She indicated that one never needed to bother about how to get sufficient savings for *large* investments. This would be true if inflation would never do any damage and could, therefore, be readily accepted.

8. *Aggregate supply and demand* [italics added]. Say's law is untenable. This was made clear by Wicksell. It was stressed by Lindahl (1929–1930) [cf. above, n. 2] and B.O. in *Economic Journal* 1929.[13] It was denied by Keynes in *E.J.* 1929.[14] [At this place Ohlin left room for about four additional lines—never finished.—*Ed.*]

9. *The uncertain future*. About the consequences for price formation, see Myrdal 1927[15] and Lindahl 1929–1930. This is one of the causes why "*ex post* results" often differed from "*ex ante* expectations." See also B.O. 1933 and 1934. [cf. n. 10 and n. 6, above]. Even earlier—around 1910—in *Ekonomisk Tidskrift* the uncertainty element was given attention by Cassel, Wicksell and others in a debate about interest policy and price level changes.[16]

10. *Interest theory* [italics added]. The supply of and demand for credit. The liquidity trap. B.O. in lecture and League of Nation-report in the year 1931, 1933 and 1934.[17]

11. *Policy problems*. The need to supplement credit policy with

13. [B. Ohlin, (i) "The Reparation Problem. A Discussion. I. Transfer Difficulties, Real and Imagined," *Economic Journal*, 1929, pp. 172–78, which is a comment on J. M. Keynes, "The German Transfer Problem," ibid., pp. 1–7, and (ii) "Mr Keynes' Views on the Transfer Problem. II. A Rejoinder," ibid., pp. 400–404.]

14. [J. M. Keynes, (i) "The Reparation Problem: A Discussion. II. A Rejoinder," *Economic Journal*, 1929, pp. 179–82, esp. p. 181, and (ii) "Mr. Keynes' Views on the Transfer Problem. III. A Reply," ibid., pp. 404–8, esp. pp. 407f.]

15. [G. Myrdal, *Prisbildningsproblemet och föränderligheten*, Uppsala etc., 1927.]

16. [The uncertainty element was *not* given attention by Cassel and Wicksell, because in their emphasis on expectations they did not observe the importance of *changing* expectations. This was instead done by Malkom B. Hamilton, a trained economist and banker, who in various papers in *Ekonomisk Tidskrift*, 1901–1914, proved to be an important forerunner of the Stockholm School with regard to uncertainty and other elements; cf. O. Steiger, *Studien zur Entstehung der Neuen Wirtschaftslehre in Schweden* etc., Berlin, 1971, ch. B.II ("The development of the Wicksellian approaches by M. B. Hamilton"), esp. pp. 78f. For a more detailed account of Hamilton and uncertainty see C. Hamilton, "Expectations and the 'Stockholm School.'" *Scandinavian Journal of Economics*, 1979, pp. 434–39.—*Ed.*]

17. [Cf. B. Ohlin, (i) "Den internationella penningpolitiken" etc., 1931, p. 23, (ii) *The Course of Phases* etc., 1931, p. 225, and (iii) *Penningpolitik* etc., 1934, pp. 42, 69, 85.]

taxation and other public finance measures. Credit policy effects were analysed by Wicksell in his pioneer book of 1898,[18] by Irving Fisher, Cassel and others later on. Financial measures, like budget deficits had also been touched upon by many economists chiefly in connection with public works, e.g. Bagge in 1925.[19] More extensively in Lindahl's book in 1930.[20] See also radical measures in lecture by B.O. June 1931 [cf. n. 4, above].

12. *The effects of economic expansion at home on the balance of payments.* This problem was extensively analysed in the British Treasury Model several years before 1930; this model was well-known to Keynes. Some aspects were analysed by Lindahl (1929–30) and by Myrdal (1933 Jan. report and the spring 1933 German paper).[21] Some additional viewpoints are to be found in report by B.O. in 1934.[22] The priority belongs to the Treasury. (A more complete combination of domestic and international aspects was presented by Meade in 1951).[23]

13. *The effects of wage level variations.* Refutal of conventional theory which maintained that *in a closed economy* wage reductions will normally increase employment.

The 'modern' theory maintained that the effects of wage reductions depend on special circumstances like the different flexibility of prices and wages, price expectations etc. Different wage development in different economic sectors can lead to different employment effects.

Some brief early observations about relative wage changes by the Stockholm school, e.g. B.O. pamphlet 1927 [cf. n. 3, above] and later. More extensive analysis in Alf Johansson: Report 193[4] and in B.O. Report 1934.[24] Conclusion: No priority for Keynes in *General Theory*. But without detailed analysis no definite conclusion about priority is possible, as other economists wrote about this question, e.g. Pigou, and—in Germany—Lederer.

18. [K. Wicksell, *Geldzins und Güterpreise*, Jena, 1898.]

19. [G. Bagge, "Produktionens reglering som medel mot arbeslöshet," *Svensk Tidskrift*, 1925, pp. 513–23.]

20. [E. Lindahl, *Penningpolitikens medel*, 1930, ch. 2, §8, on "The influence on the price level by means of public finance" (pp. 63–68); this important section was not included in the translation of the book in Lindahl's *Studies in the Theory of Money and Capital*, London, 1939.—*Ed.*]

21. [Cf. E. Lindahl, *Penningpolitikens medel*, 1930, ch. 5, pp. 135–80; not translated in his *Studies* etc.; G. Myrdal, (i) *Konjunktur och offentlig hushållning*, Stockholm, 1933, pp. 25–38, and (ii) "Der Gleichgewichtsbegriff" etc., 1933, §§76–78 (pp. 460–64), as translated in his *Monetary Equilibrium*, London, 1939, pp. 170–75. (See also Myrdal's *Finanspolitikens ekonomiska verkningar*, Stockholm, 1934, part II, ch. 5, pp. 236–56).—*Ed.*]

22. [B. Ohlin, *Penningpolitik* etc., 1934, pp. 48f., 91–94, 157–62.]

23. [J. Meade, *The Theory of International Economic Policy: I. The Balance of Payments*, 2 vols., Oxford, 1951.]

24. [Cf. A. Johansson, *Löneutvecklingen och arbetslösheten*, Stockholm, 1934, passim; B. Ohlin, *Penningpolitik* etc., 1934, pp. 60–68.]

14. The importance of declarations about the goals of monetary policy. A method *to influence expectations and actions*. An important supplement to credit and financial policy.

Wicksell emphasized. Did not Irving Fisher do the same a little later? Lindahl put more weight on this aspect of policy in his 19[29] book,[25] and later in the 1930s.[26] The Cassel, Heckscher, Wicksell [Davidson] report to the Bank of Sweden in 1931[27] recommended a stable price level program. It was accepted by the Riksdag and the Government. Priority: Stockholm more than Cambridge.

### Part II. [*Further Reflections on a Fundamental Point of Difference Between the Cambridge and Stockholm Theories*]

Will there be sufficient 'finance' for an increase in investment which is made in a situation where unused resources exist? No preceding increase in the disposition to save is assumed.

A general feeling that there will be no difficulties is characteristic of many discussions of the possibility to increase investment. This is true from the Webbs' *Minority Report* and many other recommendations that investment can be increased, e.g. through public works, without any reduction of other investment. However, the need of some theoret-

25. [E. Lindahl, *Penningpolitikens mål*, Lund, 1929, passim (proofs entitled *Penningpolitikens mål och medel: Del I* had already been circulated in 1924).—For Lindahl, the meaning with official declarations on monetary policy was "that *the risks and disturbances in economic activity following from imperfectly foreseen events should be reduced as far as possible*; cf. his *Studies* etc., 1939, p. 199 n.2.—*Ed.*]

26. [Cf. E. Lindahl, (i) "Sveriges Riksbanks konsumtions-index" (The Bank of Sweden's Consumption Price Index), *Ekonomisk Tidskrift*, 1933, pp. 83–126, esp. pp. 83–90, (ii) "The Bank of Sweden's Price Index. Its Object, Scope and Basis Explained," *The Times*, Feb. 3, 1934 (Trade & Engineering Suppl.), (iii) "Sweden's Monetary Programme. The Experiment in Operation. Its Results and Lessons," *Economic Forum* (New York), 1934, pp. 169–81, (iv) "Der Übergang zur Papierwährung in Schweden 1931," *Weltwirtschaftliches Archiv*, 1936 (I), pp. 82–95, and (v) "International Economic Reconstruction Realized through Rational Management of Free Currencies," in A. G. Gayer (ed.), *The Lessons of Monetary Experience. Essays in Honour of Irving Fisher*, New York, 1937, pp. 309–17, esp. p. 312.]

27. [Cf. L. Jonung, "Cassel, Davidson and Heckscher on Swedish Monetary Policy. A Confidential Report to the Riksbank in 1931," *Economy and History*, 1979, no. 2, pp. 85–101.—Ohlin's confusing of the late Knut Wicksell with David Davidson is not casual. On September 28, 1931, after Sweden had abandoned the gold standard the day before, the Riksbank (Bank of Sweden) and the Ministry of Finance declared that the aim of the country's monetary policy would be "to stabilize the internal purchasing power of the Swedish krona in the consumer's hands." This declaration was written by Gustav Cassel, thereby following Wicksell's old rule of a stable price level, which earlier had been heavily opposed by Davidson. In their confidential reports, written on the request of the Riksbank immediately after its declaration and containing proposals of how to realize it, Davidson, as well as Cassel and Eli F. Heckscher, supported Wicksell's rule.—*Ed.*]

ical foundation for this belief seems to have been felt by Keynes and Henderson in 1929. The reasoning in the pamphlet *Can Lloyd George Do It?* is however not quite satisfactory. Having looked at the literature, I have come to the conclusion that Kahn's paper in the *Economic Journal* (June 1931) is the first presentation of a logical theory. Unfortunately I was not aware of this fact when I wrote my paper in the *Journal of Economic Literature* in 1974, "On the Slow Development of the 'Total Demand' Idea in Economic Theory" etc. [pp. 888–96].

However, Kahn's reasoning is not as he seems to think a proof of the *sufficient* supply of 'finance.' It is just a consequence of 'Meade's relation,' and this relation is just a number of concepts, which are based on *ex post* definitions and put together in an equation.

In a similar way the theoretical motivation for the opinion that a sufficient supply of saving would be created—which opinion was generally accepted among the young economists in Stockholm in 1932, at the time when Cassel held the different opinion in a pamphlet[28]—was not a real proof but [a] putting together of definitions and concepts. Hammarskjöld at that time maintained that my theory, as presented in the early version of my [1933] paper towards the end of 1932,[29] offered no interest with regard to this question. My answer was given later with a reference to the reasoning in my paper of 1933 and to the contents of my later report and my Dublin lecture—both in 1934.[30] The analysis of the process, which takes time, is interesting because it demonstrates how the variables—saving investment, consumption, aggregate income, employment—vary in such a way that they can become compatible with one another as indicated in equations based on *ex post* concepts, e.g., how are savings and investment affected and made to differ from their *ex ante* size in such a way that they are equal *ex post*? How is aggregate income *ex post* made to agree with the sum of consumption and investment *ex post*? *There is a need of adaptation for all of them to each other*. The rate of interest is a part of this process in many cases!

I suggest that you look through my paper in *Economic Journal* in

28. [G. Cassel, *Spara eller icke spara. Frågans innebörd* (To Save or Not to Save. The Significance of the Problem), Stockholm, 1933.]

29. [An earlier draft of Ohlin's paper of 1933, entitled "Till penningteoriens centralproblem," was circulated among Swedish economists in late autumn 1932; cf. O. Steiger, "Bertil Ohlin and the Origins of the Keynesian Revolution," *History of Political Economy* 8 (1976): 353.—*Ed.*]

30. [Ohlin refers to the Finlay Lecture, entitled "The Mechanisms of Expansion," which he gave on May 16, 1934, at University College, Dublin. The outlines of this lecture which have survived are based on his *Penningpolitik* etc., 1934, part I ("General theory of expansion"); cf. Ohlin's main paper, above, nn. 46, 52.—*Ed.*]

March 1937.[31] It gives a picture of this process. In the real world both prices and quantities vary as a rule, and it is no fault to consider these variables at the same time.

My letter to Lindahl in December 1934[32] demonstrates that the concepts used in my report early in that year are fundamentally the same as in my *Economic Journal* paper [. . .] early in 1937. A comparison with my Dublin lecture also shows that I then used similar concepts and reasonings. The mutual interdependence of changes in total incomes, consumption, savings and investment in the course of the process from the planning state to the real outcome at the end of the period is made clear.

It was this interdependence which Keynes wanted to demonstrate through his oversimplified underemployment equilibrium. As I have indicated elsewhere there is no need of the idea of equilibrium. One may compare different static positions at the time when one period begins with the state when the same period ends, which is also the point of time, when the following period begins. A state of incomplete employment may last a long time—in spite of wage flexibility—or the employment may grow or fall in a coming period. The essential role played by changes in the total income, savings, investment, consumption etc. both *ex ante* and *ex post* is obvious. For many purposes the share of the extra income, which is due to increased employment, and the share which is due to a rise in the price level needs consideration. But, it is not justified to attribute the dominating role to changes in output or in investment. Different interpreters of Keynes have ascribed to him one of these two latter standpoints.

The picture of the development becomes more realistic if both the expectations and the realised results are mentioned in the account of the process. Hence, the picture I arrived at with the aid of Myrdal's fundamental distinction between *ex ante* and *ex post* and presented in the Dublin lecture and in the 1934 Report—it was worked out towards the end of 1932 and distributed among a few colleagues[33]—offers some advantages, if you compare it with the account, which Keynes gave in his simplified underemployment equilibrium, where the *ex ante* idea was only used with regard to propensity to consume, which was assumed to be less than unity.

31. [See B. Ohlin, "Some Notes on the Stockholm Theory" etc., I, 1937, part B, §§1–5 (pp. 58–68).]

32. [Letter from B. Ohlin to E. Lindahl, Dec. 7, 1934 (mimeo.), as published in German translation in O. Steiger, *Studien* etc., 1971, pp. 214–16; extensive excerpts in O. Steiger, "Bertil Ohlin" etc., 1976, pp. 360–61.]

33. [The theoretical part (I) of Ohlin's *Penningpolitik* etc., 1934, had already been worked out in his 1933 paper—without, however, the explicit use of the concepts of *ex ante* and *ex post*; cf. further n. 29, above.—*Ed.*]

Keynes' letter to Lindahl in December 1934, which is reprinted in Steiger's Doctor's Thesis,[34] makes it clear that he was aware of the distinction between *ex post* and *ex ante*. It is a great pity that he did not utilize it and thereby [make] his concepts clearer. In Kahn's 1974 *Keynes Lecture* he mentions that Keynes had read Myrdal's 1939 book *Monetary Equilibrium*,[35] which was a translation of the German 1933 paper, although considerably revised in 1938. Keynes had used his pencil to mark, particularly the things where Myrdal referred to Wicksell. Whether Keynes had seen Myrdal's paper in the Hayek volume, printed in the spring of 1933, where the distinction *ex ante* and *ex post* was made very clear and utilized to some extent, no one can tell. Keynes had a high opinion of Hayek's ability, although he was convinced that Hayek made some fundamental mistakes and it is of course quite possible that he either looked through the volume Hayek edited or that he asked some of the young Cambridge economists, who could read German easily about the ideas contained in that volume. In the early [19]30s there was a great deal of competition and sometimes a little animosity in the relation between the London and the Cambridge economists. Hence, it seems unlikely that no Cambridge economist took any interest in the collection of papers on monetary theory, edited by the leading man at the London School of Economics, namely Hayek. But this is after all only speculation, unless some Cambridge economist cooperates. Another matter is whether Keynes was made aware of Myrdal's distinction.

The reflections above are presented only because they seem to me to demonstrate that the changes in the total real income and employment were part in the account of [the] economic process during states of unemployment—as these accounts were presented in Stockholm in the years 1932 to 1934.

What about the propensity to consume? And what about the other indirect reactions of changes in the total income and employment?

In the Stockholm theory it was assumed that the increasing consumption, when a rise in the total income is expected, will amount to a smaller sum than the income growth. There would be an intention to save a part of the new income. This is one element, which helps to make the increase in real investment possible without inflation. The

34. [Letter from J. M. Keynes to E. Lindahl, Dec. 8, 1934, as reproduced in (i) O. Steiger, *Studien* etc., 1971, p. 213, and (ii) *The Collected Writings of J. M. Keynes*. Vol. 29: *The General Theory and After. A Supplement*, ed. by D. E. Moggridge, London, 1979, p. 131.]

35. [R. F. Kahn, *On Re-reading Keynes. Fourth Keynes Lecture in Economics*, London 1975, esp. p. 16 n. 3.—See also Keynes' correspondence with Myrdal and the latter's note on Wicksell, in April and June 1937, as reproduced in *The Collected Writings of J. M. Keynes*. Vol. 29, 1979, pp. 259–63.—*Ed.*]

continued development of the process of expansion would naturally depend on the relative size of this increase in consumer's demand, but it would also depend on the indirect endogenous reactions upwards of further new investments.

One cannot make the assumption that there will be during a process of expansion, e.g. during two years, a fixed ratio to save a certain percentage of the expected increase in the income. In other words one cannot assume a constant propensity to consume. Neither can one say that this [is] of vital importance for the outcome if the propensity to consume should during one part of the period be larger than one. For even [if] it should be smaller than unity, there may be indirect investment reactions whereby the sum of the growth in consumer's demand and investment demand will exceed the amount of the original expansion of investment. It is a matter of taste or preference for one pedagogical method if one prefers a description of a process without any changes in price levels. Later one adds consideration of the price movements. In Stockholm, as I have pointed out before, one prefers to take into account from the beginning both quantity and price movements. This brings the advantage that both processes of a large original increase in demand and a small one can be considered. With the Cambridge assumption of no secondary investment reactions, the conclusion will be that one regards it as vitally important if the propensity to consume is larger or smaller than unity. But this conclusion is due to the assumption to leave out of account at this stage all the secondary investment reactions.

In any case the important thing is [. . .][36]

36. [This paragraph (starting with "The important thing is") and the two following ones had already been used by Ohlin—with a few changes in style—as the last paragraphs in his main paper, §10 ("Comments on Patinkin's paper"), and are, therefore, deleted.—In the version of these paragraphs printed above, which is from a cassette, two minor handwritten corrections in the typescript (ii)—see my introduction—have been considered.—*Ed.*]

## *Appendix III*: Some Notes on the Stockholm Theory of Savings and Investment III (1937)

*Introduction by Otto Steiger*

*The earliest published documents on the relations between the Stockholm and Cambridge theories are Bertil Ohlin's famous articles "Some Notes on the Stockholm Theory of Savings and Investment" in the* Economic Journal, *March (part I) and June (part II), 1937. It may be worth mentioning that John Maynard Keynes was most interested to get this article. Only a few weeks after the publication of the* General Theory *on February 4, 1936, Keynes wrote in a letter of March 10, 1936, to Ohlin, to whom he had sent a complimentary copy of his book: "I see that as editor I am going to be involved in a delicate task to decide how much space in the Economic Journal can be reasonably devoted to my book.* But yours I should certainly like to have, and I accept it outright here and now" *(my emphasis).*

*Originally, Keynes planned to publish Ohlin's paper in the September issue of the* Economic Journal, *1936 (letter to Ohlin, June 30, 1936), but as Ohlin did not finish his work in time, he wrote to him in a letter of November 1, 1936: "I am prepared to wait for the article and publish it in the March Journal." After a meeting with Keynes in Cambridge on November 16, 1936, in connection with his Marshall Lectures on "Recent Swedish Contributions to the Economics of Unused Resources" (cf. above, Ohlin's main paper, n. 52, and a letter from Keynes to Ohlin, October 20, 1936), which contained an outline of Sections A and B of what would become "Some Notes etc.", Ohlin completed the article early in 1937 at the University of California, Berkeley. The first two installments of the paper, which reached Keynes in January and February, were printed in the March (pp. 53–69 = sections A and B, §§1–7) and June (pp. 221–40 = sections B, §§8–9, and C, §§1–2) issues of the* Economic Journal. *The title "Some Notes on the Stockholm Theory of Savings and Investment" was formulated by Keynes. Ohlin's original proposal was more in accordance with the title of his Marshall Lectures—"The Stockholm Theory of Unused Resources" (information from B. Ohlin to O. Steiger, October 16, 1977).*

*Late in March, 1937, Ohlin sent to Keynes a third installment of his article which, however, was not published. In a letter to Ohlin, April 29, 1937, Keynes explained why: "There is the [. . .] objection that I am already giving too much space to discussions about, or arising out of, my own book, which raises a delicate position for me as editor. So I hope you will forgive me if I return the enclosed to you. I may add that, in my own judgment, this in no way impairs the value of the earlier arti-*

*cles. Each of those has been dealing in a most important way with a major issue [. . .]. But your final section is a general discursive review of various passages in my book, very interesting and helpful to me personally, but much less so than the preceding sections to the general reader" (as reproduced in* The Collected Writings of John Maynard Keynes. *Vol. 14:* The General Theory and After. Part II: Defence and Development, *ed. by D. E. Moggridge, London, 1973, p. 187).*

*Enclosed with this letter were some "Notes to Ohlin's Final Section" which have been reproduced in the* Collected Writings of J. M. Keynes. *Vol. 14 (pp. 188–91) together with, however, only those passages of Ohlin's third section which Moggridge thought to be necessary for the understanding of Keynes' notes ("Addendum: Ohlin's Original Remarks," pp. 191–200) and where he missed one relevant passsage (§3; see further below, n. 1a). With this procedure, unfortunately, many passages have been deleted which not only were most interesting to Keynes personally but are also highly relevant for our understanding of Ohlin's comparison of the Stockholm and Cambridge theories. They are, therefore, reproduced in this issue of* HOPE *in their entirety for the first time, together with two very brief passages already published by Moggridge but necessary for understanding.*

*The last section of Ohlin's article consists of a typescript of 19 pages (numbered pp. 13–31) with handwritten alterations and additions which, as Ohlin informed me (October 18, 1977), were made before he sent the script to Keynes. This can be demonstrated with, e.g., Keynes' remarks on Ohlin's "reference to imperfect competition" and "Mrs. Robinson" (Moggridge, p. 190) which refer to a handwritten addition by Ohlin (typescript, p. 20; Moggridge, p. 196, but not indicated there). In any case, these insertions have been indicated in the passages here published by* **boldface type**. *Numbers in angled brackets indicate the page of the typescript ⟨13 to 31⟩.*

*Needless to say, Ohlin's references to Keynes are to the latter's* The General Theory of Employment, Interest and Money *(1936), while his references to "this paper" are to the published parts of his article in the* Economic Journal.

[C. *Some Observations on Mr. Keynes' Theory*

§1. *The characteristics of the new approach*

§2. *Keynes' equilibrium theory versus a process theory of the Stockholm type*][1]

1. [Section C, §§1–2, were published in the *Economic Journal*, June 1937, pp. 229–40.]

⟨13⟩ §3. *Further observation on Keynes' terminology and theory* **in general**

Some questions of terminology which are related to the general character of Keynes' theory will here be briefly reviewed.

*a*. The propensity to consume is defined as the relation of consumption to income, not *net* income. (In the following I do not repeat that these concepts should be *ex ante*.[2]) This is strange. For "*net income* is what we suppose the ordinary man to reckon his available income to be when he is deciding how much to spend on current consumption" (p. 57). Why should the decision to consume be correlated with changes in income, which includes "supplementary costs", i.e. the "time depreciation" of capital assets, instead of with changes in *net* income?—As far as I can see Mr. Keynes' own discussion of the motives which govern the propensity to consume and to save (in ch. 9) does run in terms of net income and net savings although he all through the book omits the word *net*. E.g. to explain why a man does not want to consume his whole income, one has to stress that he usually wants to maintain his capital and only considers consuming more than his *net* income under very special conditions. This desire to maintain capital is a fact of entirely different character than his desire to save a greater or smaller part of his net income, **which Keynes deals with in ch. 9.** For this reason it is more natural to define savings as the part of net income which is not consumed, and to keep the part of gross income which is regarded as "time depreciation" and as "use depreciation" separate from savings. This certainly agrees with the business man's way of looking at things.

*b*. Perhaps the explanation of Keynes' procedure lies in his belief that income is less "ambiguous" than net income. (See p. 60 **of this paper.**) But this opinion is untenable. To arrive at a certain sum as income, **the** revenue or proceeds must be reduced with the factor costs and the "use depreciation" or "user cost." Then net income is obtained by **deducting also** the automatic depreciation, which [is] independent of whether the asset is used or not, i.e. "time depreciation." The estimate of what the use depreciation during a future period will be

1a. [Keynes commented on this section in his "Notes on Ohlin's Final Section"; cf. *Collected Writings of J. M. Keynes*, XIV, 188–89, and my indication in the introduction above of Moggridge's editorial miss.—*Ed.*]

**2. It can be added that Keynes' "aggregate demand" *D* is "the proceeds which entrepreneurs expect to receive" from a certain employment. But in ch. 21, *D* seems to have become an *ex post* concept. Compare the observation by D. H. Robertson, *Q[uarterly]* *J[ournal of]* *E[conomics]*,** [Nov.] 1936, p. 168 ["Some Notes on Mr. Keynes' General Theory"].

is just as vague as the estimate of the corresponding time depreciation. **The *ex post* user cost for a certain period, calculated after the end of the period, may be a little less vague. But it has not the causal significance, which Keynes attributes to user cost. See § 4 below.**

*c.* What business men try to maximize is the income and the *net* income, says Keynes (p. 23). But as the difference between them—**the expected time depreciation**—is independent of their actions, it comes to the same thing, as far as their **economic policy** is concerned, to maximize net income and income.

*d.* There seems to [be] some confusion concerning those changes in realised savings, which are due to a change in the planned savings ratio, and those [. . .] due to the unexpected savings. During a slump people may plan to save a smaller proportion of their income. But this is only part of the decline in savings, for as their incomes fall short of what they expected, their "unintentional savings" are negative, e.g. when business firms lose money. Keynes believes that the planned savings ratio varies only little. Only the fact that he pays small attention to the unintentional savings—which are negative during slumps and positive during recoveries—can explain why he assumes the propensity to consume, and hence the corresponding propensity to save, to be almost constant also. Compare above about the multiplier.

[§4. *The analysis of depreciation*[3]]⟨14–17⟩

⟨18⟩ §5. *Some aspects of Keynes' theory of employment*

*a.* In §2 above I have criticised Keynes' formulation of his under-employment equilibrium theory. This is not to deny that there is a kernel of truth of the greatest importance. What is it?

Two things have been common knowledge concerning the connection between investment and employment variations, as I have already pointed out. First, that changes in total output and employment coincide with *relatively greater* changes in the volume of investment. Second, that the way to increase total employment in a depression is to increase the total investment, as this will **certainly** have favourable reactions on the employment in the production for consumption, where the reactions in the investment trades of increased consumption employment are more uncertain in a state of large surplus capacity.[4] **Kahn's theory of the multiplier gave an impetus to fruitful research in**

3. [Section C, §4, has been reproduced in *Collected Writings of J. M. Keynes*, XIV, 191–194.]

4. [The first three sentences of this paragraph ("Two things . . . surplus capacity") have already been published in *Collected Writings of J. M. Keynes*, Vol. 14, p. 194.]

**this field. But, the relation between investment and employment with reference to a *state* of activity instead of a *change* in activity was not explained. In a way this is strange. For** Wicksell had maintained that when savings equal investment, the economic situation is stable. He thought chiefly in terms of a stable price level but tacitly implied, I think, a stable volume of **output and** employment. Now it is obvious that the volume of savings varies with the national income. Hence, the conclusion would seem to follow that only if investment is as large as the savings which occur during full employment, can the latter state remain. Yet, this latter conclusion, was, as far as I know, never **drawn** explicitly, **before** Keynes **reached it through** a different kind of reasoning.

However, the relation is not so simple as Keynes indicates and as a following up of Wicksell's theory would have led us to believe. This follows from what I have said in §2 above. But it is no doubt true that there is a fairly intimate connection between the willingness to save, the percentage of national resources used for new investment and the volume of employment and output. It would take a detailed analysis of different kinds of economic development—e.g. changes in output with and without changes in general price levels—to explain what this "fairly intimate" connection really is. During certain conditions the unintentional savings—positive or negative—are important, so the connection cannot be explained in terms of planned savings only. And the character and size of these unintentional savings depend upon the economic development. **The study of these processes will be much aided by the insight gained through Keynes' equilibrium theory of employment, in spite of its oversimplification and lack of precision.** ⟨19⟩ ***On the other hand, we must be on our guard against being influenced by the tendency in Keynes' book to ignore "frictional" unemployment and to believe that all employment that matters can be obtained by influencing the volume of investment.***

[*b*.][5] ⟨19–21⟩

⟨21⟩ *c*. The disutility analysis of the supply of labour seems to me to be entirely unrealistic as far as most countries are concerned and, therefore, superfluous. Keynes' *General Theory* would have been much clearer and more general if he had been more radical in breaking away from the classical traditions in this field. After all, the minimum wage legislation—which has come into existence under political pressure from trade unions which believed that they could get the same real **weekly** wage for a shorter working week—disposes of the suggestion

5. [Section C, §5, para. *b*, has been reproduced in *Collected Writings of J. M. Keynes*, Vol. 14, pp. 195–96.]

that the workers consider the marginal disutility, when they consider how many hours to work. Furthermore, wage bargains are made for money wages. It is a well known fact that the workers representatives and the **workers** themselves **during wage negotiations** think very little about changes in costs of living, if they don't exceed a few per cent. Hence, they do not think in terms of real wages in the way assumed by the utility reasoning. Whether British trade unions are different from the Scandinavian ones in this respect I do not know. But Keynes remarks about the wage bargaining indicates that this is not so. In any case, it is preferable to treat the labour supply in very relativistic terms in a general theory, and afterwards—if necessary—add some further psychological observations about conditions in a certain country.

I pass over the difficulties connected with the looseness of the concept "involuntary unemployment" which plays a large role in Keynes' theory. It is well known by all economists that under certain **phases of a depression, (i)** workers **which are unemployed** would be willing to work for the same real wage as the existing one, and **(ii)** that a wage reduction **in this situation** might fail to increase employment. This seems to be the "involuntary" unemployment. Whether the distinction between voluntary and involuntary unemployment is a useful one would carry me too far to discuss.[6] It will be understood from the above that I prefer a reasoning which is less dependent on "real wage" considerations.

[*d.*][7] ⟨22–24⟩

⟨25⟩ § 6. *Keynes' views on the rate of interest*

As I have already, in section B, §8 of this paper indicated my general attitude towards Keynes' **interest** theory and towards interest theory in general and as, furthermore, much that I feel important has already been said **by reviewers of** ***General Theory***—notably by Mr. Robertson and Mr. Ellsworth—the following remarks will be very brief, **in spite of the fact that Keynes' difference from commonly held views is greater in interest theory than anywhere else.**[8]

[*a.* para. 1–2][9] ⟨25–26⟩

6. Compare the above-mentioned paper by [J.] Viner ["Mr. Keynes on the Causes of Unemployment," *Quarterly Journal of Economics*, Nov. 1936, pp. 147–67]. **Unemployment due to monopolistic trade union policy in the sense that *in the long run* employment would be greater if wages were lower in certain industries, may fulfil the conditions above and thus be "involuntary" *in the short run*, e.g. during the first phase of a slump.**

7. [Section C, §5, para. *d*, has been reproduced in *Collected Writings of J. M. Keynes*, XIV, 196–99.]

8. [This entire paragraph has already been published in *Collected Writings of J. M. Keynes*, XIV, 199.]

9. [Section C, §6, para. *a*. (para. 1–2) has been reproduced in *Collected Writings of J. M. Keynes*, XIV, 199–200.]

⟨26⟩ This pricing on the markets for bonds and other assets is influenced both by the willingness to save and invest and by the kind of economic process which is the result of the existing rate of interest. Consider first the willingness to save. If people decide to save more, this leads to purchases of bonds—the demand curve is shifted upwards—and, other things equal, bond prices go up. In that way, the rate of interest is depressed and the volume of investment increased, which prevents the increased savings from "running to waste," in other words, prevents that the planned savings is offset by unintentional negative savings, e.g. in connection with unexpected losses. In a similar way a change in the willingness to invest, which may take the form of a demand for credit through the supply of new bond issues, will affect bond prices directly and, thus, the interest level.—Should the rate of interest, being determined in this way, at one time lead to a rapid process of expansion of employment and output, both the ability and the willingness to save will grow. Thereby, the demand for bonds will be raised. But as supply under the influence of improving profit expectations will also rise, it is uncertain what happens to bond prices. The decisive factor will therefore—in this case—probably not be changes concerning people who provide *new* savings or want new credit but changes in the willingness of people who hold fortunes in the form of bonds etc. to continue to do so. Nevertheless, the disposition of the former category to buy bonds will play a certain role; changes in their demand may under certain conditions dominate the interest trends, affecting them directly a little and indirectly a great deal by setting up certain expectations as to the future rates of interest.

No doubt much of this could be expressed in Keynes' terminology. *Ex definitione*, it must always be true that the rate of interest is equal to the marginal liquidity preference, assuming that the yield of cash is zero (which is not always true). But Keynes' theory then becomes something rather different from what he seems to want it to be. The market for cash gets no special key position compared with the markets for different claims and other assets.

⟨27⟩ If Keynes had not, on the whole, neglected the influence on the rate of interest of changes in the processes of expansion and contraction—and of the *resulting* variations in the willingness to save and to invest—which are caused when the rate of interest is changed he would not have said, e.g.: "*Any* level of interest which is accepted with sufficient conviction as *likely* to be durable *will* be durable" (p. 203). It is true that in a depression when even a very low rate of interest cannot for some time cause a process which brings about full employment the long term rate may as well be 2% as 3% or 4%. But a 2% long term interest rate will sooner or later—at least that is the lessons of experience as I read them—bring about a revival in investment and lead to expanding output and rising prices. Then people will want to sell bonds not because they expect the rate of interest to rise but because they expect to get a higher yield on shares or other assets at present prices or because they expect share quotations to go up. Hence, bond prices will rise. One can, of course, say, that bond prices cannot rise, if a sufficient number of sufficiently rich people expect the interest level to remain low and do not expect a higher yield from other investments. But the assumption is absurd if a process is—as I have argued—started by the low rate of interest, leading after some time to large price rises.

Keynes maintains that there is a "*different* natural rate of interest for each hypothetical level of employment" (p. 242). There are two objections to this statement. First, it correlates a certain rate of interest with a certain *situation* instead of with a certain *development*. Actually, the phenomena on the markets for claims, the desire to be liquid etc. seem to me to be explainable only in terms of a process. Secondly, *any* rate of interest below a certain level—which rate is conceivable in spite of my qualification above—is compatible with full employment, although a lower rate will make the ensuing inflation of prices more rapid than a higher rate, while a still higher rate may be consistent with full employment without any rise in prices, under certain conditions as to wage policy etc. All through the book Keynes ignores the fact that full employment is consistent with different kinds of price movements, in the upward direction. Yet, this must be an important fact. I cannot but believe that is it is his failure to think in terms of processes instead of in terms of situations which is here to be blamed.

⟨28⟩ *b.* Finally, let me turn to *the practical judgments* concerning the rate of interest and the accumulation of capital which are, perhaps, the most startling part of the *General Theory*. First, is there a real danger in the world to-day that it will prove difficult to bring the rate of interest down to so low a level, that it cannot be regarded as an obstacle to full employment? Keynes mentions the cost of bringing borrower and lender together, including the risk involved. However, this margin can be made insignificant for a very large part of investment, namely public investment and housebuilding. In Sweden the margin between the effective rate of interest paid by the government and by a houseowner for a ten years first mortgage is as a rule less than a quarter of one per cent. A second factor, mentioned by Keynes, namely the uncertainty as to the future course of the rate of interest will only have little influence if a fall in this rate is considered as equally probable as a rise. There is no reason why this should not be the common opinion, once people have got used to the present 2½–3% long term rate in Great Britain and elsewhere, which is lower than the prevailing rate during the last decades. Thus, there seems to be no reason for fearing any great difficulty in making the interest fluctuate around a 3% level in wealthy countries, or even a little lower. It will, of course, be impossible to maintain so low a rate, during periods when it would lead to price increases which are considered undesirable ("inflation"). But then so low a rate of interest is not necessary to permit full employment.

A second problem raised by Keynes' theory is: will not a fall in the rate of interest, e.g. down below one per cent, seriously reduce savings? Keynes seems to think that not even a zero rate would do so. I confess that I regard the arguments advanced in well known text books are more convincing than his reasoning.[10] To discuss it would carry me too far.

Thirdly, are the outlets for new capital investments so limited that the potential supply of new savings will be used for investment—in the wealthy countries—only if the rate of interest approaches zero? If the question concerns the next decade and not the next century—about which I have no opinion—I do not hesitate to answer no. The number ⟨29⟩ of people in the working ages will continue to grow rapidly—in the absence of much greater losses through wars and epidemics than so far experienced—and this will require enormous amounts of capital in new instruments of production to provide employment and even more, perhaps, to provide houses and communications. The town building era does not seem to be finished. Besides, technical progress goes on. Some people expect it to be very rapid in the chemical industries which are notoriously capital requiring.

Thus, I cannot accept the statement that "the acuteness and the peculiarity of our *contemporary* [ital. by B. O.] problem arises, therefore, out of the possibility that the average rate of interest which will allow a reasonable average level of employment is one so unacceptable to wealth owners that it cannot be readily established merely by manipulating the quantity of money" (pp. 308f). On the contrary, given a reasonable economic policy the problem envisaged by Keynes is, in my opinion, as far as the next decade is concerned—and probably much longer—an entirely academic one of little practical significance.

Keynes advances no evidence to support the view that already during the last century before the world war, the height of the rate of interest prevented a full employment.[11] How does one know that the

10. See e.g. [G.] Cassel: *The Nature and Necessity of Interest* [1903] or *Theory of Social Economy* [1918]. Compare also [F.] Zeuthen: *Den økonomiske fordeling* [(The economic distribution), Copenhagen, 1928; published together with a paper on competition and monopoly as *Problems and Monopoly of Economic Warfare*, London, 1930.]

11. It is even less clear from where Keynes draws his knowledge concerning the liquidity preference, rate of interest, and excessive tendency to save in ancient Egypt, which

unemployment existing during the period exceeded the amount that can reasonably be explained as frictional, including thereunder the influence of great structural disturbances? In other words, would a lower interest level all through this period have led to considerably greater employment, without causing an inflation of prices which would have had to **be stopped** by means of **a rise in the** interest **rates**? This does not seem probably, particularly not as far as the last 40 pre-war years are concerned.—It is quite another matter to say that it might be a good thing, if the long term rate of interest could be reduced more quickly during depressions. But Keynes' argument does not allow the interpretation that this is what he means.

While discussing the factual basis of Keynes' position, permit me to add that available facts do not seem to indicate that the problem of how to get *an economic use* of the factors of production **and, thus, as great a quantity of goods and services as possible** is less important than the problem how to get reasonably full employment.[12] In other words, ⟨30⟩ **Keynes has not made probable that** losses **due to** an inefficient use of resources—owing to high protection e.g.—have been smaller than the losses due to **that** unemployment **which has not been of** the frictional kind. I should **suppose—although this is only a loose guess**—that in the 19th century the losses from ineffective use of the productive factors and the losses from frictional unemployment have each separately been greater than the losses through other kind of unemployment, which chiefly existed during depressions. The relative importance of the problems may have changed since the war but nobody knows. Yet Keynes seems to regard the first two of them as unimportant.[13]

§7. [*Conclusions*]

Having tested the patience of my readers so long, I want to add one thing to avoid misunderstanding. It has been my task in this paper to discuss the characteristics of Keynes' *General Theory* and some of its important weaknesses against the background of the similar theory of unused resources which has been worked out in Stockholm and which represents an alternative attempt to coordinate the theories of price, distribution, money and cycles. The criticism I have presented must

---

**permits him to suggest that this country partly owed [its] wealth to the building of pyramids!**

**12. People who refuse to agree that there are more and less "economic" ways of using factors of production and that the difference is subject to measurement must answer the question whether the chief reason, why everyone thinks full employment is desirable, is that it will give *a greater quantity* of goods and services than less full employment.**

13. See a very convincing note by Professor [F. W.] Taussig in *Q[uarterly] J[ournal of] E[conomics]*, ["Employmennt and the National Dividend," Nov.] 1936 [, pp. 198–203].

not be taken to mean that I am lacking in admiration for Keynes' achievement. It would be a narrow view indeed to take of a work of this kind, if one judged it by its weaknesses instead of by its merits as contributing to our knowledge and as a stimulus to further thinking along untrodden paths. Judged by this latter standard *General Theory* seems to me to hold an unquestionable first place in the whole post-war economics. However, even the greatest appreciations of its value cannot lead to the view that its weaknesses should be left unexposed. That I am sure is the least its author would expect or desire.

These weaknesses are, as I have tried to demonstrate, chiefly the following three: (i) The judgments concerning certain facts in the world to-day, e.g. the magnitude of the outlet for new investment at a rate of interest lower than the present one and the propensity to save, even if the rate of interest were zero and income taxes more confiscatory than to-day, are unacceptable. Without them most of the "Social Philosophy Towards Which the General Theory Might Lead" ⟨31⟩ has to be given up, at least as far as the present generation is concerned. (ii) A coordination of the theories of price, money, and cycles does, of course, lead to something rather different from the orthodox theory of price and distribution. But this does not seem to justify a denial that this theory has given significant insight into certain aspects of the economic world. It should not be criticized for being unable to do what its authors never intended it to do but tried to accomplish in the theories of money and cycles instead. (iii) In his attempt to bring about a coordination of economic theory Keynes does not—at least from the Stockholm horizon—appear to have been radical or revolutionary enough. The equilibrium method instead of a process analysis in which not more of the equilibrium idea is left than consideration of more or less stable positions, the insufficient distinction between "realisations" and "expectations," the retaining of physical marginal productivity, the disutility analysis of labour supply, in a way also the aggregate supply function, are all evidence of an exaggerated conservatism in *method* which has hampered his work.

## *REFERENCES*

Unpublished material, indicated by (*), (**), or (***), is deposited at the following institutions or is under the trusteeship of the following person:

(*) *Kungliga Biblioteket* (The Royal Library), Stockholm, collection of the late *Bertil Ohlin's papers*.

(**) *Mrs. Gertrud Lindahl*, Uppsala, collection of the late *Erik Lindahl's papers*.

(***) *Arbetarrörelsens Arkiv* (Records of the Swedish Labour Movement), Stockholm, collection of *Gunnar Myrdal's papers*.

All collections contain, of course, also material from other economists. In a few cases these sources have not survived among the original author's papers: e.g., Ohlin's 1932 draft of his famous 1933 paper on monetary theory, a copy of which has been found only among the Lindahl papers and which, therefore, is indicated by (**).

"A Bertil Ohlin Symposium" (with contributions by B. Ohlin, O. Steiger, H. Brems, D. Patinkin, and W. P. Yohe. *History of Political Economy* 10 (1978): 341–453.

Bagge, Gösta. "Produktionens reglering som medel mot arbetslöshet" (The Regulation of Production as Remedy Against Unemployment). *Svensk Tidskrift*, 1925, pp. 513–23.

Brems, Hans. "What Was New in Ohlin's 1933–34 Macroeconomics?" *History of Political Economy* 10 (1978): 398–412.

*Britain's Industrial Future. Being the Report of the Liberal Industrial Inquiry*. London, 1928.

Cassel, Gustav. *The Nature and Necessity of Interest*. London, 1903.

———. *Theory of Social Economy* (1918), London, 1923, 1932².

———. *Spara eller icke spara. Frågans innebörd* (To Save or Not to Save. The Significance of the Problem). Stockholm, 1933.

Dobb, Maurice H. Letter to Bertil Ohlin, Cambridge, Oct. 17, 1936 (*).

Erlander, Tage, *Tage Erlander 1901–1939* (in Swedish), Stockholm, 1972.

Fernholm, Tor. "Idéutveckling, ekonomisk politik och ekonomisk teori. Kommentarer till Karl-Gustav Landgren: *Den 'nya ekonomien' i Sverige*" (The Development of Ideas, Economic Policy and Economic Theory. Comments on K.-G. Landgren, *The "New Economics" in Sweden*). *Ekonomisk Tidskrift*, 1960, pp. 161–84.

Föhl, Carl. *Geldschöpfung und Wirtschaftskreislauf*. Munich, 1937.

Haberler, Gottfried. *Prosperity and Depression* (1936). Geneva, 1937, 1937².

Hamilton, Carl. "Expectations and the 'Stockholm School,' " *Scandinavian Journal of Economics*, 1979, pp. 434–39.

Hayek, Friedrich A. *Prices and Production*. London, 1931.

———, ed. *Beiträge zur Geldtheorie*. Vienna, 1933.

Hicks, John R. "A Suggestion for Simplifying the Theory of Money." *Economica*, 1935, pp. 1–19.

Johannsen, Fr. "Arbejdsstandsningen og Landets Økonomi" (Employment Creation and the Country's Economy). *Ingeniøren*, 1925, pp. 397–401.

———. "Tidens Krav" (The Demand of Our Time), *Berlingske Tidende*, March 23–25, 1927.

Johannsen, Nicholas A. J. L. *Der Kreislauf des Geldes und der Mechanismus des Soziallebens*. Berlin, 1903.

———. *A Neglected Point in Connection with Crises*. New York, 1908.

———. *Die Steuer der Zukunft*. Berlin, 1913.

Johansson, Alf. *Löneutvecklingen och arbetslösheten* (Wage Development and Unemployment). Stockholm, 1934.

Jonung, Lars. "Cassel, Davidson and Heckscher on Swedish Monetary Policy. A Confidential Report to the Riksbank in 1931." *Economy and History*, 1979, no. 2, pp. 85–101.

Kahn, Richard F. (Lord Kahn). "The Relation of Home Investment to Unemployment." *Economic Journal*, 1931, pp. 173–98.

———. "The Financing of Public Works—A Note." *Economic Journal*, 1932, pp. 492–95.

———. Letter to Don Patinkin, March 19, 1974, in "Appendix II: Correspondence between Richard F. Kahn and Don Patinkin on the 1931 Multiplier Article and the 'Cambridge Circus.' " In D. Patinkin and J. C. Leith (eds.), *Keynes, Cambridge and the General Theory* (London, 1977), p. 198.

———. *On Re-reading Keynes. Fourth Keynes Lecture in Economics*. London, 1975.

Keynes, John Maynard. "The German Transfer Problem." *Economic Journal*, 1929, pp. 172–78.

———. "The Reparation Problem: A Discussion. II. A Rejoinder." *Economic Journal*, 1929, pp. 179–82.

———. "Mr. Keynes' Views on the Transfer Problem. III. A Reply." *Economic Journal*, 1929, pp. 404–8.

———. *A Treatise on Money*. Vol. 1: *The Pure Theory of Money*. London, 1930.

———. Letter to Bertil Ohlin, Bloomsbury, Sept. 24, 1931 (*).

———. "An Economic Analysis of Unemployment." In Q. Wright (ed.), *Unemployment as a World Problem* (Chicago, 1931), pp. 3–42.

———. Contribution "III." In A. Salter, J. Stamp, J. M. Keynes, A. Clay, W. H. Beveridge, *The World's Economic Crisis and the Way of Escape. Halley Stuart Lectures 1931* (London, 1932), pp. 71–88.

———. *The Means to Prosperity*. London, 1933.

———. Letter to Erik Lindahl, Bloomsbury, Dec. 8, 1934, in (i) O. Steiger, *Studien* etc. (1971), p. 213, and (ii) J. M. Keynes, *The Collected Writings*. Vol. 29 (1979), p. 131.

———. *The General Theory of Employment, Interest and Money*. London, 1936.

———. Letter to Bertil Ohlin, Bloomsbury, March 10, 1936 (*).

———. Letter to Bertil Ohlin, Bloomsbury, June 30, 1936 (*).

———. Letter to Bertil Ohlin, Bloomsbury, Oct. 20, 1936 (*).

———. Letter to Bertil Ohlin, Cambridge, Nov. 1, 1936 (*).

———. Letter to Bertil Ohlin, Bloomsbury, Jan. 27, 1937. In J. M. Keynes, *The Collected Writings*. Vol. 14 (1973), pp. 184–85.

———. "The General Theory of Employment." *Quarterly Journal of Economics*, Feb. 1937, pp. 209–23.

———. Letter to Bertil Ohlin, together with "Notes on Ohlin's Final Section," Bloomsbury, April 29, 1937. In J. M. Keynes, *The Collected Writings*. Vol. 14 (1973), pp. 187–91.

———. Letter to Gunnar Myrdal, Cambridge, June 16, 1937. In J. M. Keynes, *The Collected Writings* Vol. 29 (1979), pp. 262–63.

———. *The Collected Writings*. Vol. 14: *The General Theory and After. Part II: Defence and Development*. Edited by D. E. Moggridge. London, 1973.

———. *The Collected Writings*. Vol. 29: *The General Theory and After. A Supplement*. Edited by D. E. Moggridge. London, 1979.

———, and Henderson, Hubert D. *Can Lloyd George Do It? An Examination of the Liberal Pledge*. London, 1929.

Landgren, Karl-Gustav. *Den 'nya ekonomien' i Sverige. J. M. Keynes, E. Wigforss, B. Ohlin och utvecklingen 1927–39* (The "New Economics" in Sweden. J. M. Keynes, E. Wigforss, B. Ohlin and the Development 1927–39). With a Summary in English (pp. 295–308). Stockholm and Uppsala, 1960.

Lindahl, Erik. *Penningpolitikens mål och medel. Del I* (Ends and Means of Monetary Policy. Part I). Lund, 1924.

———. "Penningpolitikens mål och medel. Föreläsningar vårterminen 1925 vid Uppsala Universitet" (Ends and Means of Monetary Policy. Lectures at the University of Stockholm, Spring Term 1925). Manuscript, 70 pp. (**).

———. *Penningpolitikens mål* (The Ends of Monetary Policy). Lund, 1929.

———. *Penningpolitikens medel* (The Means of Monetary Policy) (1929). Lund, 1930.

———. "Sveriges Riksbanks konsumtionsindex" (The Bank of Sweden's Consumption Price Index). *Ekonomisk Tidskrift*, 1933, pp. 83–126.

———. "A Note on the Dynamic Pricing Problem." Göteborg, Oct. 23, 1934, in (i) O. Steiger, *Studien* etc., 1971, pp. 204–11 (corr. version), and (ii) J. M. Keynes, *The Collected Writings* Vol. 29, 1979, pp. 123–31 (uncorr. version).

———. "The Bank of Sweden's Price Index. Its Object, Scope and Basis Explained." *The Times*, Feb. 3, 1934 (Trade & Engineering Suppl.).

———. "Sweden's Monetary Program. The Experiment in Operation. Its Results and Lessons." *Economic Forum* (New York), 1934, pp. 169–81.

———. "Der Übergang zur Papierwährung in Schweden 1931." *Weltwirtschaftliches Archiv*, 1936 (I), pp. 82–95.

———. "International Economic Reconstruction Realized through Rational Management of Free Currencies." In A. G. Gayer (ed.), *The Lessons of Monetary Experience. Essays in Honour of Irving Fisher* (New York, 1937), pp. 309–17.

———. *Studies in the Theory of Money and Capital*. London, 1939.

Lundberg, Erik. *Studies in the Theory of Economic Expansion*, Stockholm, 1937.

McDowell, Moore. Letter to Bertil Ohlin, Dublin, March 24, 1977 (*).

Meade, James, E. *The Theory of International Economic Policy: I. The Balance of Payments*. 2 vols. Oxford, 1951.

Myrdal, Gunnar. *Prisbildningsproblemet och föränderligheten* (The Problem of Price Formation and Changeability). Uppsala and Stockholm, 1927.

———. *Sveriges väg genom penningkrisen* (Sweden's Way through the Monetary Crisis). Stockholm, 1931.

———. "Om penningteoretisk jämvikt. En studie över den 'normala räntan' i Wicksells penninglära" (On Monetary Equilibrium. A Study of the "normal rate of interest" in Wicksell's Monetary Economics). *Ekonomisk Tidskrift*, 1931, pp. 191–302 (printed 1932).

———. Letter to Bertil Ohlin, Stockholm, June 22, 1932 (*, ***).

———. Letter to Bertil Ohlin, Stockholm, Aug. 29, 1932 (*, ***).

———. "Der Gleichgewichtsbegriff als Instrument der geldtheoretischen Analyse." In F. A. Hayek (ed.), *Beiträge zur Geldtheorie* (Vienna, 1933), pp. 361–487.

———. *Konjunktur och offentlig hushållning* (Business Cycles and Public Finance). Stockholm, 1933.

———. *Finanspolitikens ekonomiska verkningar* (The Economic Effects of Fiscal Policy). Stockholm, 1934.

———. Letter to John Maynard Keynes, Together with a Note on Wicksell on Savings and Investment and on Say's Law, Stockholm, April 24, 1937. In J. M. Keynes, *The Collected Writings*. Vol. 29 (1979), pp. 259–61.

———. *Monetary Equilibrium*. London, 1939.

———. Letter to Otto Steiger, Austin, Texas, April 5, 1978 (***).

O'Brien, George. Letter to Bertil Ohlin, Dublin, March 14, 1934 (*).
Ohlin, Bertil. *Handelns teori* (The Theory of Trade). Stockholm, 1924.
———. *Saet Produktionen i Gang* (Start Up Production Again). Copenhagen, 1927.
———, "The Reparations Problem." *Svenska Handelsbankens Index*, March 1928, pp. 2–13, and April 1928, pp. 2–33.
———. "The Reparations Problem: A Discussion. I. Transfer Difficulties, Real and Imagined." *Economic Journal*, 1929, pp. 172–78.
———. "Mr. Keynes' Views on the Transfer Problem. II. A Rejoinder." *Economic Journal*, 1929, pp. 400–4.
———. "Den internationella penningpolitiken och dess inverkan på konjunkturutvecklingen" (International Monetary Policy and Its Influence on the Development of the Business Cycle). *Förhandlingar vid Nordiska nationalekonomiska mötet i Stockholm 15–17 juni 1931* (Stockholm, 1931), pp. 11–31, 63–68, 208–10.
———. *The Course and Phases of the World Economic Depression. Report Presented to the Assembly of the League of Nations*. Geneva, 1931.
———"Prisstegringens problem. I. Replik till fil. d:r Johan Åkerman" (Problems Related to the Rise of Prices. I. Rejoinder to Dr. J. Åkerman). *Det Ekonomiska Läget*, No. 3, Aug. 1932, pp. 21–32.
———. "Kommunala finansproblem under kristider" (Fiscal Problems of Local Governments in Times of Crises). *Svenska Stadsförbundets Tidskrift*, 1932, pp. 395–400.
———. "Till penningteoriens centralproblem" (On the Central Problems of Monetary Theory). Stockholm, 1932. Typescript, 49 pp. (**); relevant passages are translated in O. Steiger, "Substantive Changes." *History of Political Economy* 10 (1978): 390–93.
———. "Ett konjunkturuppsvings förutsättningar och möjligheter. Föredrag vid 1932 års ordinarie bankmöte" (Conditions for and Possibilities of a Business Upswing. Lecture at the Annual Meeting of the Swedish Bankers' Association in 1932). *Svenska Bankföreningens Skrifter*, no. 55, (Stockholm, 1933), 21 pp.
———. "Till frågan om penningteoriens uppläggning." *Ekonomisk Tidskrift*, 1933, pp. 45–81. Translated by H. Brems and W. P. Yohe as "On the Formulation of Monetary Theory," *History of Political Economy* 10 (1978): 353–88.
———. *Penningpolitik, offentliga arbeten, subventioner och tullar som medel mot arbetslöshet. Bidrag till expansionens teori* (Monetary Policy, Public Works, Subsidies and Tariffs as Remedies for Unemployment. A Contribution to the Theory of Expansion). Stockholm, 1934.
———. "The Mechanism of Expansion." Second Finlay Lecture, University College, Dublin, May 16, 1934. Manuscript, 21 pages (*). This is identical with Ohlin's Marshall Lectures, 1936, pp. 23–43. The amended version, prepared by Ohlin, "Aspects of a Theory of Expansion," Stockholm, Spring 1977. Typescript, 12 pages (*).
———. Letter to Erik Lindahl, Stockholm, Dec. 7, 1934. Mimeo. Published in German translation in O. Steiger, *Studien* etc. (1971), pp. 214–16; extensive excerpts in O. Steiger, "Bertil Ohlin," *History of Political Economy* 8 (1976): 360–61.
———. "Recent Swedish Contributions to the Economics of Unused Resources." Marshall Lectures, Cambridge Univ. Nov. 16, 18, and 20, 1936.

Manuscript, 58 pages (*). (Pages 23–43 are identical with Ohlin's Finlay Lecture, 1934.)

"Some Notes on the Stockholm Theory of Savings and Investment I–II.", *Economic Journal*, 1937, pp. 53–69 (I), 221–40 (II).

———. "Addendum: Ohlin's Original Remarks" (1937). In J. M. Keynes. *The Collected Writings*. Vol. 14 (1973), pp. 188–91. This consists of selected parts of Ohlin, "Some Notes on the Stockholm Theory of Savings and Investment III", University of California, Berkeley, March, 1937. Manuscript, 19 pp. (*).

———. *The Problem of Employment Stabilization*. New York, 1949.

———. *Bertil Ohlins memoarer. Ung man blir politiker* (B. Ohlin's Memoirs. A Young Man Becomes a Politician). Stockholm, 1972.

———. "On the Slow Development of the 'Total Demand' Idea: Reflections in Connection with Dr. Oppenheimer's Note." *Journal of Economic Literature*, 1974, pp. 888–96.

———. "Appendix III: Some Comments on Keynesianism and the Swedish Theory of Expansion Before 1935." In D. Patinkin and J. C. Leith (eds.), *Keynes, Cambridge, and the General Theory* (1977), pp. 149–65.

———. "Bibliography [1919–1977]." *Scandinavian Journal of Economics*, 1978, pp. 93–99.

———. "Keynesian Economics and the Stockholm School. A Comment on Patinkin's Paper." *Scandinavian Journal of Economics*, 1978, pp. 144–47.

———. "Addendum to a letter to Otto Steiger." Stockholm, Jan. 9, 1979 (*).

———. Letter to Craufurd D. Goodwin, Stockholm, Jan. 9, 1979 (*).

———. Letter to William P. Yohe, Stockholm, Jan. 9, 1979 (*).

———. Letter to Don Patinkin, Stockholm, Jan. 12, 1979 (*).

———. Letter to Hans Brems, Stockholm, Feb. 20, 1979 (*).

———. Letter to Otto Steiger, Stockholm, July 25, 1979 (*).

Patinkin, Don. *Keynes' Monetary Thought. A Study of Its Development*. Durham, North Carolina, 1976.

———. "On the Relation between Keynesian Economics and the 'Stockholm School.' " *Scandinavian Journal of Economics* 1978, pp. 135–43.

———. "Some Observations on Ohlin's 1933 Article." *History of Political Economy* 10 (1978): 413–18.

———. "A Study of Keynes' Theory of Effective Demand." *Economic Inquiry*, 1979, pp. 155–76.

Patinkin, Don, and Leith, J. Clark (eds.). *Keynes, Cambridge and The General Theory. The Process of Criticism and Discussion Connected with the Development of The General Theory*. London, 1977.

Robertson, Dennis H. "Some Notes on Mr. Keynes' General Theory." *Quarterly Journal of Economics*, Nov. 1936, pp. 168–91.

"Stockholmsskolan: Idéer, tillkomst och utveckling. Ett symposium" (The Stockholm School: Ideas, Origin and Development. A Symposium). *Ekonomisk Tidskrift*, 1960, pp. 159–205, 296–300 (with contributions by T. Fernholm, E. Wigforss, E. Lundberg and G. Lindahl).

Steiger, Otto. *Studien zur Entstehung der Neuen Wirtschaftslehre in Schweden Eine Anti-Kritik*. Berlin, 1971.

———. "Bertil Ohlin and the Origins of the Keynesian Revolution." *History of Political Economy* 8 (1976): 341–66.

———. "Substantive Changes in the Final Version of Ohlin's 1933 Paper." *History of Political Economy* 10 (1978): 389–97.

———. "Prelude to the Theory of a Monetary Economy: Origins and Significance of Ohlin's 1933 Approach to Monetary Theory." *History of Political Economy* 10 (1978): 420–26.

Taussig, Frank W. "Employment and the National Dividend." *Quarterly Journal of Economics*, Nov. 1936, pp. 198–203.

Viner, Jacob. "Mr. Keynes on the Causes of Unemployment." *Quarterly Journal of Economics*, Nov. 1936, pp. 147–67.

Warming, Jens. "Beskaeftigelseproblemet" (The Employment Problem). *Gads Danske Magasin*, 1927, pp. 609–21.

———. "International Difficulties Arising Out of the Financing of Public Works During Depression." *Economic Journal*, 1932, pp. 211–24.

Webb, Sidney and Beatrice. *Reports of the Royal Commission on the Poor Laws and Relief of Distress*. Vol. III: *Separate Report* (*Being* The Minority Report *of the Poor Law Commission*). London, 1909.

*We Can Conquer Unemployment. We Mobilized for War—Let Us Mobilize for Prosperity. Mr. Lloyd George's Pledge*. London, 1929.

Wicksell, Knut. *Geldzins und Güterpreise. Eine Studie über die den Tauschwert des Geldes bestimmenden Ursachen*. Jena, 1898. Translated by R. F. Kahn as *Interest and Prices: A Study of the Causes Regulating the Value of Money*. London, 1936.

———. "International Freights and Prices." *Quarterly Journal of Economics*, Feb. 1918, pp. 404–10.

Yohe, William P. "Ohlin's 1933 Reformation of Monetary Theory." *History of Political Economy* 10 (1978): 447–53.

Zeuthen, Frederik. *Den økonomiske fordeling* (The Economic Distribution). Copenhagen, 1928. Published together with a paper on competition and monopoly as *Problems of Monopoly and Economic Warfare*, London, 1930.

# [10]

*History of Political Economy 13:2*


## Unemployment, Keynes, and the Stockholm School

*Bent Hansen*, University of California, Berkeley

After reading the Bertil Ohlin Symposium (1978) and recalling earlier contributions to the debate about Keynes and the Stockholm School, one cannot help feeling that the discussants on each side in this debate have a point. As so often in such debates, however, it would also seem that the two sides to some extent are talking beside each other. In particular, it seems to me that those who want to argue that Ohlin really had it all, and better, fail to understand what Patinkin is driving at.

There are two issues at stake in this debate. One is the genesis of Stockholm School theory from Wicksell through Lindahl, Myrdal, and Ohlin, the influence exerted by actual economic events, in particular the emergence of high-level unemployment in the twenties and early thirties, and the interaction between economic policy proposals and programs on the one hand and economic theory on the other, in Sweden and abroad. This by itself is a fascinating topic. It has been subjected to detailed investigation, initiated by Landgren (1960) and continued by Steiger (1971, 1976), Uhr (1977), and others. The conflict here is about the influence of the British and Swedish political unemployment debate upon the theoretical constructs of the Stockholm School, with the impact of Keynes' early contributions to this debate a particularly disputed problem. These relationships appear to have been fairly well disentangled in Otto Steiger's excellent study (1971), unfortunately available only in German. Steiger emphasizes the affinity of the views of Lindahl, Myrdal, and Ohlin, with Wicksell as the point of departure, "Lindahl as crucial [*entscheidenden*] stimulator, and Myrdal as well as Ohlin as correcting, completing critics" (1971, p. 169; my translation; see also Steiger 1976). I believe that Steiger's views are basically correct and shall add a little further evidence below, although I find Myrdal much more than just a correcting and completing critic.

The other issue is the theoretical model or models of the Stockholm School as compared with that of Keynes in the *General Theory*, their similarities and differences. The original authors on both sides are of little help in clarifying this issue. Each side had only limited knowledge of and insights into the views of the other side. And after the triumph of Keynesian economics, Stockholm School theory was, apart from the concepts of *ex ante* and *ex post*, for a long time relegated to the status of an almost mythological doctrine, its major works inaccessible to non-Scandinavians, with Scandinavians mostly paying lip service only to an unknown god.

Recent attempts to rehabilitate Stockholm School theory have concentrated upon Ohlin's writings and have emphasized the dynamics of the multiplier process against the background of a conventional textbook IS-LM approach to Keynesian economics, with labor market problems entirely ignored. This is unfortunate, not only because Ohlin was not really the key figure in the Stockholm School but much more because Keynes' main concern in the *General Theory* was the phenomenon of *persistent* involuntary unemployment in a capitalist market economy. To handle steady-state problems of unemployment we need some kind of steady-state or equilibrium theory dealing explicitly with unemployment. If I understand Patinkin (1979, I and II) aright, this is really what he is driving at. He does not criticize the Stockholm School for not working out the Keynesian unemployment equilibrium and its corollary the static multiplier formula just because he prefers static equilibrium to dynamic theory, but rather because he finds the dynamic theorizing of Ohlin incomplete.

In his contribution to the Ohlin Symposium, Brems (1978, p. 407) seems to argue that Ohlin was really superior to Keynes because he (Ohlin) did *not* develop the static multiplier. Ohlin, according to Brems was too realistic to follow more than a few rounds of the process. That is an unconvincing argument. We do not fully understand a dynamic process unless we understand from where it starts out, where it ultimately ends up, and the path followed all the way between. In the applications we can never know in advance how many rounds are needed in a concrete situation, and it is a poor theorist who does not complete his analysis in all directions so that the applied economist can pick up what he needs. Dynamic analysis is not complete until the corresponding steady-state model is derived. I thought it belonged to times bygone to argue about static vs. dynamic theory and to find one type of theory superior to the other one. Both are parts of a more complete theory.

The complete theory is needed because there is the problem of the persistency of unemployment and the apparent inability of the market forces to take care of unemployment and automatically establish full employment. When in Chapter 18, "The General Theory of Employment Re-stated," Keynes summarized his model, he ended up by saying:

Thus our four conditions together are adequate to explain the outstanding features of our actual experience;—namely, that we oscillate, avoiding the gravest extremes of fluctuation in employment and in prices in both directions, round an intermediate position appreciably below full employment and appreciably above the minimum employment a decline below which would endanger life [1935, p. 254].

To explain this intermediate position and not just the short-run dynamics around it was Keynes' main problem. The Stockholm School authors viewed the unemployment problem in the same way. There are short term fluctuations in unemployment (*konjunkturarbetslöshet*) and there is permanent unemployment (in addition to seasonal and frictional unemployment). The distinction appears again and again in the writings of Lindahl, Myrdal, and Ohlin, as well as the Reports of the Committee on Unemployment. It was spelled out in a review article of Myrdal's 1934 monograph *Finanspolitikens ekonomiska verkningar*, published in 1935 by Lindahl. Here he criticized the final Report for not really coming up with any policy remedies against the permanent unemployment, "the problem" as he says, "that now, since short-term unemployment (*konjunkturarbetslösheten*) has largely disappeared, appears to be the unemployment problem par préférence . . ." (1935, p. 3).

Keynes' theory was one of persistent or permanent unemployment. What was then the theory of unemployment of the Stockholm School? This is the question Patinkin is trying to get an answer to, but so far he has been crying in the wilderness. The present article aims at throwing light on this question. As an introduction it is worthwhile, however, to have a look at the Stockholm School and the multiplier.

### *The Theory of the Multiplier*

No one who has studied Myrdal's and Ohlin's monographs, presented as Supplements 5 and 7 to the main *Report II* of the Committee on Unemployment (1934) can possibly deny that these two authors, as early as 1933–34, had a fairly good understanding of the mechanisms of that kind of macroeconomic process which we know under the name of multiplier process and which conventionally is associated with Keynes' *General Theory*. Definitional subtleties apart, it is also undeniable that both Myrdal and Ohlin discussed such a macro process in terms of national income aggregates with functional forms very similar, if not identical, to those employed by Keynes two years later in the *General Theory*. To that extent, Myrdal and Ohlin did indeed anticipate Keynes' *General Theory*. And their understanding of the importance for multiplier processes of reactions speeds and lag structures and of leakages related to imports and tax payments was certainly more advanced than the *General Theory*.

The debate has centered upon Ohlin's contribution to the multiplier process. Ohlin was clearly inspired by Kahn's 1931-paper which he explicitly refers to (p. 103) and a much earlier Danish discussion of the multiplier (Steiger 1971, p. 186), and there is no doubt here about an outside influence. The debate (with Steiger—1971, p. 184—the exception) has, however, largely ignored Myrdal's contribution to the theory of the multiplier process and *his* possible sources of inspiration.[1] It was deliberate that I spoke about Myrdal and Ohlin in the preceding paragraph, and not just Ohlin, as anticipating Keynes insofar as the multiplier process is concerned. And it was not for alphabetical reasons that Myrdal was mentioned before Ohlin. Myrdal's monograph, *Finanspolitikens ekonomiska verkningar* (1934) was submitted some three or four months earlier than Ohlin's monograph, *Penningpolitik* (1934), and expanded arguments that had already been presented in January 1933 in a memorandum attached to the government's budget proposal for 1933–34. Myrdal's description and discussions of the multiplier process as set out in Part Four, Chs. 3 and 4, 1–4, show a very clear understanding of primary and secondary effects of exogenous impulses, with the rate of saving given its proper role (see in particular pp. 207–13). Myrdal gives no indication of having read Kahn's 1931 paper; the geometrical series is not mentioned, something nobody who at that time was acquainted with Kahn's paper would miss. Yet, Myrdal had grasped the basic mechanisms of the process no less than Ohlin. And at one point he is clearly superior to Ohlin. In a lucid counterargument (1934 monograph, Part Four, Ch. 4, 3) to the crowding-out argument (well known already at that time; see below), Myrdal showed how the process must *converge* with production and income expanding until savings have caught up with the original expansionary impulse (public expenditure).[2]

Moreover, Myrdal demonstrated a clear understanding of the multiplier process and its convergence even before the 1934 monograph. Steiger (1978, p. 440) has drawn attention to a place in Myrdal's 1932 Swedish article "Om penningteoretisk jämvikt" (English version, 1939, pp. 164 f.) where Myrdal discusses the effects of monetary policy

1. Landgren (1960) did not consider Myrdal's contributions, although in long discussions with him at that time I pointed out to him that any discussion of the Stockholm School without explicit consideration of Myrdal's writings was bound to be incomplete.

2. Both Myrdal and Lindahl argued in this way against the 'crowding out' argument as early as 1932.

in a depression. Myrdal shows how tighter monetary policy in a closed economy will start a downward process, ultimately converging upon an equilibrium situation with increased unemployment.

Even more interesting is the continuation of this discussion (I quote from the 1939 English edition which in this place is very similar to the original German and Swedish versions). Myrdal first tells us that so far "this is only an abstract example" (English version, 1939, p. 170), but having argued in this abstract example that credit policy may have little or no effect on the price level, he continues:

> Credit policy is, however, not without effects on social conditions, including the amount of production, its arrangement, the degree of employment, and capital values, under which monetary equilibrium is maintained or not maintained. . . . In order to illustrate better this second side of the problem I will modify my abstract example just a little. The argument will then follow quite closely circumstances which at the present time [Spring 1932] to some extent are true of a number of countries, among them my own [ibid.].

For a Scandinavian author a closed economy is always 'abstract' and 'realism' requires considering an open economy. Myrdal therefore goes on (ibid., pp. 171f.) to assume an open economy, with export volume and prices given, with import prices given, and with a trade deficit covered by sales of foreign exchange from the central bank. He assumes then that despite the prevailing depression, the credit policy is tightened so as to improve the balance of payments (the exchange rate). In the simplest case all imports are consumer goods:

> The intention of the credit policy must then be, by means of deepening the depression in this country, to reduce production, employment and hence also income so far that *because of this* the consumers' demand for *all* goods (including domestic) declines so much that the part of the shrinkage which falls on imported goods is large enough to achieve the desired effect on the balance of payments [ibid. p. 171, italics in the original].

If this is not a pretty example of the foreign-trade multiplier with prices given from abroad and production and income the equilibrating variables, I do not know what it is.

What then were Myrdal's sources of inspiration, if any? Patinkin (1979, p. 19) conjectures, following Steiger (1978, p. 440) that Myrdal, despite his explicit and emphatic denials(!), may have read and been inspired by Keynes' Harris Lectures, published in November 1931. Myrdal was, however, well acquainted with the British Liberal Party programs, both *The Yellow Book* and *We Can Conquer Unemployment* (Steiger, 1971, p. 183), and it stands to reason that he may have known Keynes & Henderson's *Can Lloyd George Do It?* in which the authors argued against the 'Treasury view' in a way similar to Myrdal's later argument against 'crowding-out' (see above). But whereas Keynes & Henderson pointed to four sources of increased saving that would help prevent 'crowding-out,' they failed to give "a demonstration that savings not only increase in those four ways, but do so to the full extent necessary for financing the additional government investment" (Patinkin, Sept. 1978, p. 216). Myrdal mentions the first one of those four sources (the dole) but then completes the argument by the demonstration that Keynes & Henderson failed to give. Whatever inspiration Myrdal may have had from the British debate, I would like, however, to point to the possibility that some inspiration may have been Swedish rather than British, Lindahl rather than Keynes. Lindahl's crucial role for the emergence of the Stockholm School is not fully appreciated by Patinkin.

In his 1932 Swedish article (p. 270) Myrdal explicitly refers to Lindahl's *Penningpolitikens medel* which was first published in 1929.[3] The reference (deleted in both German and English versions and apparently overlooked by Steiger 1978, p. 440) is to pp. 48ff. in Lindahl. I will quote *in extenso* from Lindahl because it seems to me quite likely that the notion of unemployment *equilibrium* may have entered the Stockholm School through Lindahl's carefully executed theoretical arguments.[4]

On the pages referred to by Myrdal, Lindahl discusses the effects of a permanent increase in the rate of interest in a situation with initial unemployment, case 2c. I quote (Lindahl, 1929, p. 49, my translation; brackets indicate my insertions):

> Assuming lack of flexibility in wages, the price fall [induced by the credit tightening] will lead to unemployment. Unemployment will probably be largest in the capital goods producing industries for which reason the disproportion between total demand and supply

3. *Penningpolitikens medel* was published in 1930. In 1929, however, Lindahl was competing for a chair, and following the medieval procedures at that time he had to present a new publication (*skrift*). He printed for that purpose four copies of *Penningpolitikens medel* in 1929 and later gave one of them to me. This is the copy I am quoting from. The book had been in galley proofs for some time, and the bulk may already have been written in 1927–28. The main edition of 1930 included some minor corrections to Chapters 2 and 3 and an entirely new chapter on international complications.

4. In a different context Myrdal explicitly acknowledged his appreciation of Lindahl's discussion of unemployment: "Lindahl's very interesting suggestions about the role of unemployment in the sequence. . . ." (1932 article, p. 230 n. 1).

[of consumer goods] probably will be aggravated and the price fall accelerated.[1] Because of the price fall, unemployment may arise even in the consumer goods producing industries. In this way the supply of consumer goods declines and may even fall below the initial level without the price fall coming to an end even though it may be retarded.[2]

[*Lindahl's footnotes*:] [1] It is assumed that the total wage bill for all employed workers declines so much that it compensates for the possible decline in the volume of consumer goods.

[2]In exceptional cases one can imagine that the price fall comes to an end and is replaced by a price increase: that is, if wages in the capital goods industry are fully flexible, if resources cannot be reallocated from this industry to consumer goods production, and if wages in the latter are rigid and, accordingly, give rise to unemployment. Under these assumptions it may indeed happen that supply of consumer goods is reduced more than monetary demand.

It is footnote 2 which is crucial here. Supply of consumer goods may, according to Lindahl, exceed or fall short of demand during such a downward process, leaving the possibility open for equilibrium position. Lindahl does not mention this possibility in the case referred to by Myrdal, but in the opposite case—credit expansion with a lower interest rate and initial unemployment—which Lindahl deals with in greater detail four pages before Myrdal's reference, and where the results are "just the opposite" (ibid., p. 47), the corresponding footnote 2 to case 2c reads thus:

[2]It is assumed that production of consumer goods to a relatively larger extent than the production of capital goods has been able to absorb unemployed and that wages are very rigid and accordingly do not follow the price increase for products, just as the reader is reminded about the general assumption, that resources cannot be reallocated from consumer goods production to capital goods production. Under these assumptions is it possible that the supply of consumer goods during a certain period increases as much as or more than monetary demand, after which an equilibrium may occur. If a price fall has begun it must under the assumptions made here sooner or later come to an end because it will lead to an increase in unemployment and hence a fall in consumer goods [production] [ibid. pp. 43–44].

Not only does Lindahl visualize the possibility of an unemployment equilibrium; he also argues that such an equilibrium is stable. He was explicit, however, in calling these "exceptional cases" (*undantagsfall*) and relegated them to two footnotes; in the English translation of *Penningpolitikens medel*, published as Part II of *Studies in the Theory of Money and Capital* (1939) the crucial one of these footnotes (from pp. 43–44) has even disappeared and not a trace is left of the unemployment equilibrium. Lindahl cannot have considered these cases of any great importance, and he cannot possibly have realized that he was here anticipating the *General Theory*; otherwise the footnotes of 1929 would surely have become full-blown chapters in 1939! But what Lindahl of 1929 considered "exceptional cases," and perhaps rightly so, Myrdal of 1932, possibly inspired by Lindahl at this point, understood was realistic theory for the depression.[5]

Patinkin concedes that Ohlin broadly understood the mechanism of the multiplier process but contends that Ohlin, and more generally the Stockholm School, did not anticipate the *General Theory* insofar as the Keynesian unemployment equilibrium and its corollary, the static multiplier is concerned. A quotation from Ohlin's monograph (1934, p. 33), selected by Steiger as evidence of Ohlin's having it all—the unemployment equilibrium with output and employment the equilibrating variables—requires a very generous reading to be interpreted as a Keynesian underemployment equilibrium. It argues that production may not fall below a certain very low level but does not present this low level as an equilibrium. Ohlin could rather claim that he had anticipated Hicks's trade cycle theory with its lower bound or floor for the business cycle. Moreover, as Steiger (1978, p. 440) points out, Ohlin is here strongly influenced by Myrdal.

When we turn from Ohlin to Myrdal, matters look quite different, as we have seen. Myrdal understood that multiplier processes may

5. That Lindahl was the main source of inspiration for Myrdal's 1932 article was explicitly acknowledged by Myrdal in the Swedish version: "My exposition . . . is *immanent-critical* in the sense that to begin with I accept the main line of reasoning in the Wicksell-Lindahl theory and let the argument develop under the assumption that this theory is basically correct.[2] [M.'s footnote:][2] Readers acquainted with the problems in question will easily find that the author has learnt more from Lindahl's "Penningpolitikens medel" than from any other modern work . . . [*Text:*] That I have chosen to link up with Lindahl's latest work is natural and convenient for both author and reader. "Penningpolitikens medel" must be acknowledged as one of the most important milestones of Swedish economic research, and the theoretical discussion of monetary theory benefits, indeed, from hereafter taking its point of departure in precisely this work" (1932 article, p. 193). This clear acknowledgment, with the many, many references to Lindahl's *Penningpolitikens medel* in the Swedish version, has been left out in both German and English versions, which deliberately ("Gleichgewichtsbegriff", p. 303) start out directly from Wicksell rather than Lindahl. Cross references in the German and Swedish versions of Myrdal's article, with a prefatory footnote to the Swedish version, make it clear that the two versions must have been produced or at least edited simultaneously.

converge with production and real income as equilibrating variables. I have mentioned no fewer than three examples above: two from the 1932 article, one from the 1934 monograph. One of them is discussed by Patinkin (1979, pp. 17–18) and he acknowledges that there are in that example "obvious parallels to Keynes' theory of employment." The other examples greatly strengthen the case. I for my part find it very remarkable that both Lindahl and Myrdal got around to understanding that the expansion process may *converge* under conditions of under-utilized resources because they themselves demonstrated, as their theoretical starting point, that the Wicksellian cumulative process, operating under conditions of full employment does not generally converge. When this is said, it has to be admitted also that Myrdal did not pursue the idea any further. Myrdal did not venture upon discussing the properties of an unemployment equilibrium; otherwise he would have come across the static multiplier. And it does not play any role in the analysis of his or for that matter Ohlin's later monographs. Conceived in a footnote, Lindahl's unemployment equilibrium ended in an abortion. As we shall see, however, this is not the end of the story.

*The Theory of Unemployment*

In discussing the theory of unemployment of the Stockholm School I shall take as my point of departure the second and final *Report II* of the unemployment committee, *Åtgärder mot arbetslöshet* (*Measures against Unemployment*), submitted in November 1934. The first section in the first chapter of this report aims at "giving an impression of how the degree of unemployment is determined in a given situation" (op. cit., p. 17; my translation throughout). This is to the best of my knowledge the only place in the Stockholm School literature where a deliberate attempt is made to formulate a complete model of output and unemployment. Albeit an imprecise verbal sketch, it is clearly a simple Keynesian unemployment equilibrium model that we here encounter.

Before looking at this model it is worth asking whose views it may represent. Since the committee solicited special Supplements from Myrdal, Ohlin, Johansson, and Hammarskjöld and was advised by Lindahl, amongst others, we would naturally expect its final report to reflect the theoretical views of the Stockholm School. But nothing like the model of *Report II* can be found elsewhere in the writings of the authors of the Stockholm School. It was admittedly the report of a parliamentary committee with the major parties represented, including as one of the five members the conservative party leader, professor in labor economics at the University of Stockholm, Gösta Bagge; and some kind of political consensus view dominated by Bagge, the expert in the field, might perhaps be suspected. But these were not Bagge's views, to judge from his own writings. Bagge wrote a Supplement, *Causes of Unemployment*, to the committee's *Report I*, both submitted in June 1931. I shall return to Bagge's Supplement below because, among other reasons, it is referred to as an authority by both Myrdal and Ohlin; but there is nothing in Bagge which resembles the model of *Report II*. The committee, moreover, was explicit in emphasizing that conclusions reached in the first three parts of the Report should not be considered recommendations, endorsed by the committee (ibid., p. 4).

Hammarskjöld was a secretary of the committee from 1931 and as of 1932 its only secretary; he was the main draftsman of *Report II*. The preliminary draft of Chapters 2 to 7 of *Report II* were read and commented upon by Lindahl. Through Lindahl we know that Hammarskjöld was the author of these chapters (Steiger, 1971, p. 40 n. 58), whose views they presumably reflect, as influenced perhaps by Lindahl. It stands to reason that Hammarskjöld also was the author of Chapter 1, which contains the model we are going to discuss; but I can offer no evidence to substantiate this conjecture.[6] An influence from Lindahl appears likely, but again I have no evidence to offer. It is known, on the other hand, that Hammarskjöld at this time found himself in strong opposition to Ohlin (Steiger, 1971, p. 168) and was seeking Lindahl's support.

Leaving the question of the authorship in this somewhat unsatisfactory state, let us proceed to the model. After a brief discussion of the determinants of labor supply, we are told:

> Since production can only be increased with increasing difficulty, the increment of production which will exist after an increase in demand [for products] will not be proportional. . . . The price level will therefore be higher than at a lower demand. This is the reason why the real wage, as just pointed out, in the case here discussed [increased demand for products] is lower although the nominal wage is the same . . . [*Report II*, p. 14].

What the Report is saying here is that decreasing marginal productivity of labor with constant money wages implies that increased pro-

6. In a review article Lindahl (1935, p. 1) wrote: "Also the committee's own two Reports contain theoretical and statistical investigations of high scientific standards which should be credited to . . . Dag Hammarskjöld."

(After this paragraph was written, Steiger was kind enough to let me have a copy of Lindahl's typed comments on Hammarskjöld's draft. The first two comments are impossible to identify with anything in the printed version. The third comment, however, clearly refers to the second page of the present Chapter 2. Considering the page numbers referred to by Lindahl, the first two comments must have dealt with points in the draft of Chapter 1, which, on the other hand, must have been entirely rewritten.)

duction and employment are bound to be accompanied by higher price and lower real wage. Keynes agreed, as we know.

Moreover,

> total monetary demand and the degrees to which factors of production are utilized, as well as the remuneration paid for factor services depend upon each other . . . monetary demand and capacity utilization, etc., are mutually interdependent . . . [ibid., p. 15].

In the Swedish literature of that period, 'monetary demand' always means what Keynesian theory would call total, nominal effective demand for goods and services for final use. The interdependence between employment (production) and total effective demand is, of course, the crucial idea in Keynesian underemployment equilibrium theory.

And then the demand side:

> The size of total monetary demand is *directly* determined by the size of exports, the size of investments and total demand for consumer goods. To the extent that an increase in export is followed by an increase of export prices in relation to import prices or an increase in investments is accompanied by increased productivity, these forms of increased demand differ from that discussed above [an unspecified increase in demand], the assumptions of which are fulfilled at increased consumer demand, in that they do not imply a fall in real wages. That relatively inferior resources are employed is balanced by the relatively larger quantity of import goods that can be obtained for the increased export revenues, etc.
>
> In a market with investments entirely in the hands of private entrepreneurs, the magnitude is determined by the entrepreneurs' evaluation of returns; the higher the future return on real capital is expected to be, the larger is the demand for investments at given possibilities for credit expansion. To the extent that investments take place through government decisions, investments may develop more independently of profitability.
>
> Changes in the demand for consumer goods depend, apart from monetary income formation, mainly upon changes in voluntary saving. Also the government may, of course, give rise to a considerable demand for final use.
>
> Finally we have to take into account that the existence of commodity monopolies exerts a direct influence upon the effects of monetary demand on employment [ibid., pp. 15–16].

Keynes would have little to object to this exposition of the demand side of his system, although the inclusion of exports (and perhaps the degree of monopoly, working through income distribution) would be new to him and he would probably have been smart enough to ask about imports. But the import leakage can be found elsewhere in both *Report II* and Supplements. There is no mention of money and the rate of interest and their role in the interdependency; but then there is no need for that either in an institutional setting where monetary policy pegs the rate of interest and money supply adjusts to demand for money (the old Wicksellian assumption); and there is no real balance effect built into the *Report II* system. These points are important because we should expect neither Keynes-effect (via the rate of interest) nor Pigou-effect (via real balances).

The analysis of this verbal Keynesian system, however, leaves everything to be desired. Indeed, there is no analysis of the system as such.

In analyzing the properties of the model, the Report first discusses demand-expanding measures:

> there are two basically different ways of politically accomplishing an increase of monetary demand. On the one hand one may go for encouraging exports or private demand for consumer and investment goods, and, on the other hand, the government may itself generate such demand. It must be remembered that the effects in both cases may depend on the newly hired worker's willingness to accept employment at a lower remuneration [ibid., p. 16].

We do not find the multiplier here, but the Report is explicit about the fall in real wages accompanying an expansion of the system. Keynes, of course, would agree.

The Report further discusses the effects on employment of a fall in money wages and concludes that a fall in money wages unequivocally leads to increased employment (ibid., p. 18). Although this is the result that would follow from the standard interpretation of the Keynesian model as we know it now, it does not follow from the model as presented in the Report.

The analysis fails, not because the draftsman (Hammerskjöld?) failed in setting up a complete system but because he was not capable technically of analyzing the general equilibrium system he actually set up. We should not be surprised. The year was 1934. *Value and Capital* had yet to be written, and although Wicksell was the grand master who indeed knew how to handle general equilibrium systems, his pupils (and even less Cassel's) were not well versed in formal analysis. It is characteristic that, talking about the mutual interdependency of production-employment side and demand side (see the quotation above), the Report laments that "this makes it a very difficult task to determine the effects of income changes in arguments aiming at practical conclusions *and not permitting the two sides to be separated as done here*" (ibid., p. 15; my italics). Indeed, it appears to me obvious that in the Report's discussion of both the above-mentioned cases of policy measures, demand management and wage cuts, it is a matter of *partial* analysis with "the two sides" separated.[7] In the discussion of the effects of demand-expanding policies there is no hint of the feedback to demand from increased production. And in the discussion of the effects of money-wage cuts, we are not told in the relevant paragraphs how exactly a fall in money wages should lead to increased employment. In the Report model, as presented, the only effect should be a price fall in proportion to the money-wage fall. As emphasized, both Keynes-effect and Pigou-effect are absent in the specific institutional setting. The argument about the effect of money wage cuts on p. 18 probably simply repeats an argument earlier in the chapter (pp. 11–13), where monetary demand explicitly is assumed constant despite the fall in money wages and where, of course, the result is an increase in employment, partly because at lower prices and given total nominal demand, sales must increase, partly because substitution would lead in the same direction.

My conclusion is that the author of Chapter 1 in *Report II* did succeed in formulating a Keynesian unemployment equilibrium model but did not succeed in analyzing it. I hesitate to call it *the* Keynesian unemployment equilibrium model because the alien institutional setting in regard to money and interest rate has important consequences for the properties of the model, repercussions via interest rate and real balances being excluded.

Generally, both *Report II* and the leading figures of the Stockholm School, Lindahl, Myrdal, and Ohlin, as well as Bagge in his Supplement to *Report I*, take it that rigid money wages are a necessary condition for unemployment to emerge and exist. Being almost a truism, this insight is nonetheless crucial because it directs the attention to money-wage formation and dynamics and their role in the determination of unemployment.

Detailed labor market analysis was presented by three of the authors involved in the investigations of the unemployment committee, Gösta Bagge in his supplement, *Orsaker till arbetslöshet* (Causes of Unemployment), Myrdal in his 1932 article (with little difference be-

7. Alf Johansson's volume on *Löneutvecklingen och arbetslösheten* (Wages and Unemployment), published as Supplement 6 to the main reports, does not overcome this problem either.

tween Swedish, German, and English versions), and Alf Johansson in his supplement *Löneutvecklingen och arbetslösheten* (Wages and Unemployment). Johansson's supplement is uninteresting in this context. Although he argues in terms of cost effects and demand effects of money wage changes, Johansson did not manage, indeed, did not even attempt, to set up a complete macro model of unemployment, and his analysis never got beyond casuistics. Bagge's discussion of labor demand runs mostly in terms of full utilization of resources, but when he and Myrdal do get around to discussing labor markets with unemployment, the analysis never goes beyond that of partial theory with no link-up between commodity (goods and services for final use) markets and labor market. The deficiency of the analysis of the model in *Report II*, Chapter 1, is a deficiency common to all Swedish economists at that time, whether or not they are considered Stockholm School economists.

In his monograph, Bagge discussed the conditions for unemployment to exist in both unorganized and organized markets. The analysis runs in Marshallian terms of demand and supply price of labor. Bagge was a Swedish Pigou and adhered to what Keynes called the classical view. Unemployment exists if and only if for part of the labor force, the unemployed, the supply price exceeds the demand price. In this sense unemployment is always voluntary and 'caused' by excessive wages (my translation):

> There is no special kind of unemployment with 'too high wages' and other kinds for which this is not the case. With unemployment the wage is always 'too high' in the sense that supply price exceeds demand price for a certain amount of labor. This is the case for all different 'kinds of unemployment' [*Orsaker*, p. 16].

Bagge, however, did not consider the supply (reserve) price of labor as exogenously given:

> The supply price is based on the demand price insofar as supply prices that experience proves to be higher than or lower than the marginal demand price, as a rule subsequently are lowered or raised in line with changes in the latter. The supply price at a given point of time depends upon earlier experience concerning the formation of the demand price and is already for that reason particularly traditional and rigid. The 'fair' or 'just' wage is the one the workers have got used to from earlier market situations, and it is at that wage that the large majority of workers within an occupation, an industry, or a location are willing to work . . . [ibid., p. 102].

In the longer term, unemployment should thus tend to disappear because the supply price tends to adjust to demand price. Bagge's view on unemployment is quite similar to certain modern views on 'aspiration levels' and the like (Holt 1970, pp. 61–66) as an explanation of the existence of unemployment and rigid wages. In organized markets with money wages determined by collective agreement, Bagge takes it that the actual market wage is the supply price of labor (*Orsaker*, p. 105).

Keynes' famous definition of *involuntary* unemployment (Keynes 1935, p. 15) assumes that at the employment margin, supply price falls short of both going market wage and demand price so that at a small decrease in market wages, not only demand for labor but also supply of labor willing to work would exceed actual employment. There is nothing like Keynes' involuntary unemployment to be found in Bagge, and the same is the case, as we shall see now, with Myrdal's discussion of unemployment.

Myrdal discussed the conditions for unemployment to exist in equilibrium and linked it to the existence of 'bilateral monopoly' in the labor market (1939, pp. 143–45). He acknowledged the possibility of monopolistic price formation generally and offered a definition:

> By monopolistic price formation I mean in this connexion all the cases where the supply or demand price of a good can be held, not merely temporarily but for some time, at a level such that not the entire quantity of the good is demanded or supplied; or such that the supply or demand does not extend to an amount which in the ruling situation—with regard to the corresponding supply and demand curves—would be profitable to the suppliers or demanders if no account was taken of the reaction of demand and supply to their own actions (which would be the case under 'perfect competition'). These assumptions of monopolistic action are fulfilled to a high degree in the labour market . . . [ibid., p. 143].

He then assumed 'bilateral monopoly' in the labor market and defined a so-called "monopolistic intensity" on both sides which

> is a result of the strength and the will to maintain a certain supply or demand without making price concessions, or to maintain a certain price without concessions of supply or demand, and it is measured by this difference arising out of the disequilibrium of supply and demand [ibid., p. 145].

I think that Myrdal's 'bilateral monopoly' can be illustrated in a simple demand and supply diagram with both ordinary 'competitive' demand and supply curves, D and S, and 'monopolistic' curves, MD and MS, with the horizontal distances between MD and D, and MS and S, respectively, measuring the 'monopolistic intensity' on each side. While the competitive equilibrium would be in A, the 'bilateral monopoly' will settle down at MA.

Myrdal discusses the consequences of such wage formation at some length (ibid., pp. 143–58) and points out that in equilibrium unemployment equal to MA–S′, and potential vacancies equal to MA–D′ must exist. How then this partial labor market equilibrium under monopolistic conditions fits into a general equilibrium model, Myrdal does not enter upon, although he claims that there must be 'supply monopoly' in the commodity markets corresponding to the 'demand monopoly' in the labor market. It is a question of how the levels of the curves, in particular the demand curve, are determined and this, of course, again is the "very difficult task" which *Report II* failed to handle.[8] It seems to me, however, that what this model aims at is to determine an equilibrium level of unemployment that is involuntary only in the sense that individual workers would prefer work to unemployment at the equilibrium money wages and prices. The assumption is not that labor supply is withdrawn from the market to prevent money wages from falling: "For labour . . . the supply of which cannot be limited in a monopolistic fashion, this disequilibrium appears directly in the form of unemployment" (ibid., p. 156). There is equilibrium in the sense that money wages do not tend to change, yet there is labor market disequilibrium with actual, unsold labor supply and potential, unfilled vacancies on the employer side. Myrdal qualifies the analysis by the

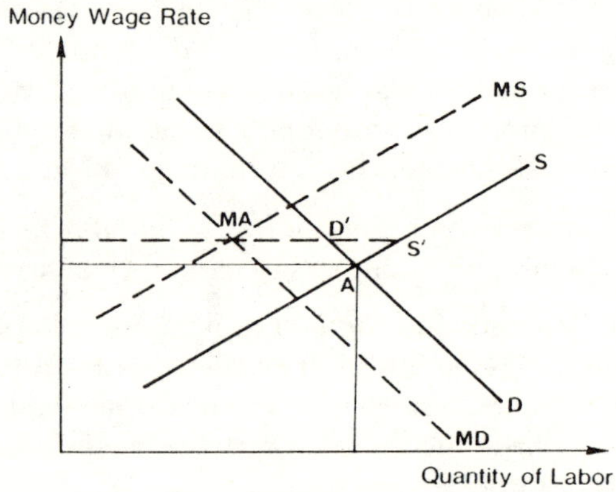


Figure 1.

8. Myrdal has in his 1934 monograph a general reference to Bagge's abovementioned Supplement from 1931. Myrdal is here talking about saving and capital formation as determinants of demand for labor (1934 monograph, p. 75).

condition that "a greater amount of labour would be demanded at a lower wage," hereby perhaps opening up the possibility that a wage cut might not lead to increased employment (ibid., p. 144). Unemployment is involuntary in the sense that the unemployed would prefer to work at going wages; yet it is voluntary in the sense that workers prefer to be unemployed rather than bidding down money wages and thus becoming employed.

Myrdal, unfortunately, does not specify the institutional setting. He talks about "the monopoly of the workers" (ibid., p. 144, for instance) and unemployment as a "cost, which the working class pays in its wage struggle" (ibid., p. 155), but does not make it clear whether workers (and employers) are organized. If all workers were unionized, the situation would be pretty clear; the union (in negotiations with the employer side) would fix money wages which all union members would respect even if they were to go unemployed. Considering Myrdal's Swedish background, this may be the setting he has in mind. But what about non-unionized workers? Do they refrain from bidding down money wages out of loyalty to the unions or, more generally, to the cause of the working class? Or would Myrdal here endorse Bagge's views? We are right up in the problems raised by the modern discussion about money wage stickiness and involuntary unemployment.

It is interesting and important, though, that Myrdal conceives of his equilibrium situation as determining a kind of 'natural' level of unemployment in the sense that if unemployment deviates from the equilibrium position, then money wages will tend to increase or fall and will continue increasing (falling) as long as demand management policy (monetary policy in Myrdal's paper) keeps unemployment too low (high). The "attempt would lead to a Wicksellian cumulative process . . . this process could not be stopped as long as unemployment was kept below that level at which the monopoly is satisfied; it would accelerate all the more" (ibid., p. 153, and p. 25 concerning acceleration via expectations). The "monopolistic price struggle and the tension between demand and supply arising from it, cannot be abolished simply by monetary policy, since one cannot assume that, in the long run, monetary policy can diminish or abolish monopoly power" (ibid., p. 154). Both the parallel and the contrast to Friedman and *his* 'natural' unemployment are striking.[9]

9. There were men before Agamemnon—and there were expectational accelerationists before Friedman. Myrdal was not the only one and not even the first. As he explicitly acknowledges (1939, p. 25), the idea seems to have originated in Lindahl's *Penningpolitikens medel* (1929). Joan Robinson spelled out the idea in some detail a few years later (1938, pp. 21–22) and after the war, Lindahl developed the idea further (1957, pp. 10–12, 18–21).

In allowing for deviations from the 'monopolistic' equilibrium level of unemployment, Myrdal obviously assumes that the labor market does not move instantaneously from one equilibrium position to another. Also, the monopolistically determined wages are sticky, something which does not follow directly from the model as presented in Figure 1. Myrdal is fully aware of this problem and says:

> In reality, however, this difficulty is not as great as it appears. For at least in the short run the changes of monopolistic pressure, i.e., acceptance of a certain change of demand or supply without making price concessions, or maintenance of a certain price in spite of supply or demand concessions, are largely connected with the 'external' [i.e., exogenous, such as monetary policy] causes of price changes. An increased intensity of the price struggle usually arises from the fact that one wants to maintain a certain price despite changes in the market situation. The workers, e.g., in the first instance consider monetary wages, not 'real wages.' . . . The change in pressure is only one of the causes of the stickiness . . . . stickiness of price is not based exclusively upon the specific variability of the monopoly element proper or its pressure in the market. Other relevant causes . . . are: Fixed price contracts, imperfect knowledge of other markets, customs and conventions . . . and similar influences [ibid., pp. 157–58].

And in another context:

> Experience indicates that whichever party on the labour market finds himself on the defensive fights most obstinately. Thus, in other words, the monopolistic pressure of the workers grows if a reduction in money wages is threatened. That is only another way of saying *the workers are ready to put up with greater unemployment than before* [ibid., pp. 163–64; my italics].

Although one might argue that Myrdal here does little more than shift the problem to the "variability of the monopoly element," he does introduce short term "money illusion" on the labor side (à la Keynes) and he is certainly aware that price stickiness is a phenomenon that calls for explanation. There is little doubt that unemployment is voluntary and it seems to me that Myrdal does little more than elaborate upon Bagge.

In the 1934 monograph, Myrdal explicitly refrains from discussing the general problem of how unemployment arises during a recession. He assumes that unemployment exists intially and says: "The theoretical mechanism of price formation behind such a development shall not be described more in detail . . ." (ibid., p. 160), but it would seem that he is just referring to his general views on such matters, and one would assume that these would be the views expressed in the 1932 article and its various versions.

We are left then with Ohlin. In the third part of his 1934 monograph, "Expansion, Structural changes, and Unemployment," Ohlin discusses "structural changes," which are defined as "a change of the circumstances which determine price formation under static assumptions . . ." (p. 153), and he declares that "unchanged employment during a period with structural changes requires usually either that labor is moved from one point to another or that the price of labor is fully flexible upwards or downwards.[1]" (p. 153); and in the footnote 1, "Generally it is the case that the larger mobility and wage flexibility are, the smaller and of the shorter duration will unemployment be at structural changes. . . . Concerning these matters, reference can be made to Bagge: Causes of Unemployment. Report I of the Committee on Unemployment, Supplement 1, 1931."

Dynamically, however, Ohlin denied that at flexible money wages unemployment would be nonexistant or, if actually existing initially, would tend to disappear. He discusses the effects of money-wage changes in situations with unemployment (Ohlin, 1934 monograph, ch. 3, paras. 4 and 7) and concludes that depending upon time lags, speeds of reaction, and expectations, anything can happen.[10] (This, incidentally, is quite typical of the dynamic 'analysis' of the Stockholm School. Anything can happen and there is no statement that can be refuted empirically except that time lags, etc., are important.) From our point of view it is crucial that in these paragraphs there is no mention of effects on effective demand via the rate of interest (the Keynes-effect) or via real balances (the Pigou-effect). Ohlin operates with both institutional and market rates of interest and in his analysis such effects should not be excluded a priori. This is particularly interesting because in the two separating paragraphs (5 and 6), Ohlin discusses the effects of changes in savings and here explicitly introduces effects via changes in interest rates called forth by differences between demand and supply for loanable funds created by the change in savings *ex ante*.

As already mentioned, Lindahl in a review article (1935) of Myrdal's 1934 monograph criticized the final Committee Report for not having dealt with the problem of permanent unemployment in a satisfactory way. Lindahl's criticism is not quite justified. In principle, *Report II* says (p. 20), there are four different ways of increasing the demand for labor:

10. Alf Johansson's monograph (1934) strongly emphasizes the risk of negative effects of wage cuts, and Myrdal also, in an early contribution (see Steiger, p. 180), makes this point.

a lowering of money wages or possibly other administered [*bundne*] prices, alternatively such changes in market conditions that price flexibility is increased;

a subsidization policy which at unchanged prices on various productive resources lowers costs of production through an income transfer, for instance through taxation;

promotion of real capital formation or an improvement of the quality of land and labor; and

a direct increase of total monetary demand, a solution which does not lead to a corresponding increase in employment, however, unless it is combined with an improvement of the relation between export and import prices, improved quality of labor or, alternatively . . . a lowering of real wages in particular.

These are recommendations that would follow from a standard Keynesian model. But it should be noticed that the first three ways of increasing demand for labor, lower money wages, subsidization, and increased marginal productivity of labor, all seem to assume given total monetary demand. From a Keynesian point of view this looks again like partial analysis; but it could also be a lapse into traditional neoclassical unemployment analysis (Bagge?). Lindahl's own recommendation (1935, pp. 8–9) was to promote real capital formation, in particular through removing tax disincentives to both savings and investments, the former through shifting personal taxation towards consumption taxes, the latter through lower taxes on corporate business income.

## *Conclusions*

Both sides of the debate have a point. While Patinkin certainly is right that Ohlin was far from having anticipated Keynes' *General Theory*, he does not, in my opinion, fully appreciate the understanding of underemployment equilibria actually reached by Swedish economists during the years 1929 to 1935, nor the degree to which this understanding arose as the result of original contributions from and interaction between Swedish economists. In particular, he does not fully appreciate the roles played by Lindahl and Myrdal in the genesis of the Stockholm School. Language may be a problem.

1. While both Ohlin and Myrdal demonstrated clear understanding of the dynamics of the multiplier process, only Myrdal had a full understanding of the *convergence* of the process. Myrdal may here have been inspired by Lindahl, who did visualize the possibility of underemployment equilibria as early as 1929.

2. A complete Keynesian underemployment model was sketched by the draftsman, most probably Hammarskjöld, of Chapter I in the fi-

nal *Report II* of the unemployment committee. The draftsman failed, however, to analyze his model correctly.

3. The equilibrating mechanisms of Keynes-effect and Pigou-effect appear nowhere in the writings of the Stockholm School (including the Reports of the unemployment committee). This, however, is related to the underlying institutional assumptions about the monetary system, with a central bank setting the rate of interest and letting money supply adjust rather than fixing money supply with the rate of interest adjusting. This is the assumption underlying the Wicksellian cumulative process, and it was the realistic assumption in a Continental-European context.

4. While the authors of the Stockholm School had a full understanding of the crucial importance of wage rigidity as a condition of unemployment, nowhere did they succeed in linking the labor market analysis with the multiplier analysis. The analysis of unemployment did not go beyond what Keynes called the classical theory of unemployment, with Bagge the Swedish Pigou.

5. Keynes tried hard to convince his readers that it is not wage stickiness as such which is the ultimate cause of unemployment, but rather insufficient effective demand. Keynes tried to argue that wage reductions might lead to a downward deflationary process through adverse expectations, without any fall in unemployment. Ohlin's dynamic arguments about money-wage changes and their effects upon employment resemble very much those of Keynes. Myrdal and Johansson also argued in this way. But then, it is not these expectational ad hoc arguments that are nowadays associated with Keynes' *General Theory*.

The Stockholm School was a fairly advanced edifice of its own—but the complete edifice of the *General Theory* was beyond its reach.

This article grew out of discussion with Patinkin at Berkeley in the fall of 1979 about the Stockholm School. Patinkin urged me to write down my views on some topics that came up in our discussions. I am grateful to Patinkin for critical remarks on both an earlier draft and this version. Steiger read the early draft. I am grateful for his very extensive comments, several of which are incorporated in this version, and for the new information supplied. Patinkin and Steiger do not in all details agree with my views on the Stockholm School.

*REFERENCES*

Bagge, Gösta, *Orsaker till arbetslöshet*, Arbetslöshetsutredningens betänkande, I, bilaga I, 1931, S.O.U. 1931:21. Stockholm, 1931.

Brems, Hans, "What Was New in Ohlin's 1933–34 Macroeconomics?" *History of Political Economy* 10 (1978): 398–412.

Johansson, Alf, *Löneutvecklingen och arbetslösheten*, S.O.U. 1934:2. Stockholm, 1934.

Keynes, J. M., *The General Theory of Employment, Interest, and Money*. New York, 1935.

Landgren, K.-G. *Den 'nya ekonomien' i Sverige*. Stockholm, 1960.

Lindahl, Erik, *Penningpolitikens medel*. Lund, 1929.

———, *Studies in the Theory of Money and Capital*, London, 1939.

———, *Spelet om penningvärdet*. Stockholm, 1957.

———, "Arbetslöshet och finanspolitik," *Ekonomisk Tidskrift* 37, Häft 1–2 (1935): 1–36.

Myrdal, Gunnar, *Prisbildningsproblemet och föränderligheten*. Uppsala, 1927.

———, "Om penningteoretisk jämvikt. En studie över den 'normala räntan' i Wicksells penninglära," *Ekonomisk Tidskrift* 33, Häft 5–6 (1931): 191–332. Cited as "1932 article."

———, "Der Gleichgewichtsbegriff als Instrument der geldtheoretischen Analyse," in Hayek, ed., *Beiträge zur Geldtheorie* (Vienna, 1933), pp. 361–488. Cited as "German version, 1933" of "1932 article."

———, *Monetary Equilibrium*, London, 1939. Cited as "English version, 1939" of "1932 article."

———, *Finanspolitikens ekonomiska verkningar*, S.O.U. 1934:1. Stockholm, 1934. Cited as Myrdal's "1934 monograph."

Ohlin, Bertil, "Till frågan om penningteoriens uppläggning," *Ekonomisk Tidskrift* 35, Häft 2 (1933): 45–81.

———, *Penningpolitik, offentliga arbeten, subventioner, och tullar som medel mot arbetslöshet, Bidrag till expansionens teori*, S.O.U. 1934:12. Stockholm, 1934. Cited as Ohlin's "1934 monograph."

Patinkin, Don, *Anticipations of the General Theory*, I and II. Unpubl. 1979.

———, "Keynes and the Multiplier," *Manchester School*, Sept. 1978, pp. 209–23.

Robinson, Joan, *Essays in the Theory of Employment*, London, 1937.

Steiger, Otto, *Studien zur Entstehung der Neuen Wirtschaftslehre in Schweden. Eine Anti-Kritik*. Berlin, 1971.

———, "Prelude to the Theory of a Monetary Economy: Origin and Significance of Ohlin's 1933 Approach to Monetary Theory," *History of Political Economy* 10 (1978): 420–47.

"A Bertil Ohlin Symposium," *History of Political Economy* 10 (1978): 353–453.

Uhr, C., "Economists and Policy Making 1940–46: Sweden's Experience," *History of Political Economy* 9 (1977): 89–121.

*Arbetslöshetens omfattning, karaktär och orsaker*, Arbetslöshetsutredningens betänkande, I, S.O.U. 1931:20. Stockholm, 1931. Cited as *Report I*.

*Åtgärder mot arbetslöshet*, Arbetslöshetsutrendningens betänkande, II, S.O.U. 1935:6. Stockholm, 1935. Cited as *Report II*.

# Name Index

# Pioneers in Economics

**Section I: The Forerunners of Classical Economics**

1. The Historiography of Economics
2. Aristotle (384–322 B.C.)
3. St Thomas Aquinas (1225–1274)
4. The Early Mercantilists
*Thomas Mun (1571–1641), Edward Misselden (1608–1634), Gerard de Malynes (1586–1623)*
5. The Later Mercantilists
*Josiah Child (1603–1699) and John Locke (1632–1704)*
6. Pre-Classical Economists Volume I
*Charles Davenant (1656–1714) and William Petty (1623–1687)*
7. Pre-Classical Economists Volume II
*Pierre le Pesant Boisguilbert (1645–1714), George Berkeley (1685–1753), Baron de Montesquieu (1689–1755), Ferdinando Galiani (1727–1787), James Anderson (1739–1808), Dugald Stewart (1753–1828)*
8. Pre-Classical Economists Volume III
*John Law (1671–1729) and Bernard Mandeville (1660–1733)*
9. Richard Cantillon (1680–1734) and Jacques Turgot (1727–1781)
10. François Quesnay (1694–1774) Volumes I and II
11. David Hume (1711–1776) and James Steuart (1712–1780)

**Section II: The Golden Age of Classical Economics**

12. Adam Smith (1723–1790) Volumes I and II
13. Henry Thornton (1760–1815), Jeremy Bentham (1748–1832), James Lauderdale (1759–1839), Simonde de Sismondi (1773–1842)
14. David Ricardo (1772–1823)
15. Jean-Baptiste Say (1776–1832)
16. Thomas Robert Malthus (1766–1834) and John Stuart Mill (1806–1873)
17. Ramsay McCulloch (1789–1864), Nassau Senior (1790–1864), Robert Torrens (1780–1864)
18. Thomas Tooke (1774–1858), Mountifort Longfield (1802–1884), Richard Jones (1790–1855)

19. William Whewell (1794–1866), Dionysius Lardner (1793–1859), Charles Babbage (1792–1871)

20. George Scrope (1797–1876), Thomas Attwood (1783–1856), Edwin Chadwick (1800–1890), John Cairnes (1823–1875)

21. James Mill (1773–1836), John Rae (1796–1872), Edward West (1782–1828), Thomas Joplin (1790–1847)

22. James Wilson (1805–1860), Issac Butt (1813–1879), T. E. Cliffe Leslie (1827–1882)

23. Karl Marx (1818–1883)

**Section III: Neoclassical Economics and its Critics**

24. Johann von Thünen (1783–1850), Augustin Cournot (1801–1877), Jules Dupuit (1804–1866)

25. Leon Walras (1834–1910)

26. Carl Menger (1840–1921)

27. Eugen von Böhm-Bawerk (1851–1914) and Friedrich von Wieser (1851–1926)

28. Knut Wicksell (1851–1926)

29. Alfred Marshall (1842–1924) and Francis Edgeworth (1845–1926)

30. Gustav Schmoller (1838–1917) and Werner Sombart (1863–1941)

31. Dissenters
*Charles Fourier (1772–1837), Henri de St Simon (1760–1825), Pierre-Joseph Proudhon (1809–1865), John A. Hobson (1858–1940)*

32. Thorstein Veblen (1857–1929)

33. Wesley Mitchell (1874–1948), John Commons (1862–1945), Clarence Ayres (1891–1972)

34. Henry George (1839–1897)

35. Vilfredo Pareto (1848–1923)

**Section IV: Twentieth Century Economics**

36. Arthur Pigou (1877–1959)

37. Frank Knight (1885–1972), Henry Simons (1899–1946), Joseph Schumpeter (1883–1950)

38. Edward Chamberlin (1899–1967)

39. Michal Kalecki (1899–1970)

40. Harold Hotelling (1895–1973), Lionel Robbins (1898–1984), Clark Warburton (1896–1979), John Bates Clark (1847–1938), Ludwig von Mises (1881–1973)

41. Irving Fisher (1867–1947), Arthur Hadley (1856–1930), Ragnar Frisch (1895–1973), Friedrich von Hayek (1899–1992), Allyn Young (1876–1929), Ugo Mazzola (1863–1899)

42. Harry Johnson (1923–1977)

43. Bertil Ohlin (1899–1979)

44. Piero Sraffa (1898–1983)

45. Joan Robinson (1903–1983) and George Shackle (1903–1992)

46. John Maynard Keynes (1883–1946) Volumes I and II